TRADE UNIONISM IN AUSTRALIA
A history from flood to ebb tide

In the late 1960s Australian unionism was on the flood tide: growing in strength, industrially confident and capable of shaping the overall political climate of the nation. Forty years on, union membership and power is ebbing away despite community support for trade unionism and the continuing need for strong unions. Even the unprecedented mobilisation against WorkChoices, which defeated a government and lost the prime minister his own seat, has done little to turn the tide.

With compelling rigour, Tom Bramble explores the changing fortunes of what was once an entrenched institution. *Trade Unionism in Australia* charts the impact on unions of waves of economic restructuring, a succession of hostile governments and a wholesale shift in employer attitudes, as well as the failure of the unions' own efforts to boost membership and consolidate power. Indeed, Bramble demonstrates how the tactics employed by unions since the early 1980s may have paradoxically contributed to their decline.

Ultimately this timely book traces union-led action from the workplace to the political sphere over a period of significant change, and concludes by pointing to strategies for a renewal and revival of Australian unions.

Tom Bramble is Senior Lecturer in Industrial Relations, School of Business, University of Queensland and has been a union activist. He has lectured in Industrial Relations at tertiary level for more than 20 years.

T0323344

TRADE UNIONISM IN AUSTRALIA

A history from flood to ebb tide

TOM BRAMBLE

CAMBRIDGE
UNIVERSITY PRESS

CAMBRIDGE UNIVERSITY PRESS
Cambridge, New York, Melbourne, Madrid, Cape Town, Singapore, São Paulo, Delhi

Cambridge University Press
477 Williamstown Road, Port Melbourne, VIC 3207, Australia

Published in the United States of America by Cambridge University Press, New York

www.cambridge.org
Information on this title: www.cambridge.org/9780521888035

First published 2008

Cover design by Liz Nicolson, designBITE
Printed in Australia by Ligare

A catalogue record for this publication is available from the British Library

National Library of Australia Cataloguing in Publication data
Bramble, Tom.
Trade unionism in Australia : a history from flood to ebb tide / Tom Bramble.
9780521716123 (pbk.)
9780521888035 (hbk.)
Includes index.
Bibliography.
Labour unions – Australia – History.
331.880994

ISBN 978-0-521-88803-5 hardback
ISBN 978-0-521-71612-3 paperback

CONTENTS

FIGURES AND TABLES

Figures

Tables

ACRONYMS

Acronym	Full title
ABC	Australian Broadcasting Corporation
ABCC	Australian Building and Construction Commission
ABOA	Australian Bank Officials' Association
ACCI	Australian Chamber of Commerce and Industry
ACOA	Administrative and Clerical Officers' Association
ACSPA	Australian Council of Salaried and Professional Associations
ACTU	Australian Council of Trade Unions
AEU	Amalgamated Engineering Union
ALAC	Australian Labor Advisory Council
ALP	Australian Labor Party
AMC	Australian Manufacturing Council
AMIA	Australian Metal Industries Association
AMIEU	Australasian Meat Industry Employees' Union
AMWU	(before 1995) Amalgamated Metal Workers' Union
AMWU	(after 1995) Australian Manufacturing Workers' Union
APESMA	Association of Professional Engineers, Scientists and Managers Australia
APPM	Associated Pulp and Paper Mills
ARU	Australian Railways Union
ASE	Australasian Society of Engineers
ASIO	Australian Security Intelligence Organisation
AWA	Australian Workplace Agreement
AWU	Australian Workers' Union
BCA	Business Council of Australia
BHP	Broken Hill Proprietary Company Limited
BLDC	Builders Labourers for Democratic Control

BLF	Builders Labourers' Federation
BWIU	Building Workers' Industrial Union
CAGEO	Council of Australian Government Employee Organisations
CEEP	*Commonwealth Employees (Employment Provisions) Act 1977*
CERR	*Commonwealth Employees (Redeployment and Retirement) Act 1977*
CFMEU	Construction Forestry Mining and Energy Union
CMC	Council for Membership Control (AWU)
CPA	Communist Party of Australia
CPA(M-L)	Communist Party of Australia (Marxist-Leninist)
CRA	Conzinc Rio Tinto of Australia Ltd
DLP	Democratic Labor Party
ECCUDO	Electricity Commission Combined Union Delegates Organisation
EPAC	Economic Planning Advisory Council
ETU	Electrical Trades Union
FCU	Federated Clerks' Union
FEDFA	Federated Engine Drivers and Firemen's Association
FIA	Federated Ironworkers' Association
GMH	General Motors-Holden's Limited
HEWRR	Higher Education Workplace Relations Requirements
IRB	Industrial Relations Bureau
IRC	Industrial Relations Commission
JIR	*Journal of Industrial Relations*
LHMU	Liquor, Hospitality and Miscellaneous Union
MIM	Mount Isa Mines Limited
MTEA	Metal Trades Employers' Association
MTIA	Metal Trades Industry Association
MUA	Maritime Union of Australia
NDA	National Day of Action
NFF	National Farmers' Federation
NTEU	National Tertiary Education Union
NUW	National Union of Workers
OECD	Organisation of Economic Cooperation and Development
PKIU	Printing and Kindred Industries Union
RAAF	Royal Australian Air Force
SDA	Shop Distributive and Allied Employees' Association

SEC	State Electricity Commission
SEQEB	South East Queensland Electricity Board
SPA	Socialist Party of Australia
SUA	Seamen's Union of Australia
TLC	Trades and Labor Council
TUTA	Trade Union Training Authority
TWU	Transport Workers' Union
VBEF	Vehicle Builders Employees' Federation
VSTA	Victorian Secondary Teachers' Association
WIRA	Waterfront Industry Reform Authority
WWF	Waterside Workers' Federation
YRW	Your Rights at Work

PREFACE

This book represents a first attempt to tell the story of trade unionism in Australia between the 1960s and 2000s in the context of the class struggle between capital and labour. It is framed within a Marxist perspective; that is, a perspective that takes as its starting point the struggle by the working class for its own liberation. My understanding of the shifting contours of this struggle is shaped not only by my own involvement since the mid 1980s, but also by discussions with many hundreds of participants. These have included unionists, employers and political activists. I would particularly like to thank my comrades in Socialist Alternative who have taught me so much and whose thinking has made a major contribution to this book.

This book has benefited greatly from comments and suggestions by Mick Armstrong, Kaye Broadbent, Diane Fieldes, Phil Griffiths, Rick Kuhn, Tom O'Lincoln, Louise O'Shea and Liz Ross. Louise O'Shea also provided invaluable research assistance. The University of Queensland gave me the time free from teaching, and the University of Melbourne supplied me with the space and facilities to get this book started in the first half of 2007, for which I would like to thank them. During my sabbatical at Melbourne University, Christina Cregan was a valued source of encouragement. For permission to use materials or for assistance in their use, I am grateful to the Australian Bureau of Statistics (www.abs.gov.au), Stephen Bell, Frank Stilwell and Margaret Gardner. Finally, I would like to thank Debbie Lee and all at Cambridge University Press for their assistance during production of this book and Frances Wade for her care in editing the manuscript.

I would like to dedicate this book to my parents, Harry and Margaret, for raising me, and to Kaye for her love and support and for giving me the impetus to write it.

INTRODUCTION

Two vignettes

Thursday 15 May 1969, Industrial Court, Melbourne

Thousands of workers take to the streets. Discarded and ineffectual police barricades trace their march route. The atmosphere is saturated with defiance and anticipation. A figure emerges from the Industrial Court: 'Clarrie's been sent down!' and the crowd erupts.

Over the next six days, Victoria will experience the largest general strike in its history. Power and gas supplies will be disrupted, television broadcasts will cease and public transport will stop running in protest at the jailing of Tramways Union leader Clarrie O'Shea. Workers from as far afield as Townsville, Hobart and Sydney will walk off the job in solidarity. Decades of massive fines and jailing of union leaders will be brought to an abrupt end. An era of working-class militancy will be unleashed.

For the union leaders, turmoil ensues. Confronted with the very actions that they have attempted to avoid for years, they now face a choice – lead from the front or be swept to the back. Leaders of the left-wing metal trades unions, who previously accepted and attempted to pay the crippling fines, are now prepared to take action.

The right-wing leaders who have supported the penal powers – seeing them as a useful tool by which to contain industrial action and to discipline militants – are dismayed by the explosion of working-class activity. Yet they are powerless to contain it. Instead, the right-wing ACTU, along with the leaders of the New South Wales and Victorian labor councils, are forced to condemn the penal powers and urge unions not to pay fines.

Even the ALP is affected. At its 1970 conference it reverses its long-standing support for the powers and commits to their repeal.

O'Shea is released from jail the following Wednesday. The penal powers are rendered dead.

The Your Rights at Work campaign, 2005–07

It is now 2005 and a conservative Government passes laws to criminalise union activity and persecute militants.

Overwhelming opposition to WorkChoices is evident in demonstrations of hundreds of thousands of workers organised by the ACTU and its affiliates. Workers have suffered years of attacks on their rights and they are determined to resist this latest and most savage round.

The anger is there, but the union mobilisations are stage-managed, electorally oriented affairs, featuring slick broadcasts of pre-recorded addresses, stand-up comedians and musical video clips. The message throughout is the need for a change of government, not militant action by workers.

No union or union leader, even in Victoria whence some of the first calls for demonstrations came, is willing to challenge this agenda or call for strikes. Instead they, along with the ACTU and the labor councils, argue that such action would 'play into the hands of the Coalition'. So after choking up the central business district of every capital city in protest against WorkChoices, workers return to work.

The conservative Government survives the immediate challenge with its laws intact, and the union leaders are free to pursue their electoral strategy without organised opposition from a dissatisfied rank and file.

No shopfloor organisation exists to pressure the union leaders, either right or left, to take more serious action and to give voice to workers' desires to see WorkChoices scrapped immediately.

With no pressure from industrial action, an organised rank and file, or left-wing union leaders, Labor's industrial policy shifts consistently to the right over the course of 2007. When it wins government in November 2007, it does so on a platform that retains many of the policies introduced by the Coalition, including much of WorkChoices.

Working conditions are under continuing threat.

These two episodes illustrate the sharp change in the fortunes of Australian unionism between the late 1960s and early 1970s and the 2000s. Underpinning the transition was a change in the terrain of class struggle in Australia – in the confidence of rank-and-file workers, the organisation of union militants, the attitudes of the union leaders, and the strategy of the government and employers.

The earlier period was marked by rising working-class confidence and assertiveness, a belief that taking on the boss was the way to get what you wanted, and *demands* on the ALP to act. The latter years were characterised by the domination of the union leaders, a lack of confidence to organise outside the boundaries of the law and a *dependence* on the ALP to save the unions.

This book tells the story of how and why unions in Australia underwent this transformation.

Outline of this book

After reviewing the story of unionism in the postwar decades through to 1967 in Chapter 1, this book will tell the history of Australian unionism between the 1960s and the 2000s in three phases. The first phase, which is discussed in Chapter 2, may be described as the *flood tide*. The flood tide occurred in the period 1968 to 1974 when Australian unions began an offensive for higher wages, improved working conditions and political reform. Nearly 30 years of full employment and a rapidly expanding workforce created the conditions for a union upturn. With tight labour markets unions began to use the strike weapon in earnest. As described earlier, in 1969 the government's restrictive 'penal powers' were smashed by a general strike based in Victoria. This unlocked the floodgates and for the next five years workers conducted one of the biggest waves of strikes in Australian history. Industrial militancy spread from blue-collar to white-collar workers, particularly in the public sector. Strikes were accompanied by a political radicalisation based around the war in Vietnam but spreading to a host of other issues. Union membership surged by more than 20 per cent and union coverage rose by 5 percentage points.

The flood tide came to a halt in 1974–75 through a combination of economic crisis and the failure of the unions to halt a coup against the Whitlam

Government, both of which are discussed in Chapter 3. The resulting *stand-off* between capital and labour continued for another eight years. Chapter 4 outlines the various stages in the struggle that unfolded between the unions and the Fraser Government at this time. Neither side made a decisive breakthrough and in 1980 unions went back on the offensive with a wages push that destroyed the economic and industrial relations credibility of the Fraser Government. However, as a result of a series of partial defeats suffered by unions in the latter half of the 1970s and a significant shift to the right in the ranks of the union leaders, who increasingly began to trade wage rises for no-strike agreements, the ground was laid for retreat.

The ALP–ACTU Accord marked the beginning of the *ebb tide*, which is described in Chapters 5 and 6. Chapter 5 discusses the genesis of the Accord and its first seven years of operation. Under the Accord, union leaders increasingly became industrial disciplinarians, driving an agenda of wage cuts and productivity increases. While union leaders were involved in peak discussions with government and employer representatives, the grassroots of the union movement were in marked decline. Employers, backed by conservative state governments, became increasingly emboldened to challenge the unions in the 1990s. This, together with the continuing productivity drive by union leaders and the federal government, is discussed in Chapter 6.

Chapters 7 and 8 review the operations of Australian unions under the conservative Howard Government. Chapter 7 covers the first three terms of this government, from its election in 1996 to 2004. This period is characterised by the determined efforts of the Howard Government to attack union power by a variety of legislative and political means. It encompasses the passage of the Workplace Relations Act of 1996, the waterfront dispute of 1998 and a series of industry-specific measures directed by successive industrial relations ministers and aimed at undermining unionism in its remaining strongholds. Chapter 7 also considers efforts by the ACTU to halt the slide in union coverage.

Chapter 8 focuses on the union campaign against the WorkChoices legislation, which was passed by the Howard Government in its fourth term in office (2004–07). WorkChoices was the most draconian anti-union legislation passed by an Australian government for many decades. It also sought to force down the wages and working conditions of the working class more generally. Unions responded with the Your Rights at Work campaign, which played a very important role in the defeat of the Howard Government at the 2007 election.

The concluding chapter, Chapter 9, provides an overview of the 40-year period, drawing together the threads and recapitulating the main arguments. It then discusses the prospects for Australian unionism after the election of the Rudd Labor Government in November 2007.

Chapter One

TRADE UNIONISM IN THE POSTWAR BOOM, 1945–67

The flood tide of 1968–74 arose out of the contradictions of Australia's postwar economic boom and the politics of the Cold War.

The postwar upsurge

In 1943, after a sharp drop at the height of the Pacific War in 1941–42, the strike rate in Australia began to recover quickly (see Figure 1.1). Workers went on the offensive for higher wages, better working conditions and an end to the speed-up of work associated with wartime conditions. The strike rate then exploded as the war ended. Workers were determined to make good the losses that they had experienced during the war and the Great Depression that had preceded it. Now it was time to turn the screws on the employers. They met stiff opposition not just from the employers but also from the new Labor Prime Minister, Ben Chifley, who was determined to continue the program of wartime austerity prosecuted by his predecessor John Curtin. However, workers were not to be deterred. Strikes broke out in a wide range of industries. Large May Day rallies marched through the streets in a parade of strength. Working-class women stormed shops protesting against the high price of goods.

Amid a range of workers' demands, two emerged as central: a 40-hour working week and an increase in wages. The breakthrough came with a successful six-month strike by Victorian metalworkers in 1946–47, which

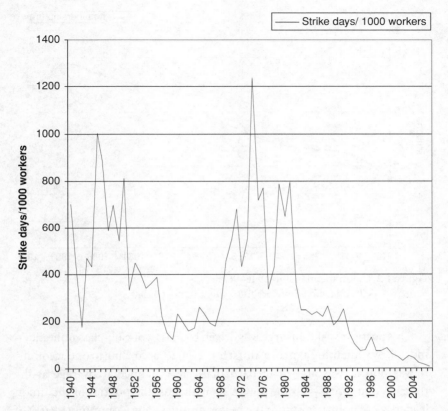

Figure 1.1 Strike rate 1940–2007
Sources: Strike rate for period 1945–66 calculated from civilian workforce data
sourced from the ABS *Year Book Australia* (various editions), cat. no. 1301.0 and
strike days sourced from S. Deery & D. Plowman, *Australian Industrial Relations,*
3rd edn, McGraw-Hill, Sydney, 1991, pp. 66–7
Strike rate for period 1967 to 1984 sourced from S. Deery & D. Plowman, *Australian
Industrial Relations,* 3rd edn, McGraw-Hill, Sydney, 1991, p. 62
Strike rate for period 1985–2007 sourced from ABS *Industrial Disputes,* cat. no.
6321.0

overcame all efforts by the state and federal Labor governments to defeat
it. Notable among these was the Chifley Government's decision in 1947 to
grant powers to the Arbitration Court to fine unions for taking strike action
(the 'penal powers'). Union membership rose by one-third between 1946
and 1951 as thousands of soldiers returned to civilian occupations and as
strikes drew in new recruits. Coverage rose from 51 per cent to 60 per cent.

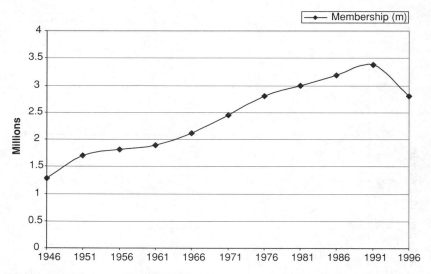

Figure 1.2 Union membership 1946–96
Source: ABS *Trade Union Statistics Australia,* cat. no. 6323.0

This postwar strike upsurge was driven by mass working-class militancy – indeed, by something akin to a 'thirst for revenge', according to one account.[1] It was not, as was argued in particularly fervent media coverage at the time, a communist grab for power. Nonetheless, the politics of the union leaders were not irrelevant to the major disputes. The Communist Party of Australia (CPA) had strengthened its influence in the trade unions during the war and led some of the country's most significant unions, including the Waterside Workers' Federation (WWF), the Seamen's Union (SUA), the Federated Ironworkers' Association (FIA) and the Australasian Coal and Shale Employees' Federation (ACSEF, better known as the Miners' Federation).[2] The party also played an important role in unions covering engineers, boilermakers, shipwrights, sheet metal workers, the building trades and the sugar mills of north Queensland, among others. At the 1945 ACTU Congress CPA members and their allies came within a whisker of having a majority of delegates, and the CPA candidate for president was only narrowly defeated.

In the immediate aftermath of the war, the CPA maintained a policy of support for the Labor Government. With the onset of the Cold War in 1947–48, however, Moscow ordered the world's communist parties to undertake a

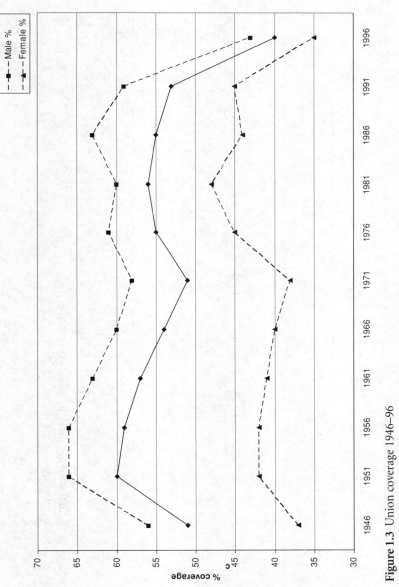

Figure 1.3 Union coverage 1946–96
Source: ABS *Trade Union Statistics Australia*, cat. no. 6323.0

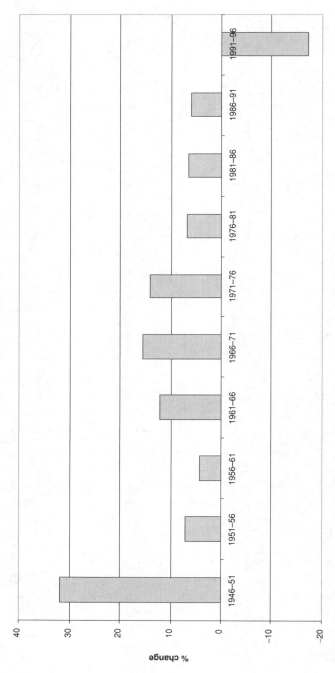

Figure 1.4 Percentage change in union membership 1946–96 (five-year periods)
Source: ABS *Trade Unions Statistics Australia*, cat. no. 6323.0

'left turn'. The social democratic parties, such as Australia's Labor Party, were treated no longer as allies but as bitter enemies. The Russian leadership forecast a major world depression, which would see a sharp leftward swing in the working classes of the West and a further rightward swing by social democracy; the reformist parties would therefore stand 'exposed' in the eyes of the masses and the communist parties would win their support. The CPA now sought to mount a challenge to the ALP for leadership of the Australian labour movement.

Both propositions – that a depression was looming and that the ALP would stand exposed for its right-wing policies – made sense to many trade unionists. The former was a widespread belief held by many mainstream economists, and it was not as though the ALP was doing anything in office to refute the notion that it was a right-wing party that served the interests of business. Its record in the 1946–47 metal trades strike was one example. The Labor Government in Queensland used draconian powers in its attempt to smash a rail strike in 1948. Challenging ALP governments was in this sense the only option possible for militant workers, short of complete capitulation.

The CPA played a prominent role in organising the Queensland railway workers and also in the 1948 Victorian transport workers' strike. Both were successful in winning many of the workers' demands. The ALP, along with the press and the employers, responded by increasingly ramping up Cold War propaganda against the CPA. In short, the new turn in Communist policy appeared to fit the unfolding situation.

It was in this context that the Miners' Federation, led by the CPA, embarked on a major strike. On 27 June 1949 more than 20 000 coal miners struck for a 35-hour week, a 30-shilling increase in wages, and long service leave. The Chifley Government responded swiftly, passing legislation that made it illegal to give strikers and their families financial support; seizing union funds; jailing seven strike leaders; setting the Commonwealth Investigation Service (the predecessor of ASIO) onto the union; and threatening to put 'communists and their sympathisers' into prison camps. Chifley told the Labor caucus that 'The Reds must be taught a lesson'. The ACTU fully backed the Government. Finally, and for the first time ever in peacetime, Labor sent troops in to break the mineworkers' strike on 1 August. Two weeks later the miners' strike crumbled.

The 1950s retreat

The impact of the Cold War

The Chifley Government's agenda of economic austerity, union-busting and prosecution of the Cold War at home did not save it from electoral defeat in 1949. Indeed, by its enthusiastic attacks on the CPA, Labor helped to steer mass politics to the right, and by its persecution of militant unionists it demoralised its own support base. The death knell of postwar militancy was finally sounded with the defeat of a long and large-scale Victorian public transport strike in 1950. The conservatives won power and held it for the next 23 years.

The Menzies Government set out to put a lid on the wages share of national income and to suppress militant unionism. It was broadly success-ful in achieving these two aims, at least until the late 1950s. The wages share of national income dropped sharply between 1949 and 1952, the result of the scrapping of price controls and a succession of regressive budgets. In 1953 the Arbitration Court ended automatic quarterly indexation of the Basic Wage, which meant that wages were no longer guaranteed against inflation.[3]

Menzies attacked militant unionism on a range of fronts: anti-union laws, legislation to ban the CPA, the use of troops during strikes on the waterfront, the jailing of union leaders, and deregistration of militant unions such as the Building Workers' Industrial Union (BWIU). The most far-reaching measure was an extension of the penal powers. In 1951 the Menzies Government amended the Conciliation and Arbitration Act to allow for the introduction of bans and limitations clauses in all awards. The typical clause prescribed that:

> No organisation party to this award shall in any way, whether directly or indirectly, be a party to or concerned in any ban, limitation, or restriction upon the performance of work in accordance with this award.[4]

In short, this was a 'no-strike' order.

Although bans clauses were in the first instance only intended to be temporary and to lapse after six or twelve months, they became a permanent feature of the all-important Metal Trades Award, which was the benchmark award in the postwar decades.

In 1956, when the Arbitration Court was split into two bodies, the Arbitration Commission and the Industrial Court, the latter was given the power to enforce awards and impose penalties. Under section 109 of the amended Act, the Court, headed by the former Attorney-General in the Menzies Government, the arch-conservative Justice John Spicer, had the power to order compliance with the bans clause. Violating an order under section 109 (for example, organising a strike) constituted contempt of court and could bring maximum penalties of £500 (in the case of an organisation), £200 (in the case of an employer or the holder of union office) and £50 (in the case of a rank-and-file union member) for *each day* of the contempt.

The bans clauses offered advantages to the Menzies Government that jailing union leaders did not. The latter action created an important propaganda opportunity for the unions: in the name of 'freedom', which Menzies was purporting to promote by his Cold War agenda, trade unionists were being jailed. The bans clauses, by contrast, were put into effect by the Arbitration Commission and enforced by the Industrial Court, which were nominally at arm's length from the government. Further, the measure involved bleeding the unions financially, which lacked the dramatic effect of marching union leaders into jail.

Menzies had allies. With the Cold War in full swing the US State Department, big business interests, the RSL and the Catholic Church went on the offensive against the left. A chief mover was the 'Movement' led by Bob Santamaria and sponsored by the Roman Catholic church hierarchy, which still had substantial sway with the working class at this time. The Movement aimed to crush Communist influence and, ultimately, to convert the Labor Party into a right-wing Christian farmer–worker party.

Santamaria won the support of a number of ALP-aligned union leaders who were not associated with the Movement but who also wanted to destroy the influence of the Communist Party. The result was the formation of anti-communist ALP 'Industrial Groups' in a wide variety of trade unions. One important player was New South Wales Labor Council assistant secretary Jim Kenny, a fervent supporter of Santamaria with strong links to US Republicans, including Richard Nixon and Dwight D. Eisenhower.[5] In the early 1950s the Groupers and their supporters won major battles inside unions against the Communist Party, most notably in the FIA. In addition, they won leadership positions in the Federated Clerks' Union (FCU), the Australian Railways Union (ARU), the Amalgamated Society of Carpenters and Joiners (ASC&J) and some branches of the WWF, the BWIU and the public service unions.

Using their leadership of several large unions and their influence in the NSW Labor Council as a power base, the Groupers began to attack not just Communist influence but also any figure in the ALP and the unions who would not denounce communism. By 1954 the Groupers were in a position to challenge the mainstream ALP leadership under Herbert 'Doc' Evatt, who had become leader on the death of Chifley in 1951. Evatt and significant numbers of union leaders took fright. Many union leaders, including Tom Dougherty from the powerful right-wing Australian Workers' Union (AWU) and Melbourne Trades Hall secretary Vic Stout, had been happy to see the 'Coms' thrown out, but the Groupers were now threatening their positions as well. Evatt and the union leaders were supported by left-wing Labor leaders, such as Eddie Ward and Clyde Cameron, and other senior Labor figures, such as future leader Arthur Calwell. Together they launched a counter-offensive.

This fight culminated at the March 1955 Federal Party Conference, where the entire Victorian executive of the ALP, which had been captured by the Groupers, was expelled and the Industrial Groups disendorsed. At the last moment leading figures in the NSW Labor Council, including assistant secretary Jim Kenny, drew back from the brink, opting to 'fight from within', as did the FIA's Laurie Short and John Ducker. Necessary though the fight was, if the Labor Party were to remain a social democratic party and not retreat and become a shadow of the Coalition parties, the immediate result of the Split was devastating. The Victorian Labor Government promptly collapsed, and it was followed into the wilderness by the Queensland Labor Government, which had been in power with only a short interruption since 1915. The Labor Split led to the creation of the Democratic Labor Party in 1957, and DLP preferences to the Coalition kept federal Labor out of office for a further 15 years.

The Menzies Government's attacks on workers and its militarist posture had won it little support in working-class communities. At the 1951 and 1954 elections the Labor Party more than recovered the votes that it had lost in 1949, and in 1954 it polled 50 per cent of the primary vote for only the second time in its history. However, Menzies used the Split, the Petrov affair of 1954 and an economic recovery to win a big swing towards the conservatives at the December 1955 election. Labor lost more than

5 per cent of its primary vote and a further 2 per cent at the 1958 federal election.

In the new right-wing climate thousands of worker militants dropped out of politics or drifted into inactivity. The attraction of radical politics waned when it appeared that the system could deliver growth and personal advancement on a long-term basis. Rising wages, cheap land, full employment, plenty of overtime and low interest rates meant that the quarter-acre block became a realistic proposition for many blue-collar workers. Car ownership allowed workers to commute long distances to work, and contributed to the dissolution of the political culture that had characterised some tight-knit inner-city working-class communities in the inter-war decades, such as Balmain and East Sydney in Sydney and Richmond and Collingwood in Melbourne. The nuclear family increasingly became the central point of working-class identity with a rising birth rate and, for a period, a steady reduction in the age of marriage and the arrival of first children. Religious observance revived in the 1950s after many years of decline.

The repressive measures adopted by the Menzies Government and the Industrial Court seemed to work. The strike rate, which had fallen sharply after the defeat of the coal miners in 1949 and then stabilised for five years, fell again between 1956 and 1959 (see Figure 1.1). Union membership, which had grown by one-third between 1946 and 1951, rose by only 7 per cent over the next five years and by only 4 per cent between 1956 and 1961 despite rapid growth in the workforce (see Figure 1.2).

It was not that most working-class families came to love the Menzies Government. Far from it – the conservatives and 'Pig Iron Bob' (as Menzies was known) were despised by most class-conscious blue-collar workers. However, the radical impulse that had driven important sections of the working class who had been fired up by the experience of bitter strikes in the late 1920s, the Depression and the rise of fascism in Europe, dwindled in this period.

The role of the union leaders

In the latter half of the 1950s and 1960s there were three broad currents among Australian union leaders: the 'moderates', the far right and the left. The moderates, who were based in the right wing of the ALP for the most part, became the dominant current in the union movement. They controlled the labor councils in the two biggest states, Victoria and New South Wales, as well as in Tasmania. They also dominated the floor of ACTU congresses and the ACTU executive. Key figures from this current included ACTU president Albert Monk, ACTU secretary Harold Souter and Melbourne Trades Hall secretary Vic Stout. They rested on a base of mostly small unions that had little record of industrial struggle but exercised a disproportionate role in the peak councils.

These leaders were for the most part hostile to union militancy. They had endorsed Chifley's efforts to break the Victorian metal trades strike and the 1949 coal miners' strike. They formally opposed the bans clauses but did nothing to challenge them, seeing them as necessary for controlling working-class militancy. Similarly, the NSW Labor Council did nothing to challenge the State Labor Government's penal powers, which were used with devastating effect by the Broken Hill Proprietary (BHP) against unions in the steel industry.[6] The moderate leaders looked to peaceful negotiations and representations to tribunals and wages boards to win wage rises and resolve grievances. In 1952, at the very time when the Menzies Government was launching a series of attacks on militant trade unionism, the ACTU accepted an invitation to participate in the Government's new Advisory Committee together with employers.

The 'moderate' union leaders provided employers with an important bulwark against strikes. At the Ford Motor Company the Vehicle Builders union (VBEF) leaders signed up to a disputes procedure that stipulated:

> Pending settlement of any dispute . . . employees of the Companies [Ford Manufacturing Company and the Ford Motor Company] shall remain at work and not restrict the extent of their work; and the Union, its executive, Officials and Stewards will take every action within their power to enforce this provision.

Clauses 10 and 11 of the agreement required a secret ballot prior to any industrial action and also provided for 'the company nominating as observers any responsible members of the staff and to have its public auditors certify to the correctness of the ballot'. Twenty of the 24 clauses of Ford's grievance procedure spelled out restrictions on the union's freedom to strike.

In return for their role as industrial disciplinarians, the moderate union leaders were propped up by closed shop or union preference arrangements that facilitated the growth of membership. The closed shops guaranteed a rising income for the union and a means for the leadership to discipline recalcitrant members, since cancellation of membership could lead to termination of employment. Furthermore, it was common for employers and union leaders to connive in the sacking of 'troublesome' union militants.

Little effort was made by these leaders to encourage activism. They saw the job of delegates simply as one of collecting union dues, recruiting new members (in the absence of a closed shop) and guarding against breaches of the award. Shop stewards were not seen as an active force in their own right. A 1954 survey by the Federal Department of Labour and National Service revealed:

> . . . a very poor development of shop organisation in which the workers could responsibly participate, and very few effective means where the workers could treat local job problems at the place of employment.[7]

This situation prevailed for many years. In 1967 Kevin Hince described the situation as follows:

> In Australia, the accepted procedure is that union activity is carried to the shopfloor by the officers of the union branch . . . Where a dispute occurs at the place of work, any official union action will stem from the branch and from branch officers who are brought in from outside the place of work . . . Shop stewards are rarely part of the official union organizational structure and they are rarely delegated more than a limited role in the activities of the organization.[8]

Crucial to understanding the stance of these leaders was the fact that, for the most part, they led unions with little experience of strikes and militancy – for example, the Australasian Society of Engineers (ASE), the Bank Officials (ABOA), the Insurance Clerks, the federal public service unions – or unions that had militant pasts but whose traditions had been destroyed, for example the Timber Workers and the AWU. The passive leadership of most moderate union leaders reflected a lack of pressure on them from members and the personal benefits that they accrued from playing the role of 'labour statesmen' – respect from employers and power and influence within the ALP. In many cases loyalty to the party was rewarded by plum jobs on retirement: parliamentary seats or public sector sinecures. Leaders of the NSW Labor Council were gifted seats in the state's upper house even while they held their union positions.

Not all of the politically moderate union leaders were industrially quiescent. An important minority did not hesitate to use strikes to advance campaigns for industrial gains. These included the leaders of the Transport Workers' Union (TWU), the Storemen and Packers and the Electrical Trades Union (ETU). The strategic power of members of these unions helps explain their record. With the rise of trucking, the growth of the capital cities and the increasing integration of the Australian states into a national economy, workers in the transport and distribution industries held immense strategic power. The same applied to electricians who, like the metal tradesmen, played an indispensable role in every industry across the country.[9] Members of these unions were not afraid to strike to win improved wages and conditions. The leaders of these unions could not simply squash strikes and keep their positions – they bent to the prevailing militancy of their members. Furthermore, their role in leading strikes also won them a following among union members, earned them kudos among their colleagues and forced employers to take them more seriously than they did leaders of more docile unions.

Standing to the moderate leaders' right were the Grouper (later National Civic Council) leaders. The Groupers were ensconced in the leadership of several large unions and also contested CPA influence in the Engineers (AEU). Initially the Groupers' industrial practice had been virtually indistinguishable from that of the other currents. Where the members were passive and where there was no strong tradition of local activism, as in the Shop Assistants' and Warehouse Employees' Federation and the FCU, the Grouper union leaders pursued a conservative anti-strike strategy and pointed to the punitive and restrictive apparatus of arbitration to justify their inactivity. Where, however, members were prepared to fight and had some capacity to do so, as was the case with the Engineers, the Miners' Federation and the WWF, and in some areas of the FIA and FCU (on the waterfront), the Grouper officials showed themselves to be just as prepared to fight as those from the CPA.[10] The situation changed following the 1955 ALP Split, however. With the hardening of antagonism between the DLP and moderate ALP union leaders, the former became a much more hard-line anti-strike current.[11] Their fortunes in the Engineers and other militant unions rapidly declined and the left was thereafter able to dominate these unions.[12]

Finally, there were the CPA union leaders and their allies in the left of the ALP. In line with the media, the employers and the Menzies Government, right-wing union leaders during the 1950s and 1960s blamed 'Communist agitation' for strikes. There appeared to be some basis for this allegation: workers in the coal mines and the metal trades, on the waterfront and in shipping – four sectors where the CPA had an important influence – were by far the most ready to strike, accounting for two-thirds of all strike days in the 1950s.[13]

Nonetheless, the truth was rather more complex. In the coal mines, shipping and the waterfront, CPA militants had helped to rebuild unions after the smashing defeats of the 1920s and early 1930s. As they did so they earned respect among militant workers; hundreds joined the party in the 1930s and 1940s. Over time, the CPA was able to use this support to win leadership positions in several unions. Militant figures such as Ted Rowe of the AEU, Jim Healy of the WWF and E.V. Elliott of the Seamen's Union therefore *emerged from* a culture of workplace militancy; they did not *create* it.

The practice of the CPA leaders shifted to the right in the 1950s. This was partly in response to a general shift in Communist policy internationally, following direction from the Soviet Union. However, the party's analysis of the causes of the mine workers' defeat in 1949 was an additional and important factor.[14] The CPA committed many errors in its leadership of the strike. It sought to invest in the strike a political content that was alien to the motivations of most rank-and-file coal miners. It created a sense of overconfidence among the mineworkers by suggesting that only a short strike was needed to get the Labor Government to pressure the employers into conceding their claim. It sought to bureaucratically manage the strike, refusing to call mass meetings to allow the workers to have any say in the progress of the strike, suppressing information about Court proposals to bring about a compromise resolution, and manipulating meetings in order to extend the strike at a time when most workers were in favour of calling it off.

However, the CPA failed to draw these lessons. It focused overwhelmingly on the fact that the strike was too ambitious and 'ultra left', given the party's state of isolation. Thus it drew only conservative conclusions about the need to moderate its approach in order to patch up relations with the Labor Party. Having swung from right to left in the late 1940s, the party now swung back to the right and increasingly accommodated itself to the ALP. In 1950 the Victorian party secretary, Ted Hill, declared: 'It is clear that the struggle for working class unity is a struggle not only against the Chifleys and the Evatts but against the Monks and the Broadbys.'[15] Four years later, Hill was quoting with approval national secretary Lance Sharkey's declaration that 'The Communist Party stands for the broadest united front with the ALP rank and file and also with those ALP leaders who fight for a progressive policy for the Labour movement.'[16]

From 1951 CPA unionists pursued a strategy of 'unity tickets' in union elections on the basis of whatever lowest common denominator could be agreed to with the ALP.[17] Even though the ALP hierarchy sought to ban such 'unity tickets', it was not successful in stamping them out and by 1958 a series of electoral successes achieved by 'unity ticket' methods had allowed the CPA to make up much of the ground that it had lost in union elections in the late 1940s and early 1950s.

The party's success in winning leadership positions was not, however, matched by a flourishing base of supporters in the factories, mines and waterfront. It was rather the opposite. Party activists were knocked about by the general rightward shift in society in the 1950s and found it difficult to find an audience for socialist politics. The CPA could have sought to retreat in good order but was incapable of doing so, since its leadership still clung to two fatal beliefs – that the party was on the verge of a breakthrough to mass membership and that the economic collapse predicted annually since 1945 was just around the corner. Party loyalists were further stunned in 1956 by the Soviet Premier Nikita Khrushchev's revelations about the Stalinist regime in the Soviet Union and the subsequent Soviet invasion of Hungary. Many members had held on through the hard times of the 1950s secure in the belief that, if things were tough in Australia, at least communists were making ground on a world scale. For many, the Khrushchev revelations knocked away this last item of faith and seemed to suggest that any project for radical change could only end up with disastrous results.[18] The party had declined from 16 000 shortly after the war to 8000 by 1955. Following the events of 1956, membership shrank to just 6000.

With the CPA militants increasingly thin on the ground in the work-shops and with communist politics increasingly sidelined in the conservative political climate of the 1950s and early 1960s, the party's role in the unions became increasingly bureaucratic, its members holding high office but with few party members at the grassroots to sustain it. Far from retreating from the bureaucratic methods revealed in the coal miners' strike, the party went on to build up a cult of leadership involving its senior union leaders, including Ernie Thornton (until his resignation in 1950), Jim Healy and E.V. Elliott. The CPA's bureaucratic modus operandi, its cult of leadership, its desire to accommodate to mainstream ALP union leaders and the decay of its factory cells, together with the tendency inherent in holding union leadership positions towards industrial caution, all came together to foster a conservative practice on the part of the CPA union leaders.[19]

Far from fomenting constant strikes in the 1950s through to the mid 1960s, the practice of left-wing union leaders was not fundamentally dissimilar to that of the moderate union leaders in this period. Both utilised strikes and arbitration to pursue their interests – the left leaders with a bias to the former and the conservative leaders to the latter – but there was no *qualitative* distinction between the two. Both were committed to playing within the 'rules of the game'. For example, the industrial strategy pursued by the Engineers in the late 1940s remained the same, regardless of whether the CPA or the Groupers had temporary majorities on the Commonwealth Council.[20] The CPA officials, as much as the conservative union leaders, worked within the parameters of the arbitration system most of the time, but were also prepared to use the strike weapon, particularly when under pressure from rank-and-file members, to win gains. When action by members threatened to bring on Court-imposed fines against the AEU, however, the CPA and the Grouper leaders alike ordered the workers back to work.[21]

Just as there were industrially militant unions with politically moderate union leaders, so there were industrially quiescent unions with left-wing leaders. The New South Wales Teachers' Federation is one such case. Led by prominent CPA member Sam Lewis from 1946 to 1967 (with brief interludes), the Federation relied mostly on lobbying government ministers and appearances before the Teachers' Tribunal, and did not mount a state-wide strike until 1968. Likewise, the Miscellaneous Workers' Union (MWU), led by the left-wing Labor figure and ally of the CPA, Arthur Gietzelt, rarely struck.

A split in the CPA in 1963, which led to the formation of the CPA(M-L) – the Communist Party of Australia (Marxist-Leninist), often referred to as 'Maoists' – did not fundamentally change the situation. Several union leaders who were to play important roles in the upsurge of unionism in the late 1960s, including the Tramways Union's Clarrie O'Shea, the Waterside Workers' Ted Bull and the Builders' Labourers' Norm Gallagher, joined the CPA(M-L). Although the CPA leaders espoused more radical rhetoric and condemned the CPA union leaders as 'reformists', their practice followed within the same broad parameters.

The ideology of the leaders was by no means irrelevant in determining their actions, but the dominant factor was the relative pressure from employers, tribunals, courts and governments to discipline rank-and-file workers on the one hand and, on the other, from the members themselves.

It is important to draw a distinction between the CPA union leaders and CPA organisers and workplace activists. The organisers and activists were in much closer contact with rank-and-file workers and less subject to the conservative influences of holding office. Although making few inroads in terms of building party membership, workplace CPA activists played an important role in rebuilding workplace organisation. In the New South Wales power industry, for example, CPA members worked alongside left-wing ALP members and other workers with mainstream Labor sympathies to establish a network of workplace committees known as the Electricity Commission Combined Union Delegates Organisation (ECCUDO), covering 32 power stations.[22] The same array of forces was responsible for building activism among rank-and-file workers on the waterfront, in the construction industry among tradesmen and labourers, and in the metal trades.

The working-class revival of the 1960s

With the defeat of the postwar union upsurge and the general shift to the right in Australian society in the 1950s, the strike rate declined. However, the economic boom played a contradictory role. On the one hand it contributed to quiescence in the working class. On the other, it also produced conditions that bred frustration alongside an enhanced capacity to resist. From the early 1960s, the strike rate began to revive as the capacity to resist came to the forefront (see Figure 1.1).

The restructuring of the working class

The long economic boom contributed to a significant restructuring of the Australian working class. A central role in the economic growth of this period was played by the manufacturing industry, encouraged first by wartime production and then by major infrastructure projects, including the Snowy Mountains Hydro-Electric Scheme, the mechanisation of agriculture, and rising consumer demand for household goods and transportation. Manufacturing output and capital investment rose at an annual rate of 6 per cent in the 1950s, and output per worker by nearly 4 per cent.

The expansion of manufacturing brought a growth in mass production, hitherto limited mostly to the clothing, textile and boot industries, the Port Kembla steelworks and some big meatworks. The vehicle industry was exemplary, with General Motors-Holden's (GMH), Ford and Chrysler establishing large factories that employed thousands of workers in Sydney, Melbourne and Adelaide. The growth of vehicle manufacture was a powerful stimulus for basic iron, steel and foundry products, aluminium and plastics, textiles and electrical products. Factory employment grew by one-third between 1953–54 and 1966–67 to 1.3 million.[23] The metal and engineering industry accounted for two-thirds of this increase, and employment in the vehicles and electrical goods sectors nearly doubled.[24] Employment in chemicals and oil refining also rose strongly, as it also did in power generation, where the old, small metropolitan power stations were shut down in favour of large stations situated next to the coalfields. Other areas of blue-collar work saw a similar process of concentration. Mail sorting was centralised in large metropolitan sorting centres such as the Sydney Mail Exchange in Redfern. City centre building sites brought together thousands of construction workers using new technology to erect high-rise office buildings.

There were of course countervailing tendencies. Restructuring did not just expand the workforce in some areas but also cut it in others, significant examples being in coal mining and on the waterfront, where mechanisation, containerisation and consolidation led to sharp declines in the workforce. Nonetheless, it did not weaken the strategic power of unions in these sectors. If anything, it increased it as it gave workers control over expensive capital equipment.

The increase in white-collar workplaces was even more rapid. Some of this growth was in areas directly ancillary to manufacturing, with large increases in administrative, scientific, technical, professional and managerial employment. The rise of large enterprises also necessitated an enhanced financial sector, and as regional banks gradually merged or were taken over, employment in the already large banks grew especially quickly. Expanded support industries were needed to educate and care for workers and their families, with the result that employment in health and in education grew. Finally, as state and federal governments expanded their functions to cater for the increasingly diverse and sophisticated economy, public service employment also rose.

White-collar workers were increasingly drawn out of small workplaces employing half-a-dozen or fewer staff into larger workplaces employing hundreds, if not thousands. Banks and public services moved into office blocks that concentrated white-collar workers in unprecedented numbers. Supermarkets replaced corner stores. Single-teacher schools in country and regional areas were shut down and the teaching workforce shifted into metropolitan schools with dozens or hundreds of staff and thousands of students.

The familial and patriarchal relations common in small business gave way to bureaucratic management. For many white-collar employees the boss was now a distant figure and workers were now more open to taking collective action to improve their lot. The Australian Council of Salaried and Professional Associations (ACSPA), which was founded in 1956, reflected this trend, and from the early 1960s began to cooperate with the ACTU in industrial campaigns. In 1965 the Victorian Secondary Teachers' Association (VSTA) held a stop-work meeting to discuss dissatisfaction with the Teachers' Tribunal and in 1967 the Australian Insurance Staffs' Federation (AISF) began to actively canvass striking.

Labour shortages during the postwar boom drew hundreds of thousands of women into the paid workforce. The proportion of women in paid employment doubled from 20 per cent at the end of World War II to more than 40 per cent by the end of the 1960s.[25] The proportion of married women in paid work rose from 3 per cent in 1947 to 16 per cent in 1966. Women flocked to office jobs, but usually only into the most junior positions. The number of female typists, secretaries and stenographers increased from 71 000 to 163 000 between 1947 and 1966.[26] The booming retail sector also drew in tens of thousands of women workers, as did domestic work.

A further structural factor shaping the working class was the relative decline of the skilled trades in manufacturing enterprises under the impact of automation and standardisation. For example, between 1947 and 1966 the number of fitters and turners rose from 50 000 to just over 80 000, a jump of 62 per cent. However, the number of process workers and machinists rose over the same period by 265 per cent from just under 25 000 to 90 000.[27] Technological change also had an impact in the building and construction industry. The increased use of concrete put builders' labourers in a powerful position, as whoever controlled the concrete pours controlled the building sites. High-rise buildings also put crane drivers, scaffolders and riggers in a strong position to halt projects. As a result of these changes the power of the Builders Labourers' Federation (BLF) was enhanced.

As workers were drawn into mass production many grievances presented themselves. The vehicle assembly plant provides some insights into the problems encountered by many factory labourers. One of the most common complaints was the relentless machine pacing of work. The VBEF complained about 'excessive time studies which have led to ever-increasing speed-up methods, resulting in piece work for award rates of pay' and noted that 'intensified introduction of mechanisation and automation is developing many operations into soul-destroying occupations performed at ever increasing speeds.'[28] Workers were not able to take breaks from the assembly line without management approval, forcing workers at the Ford Broadmeadows (Victoria) plant, for example, to urinate into milk bottles. Tea breaks were a rarity in the industry until the 1960s, which meant that workers had to drink their tea while working.

An attendance and merit bonus system was introduced at Ford and these bonuses presented a significant component of the vehicle workers' wage. They were, however, subject to a wide range of penalties. Workers could lose a large percentage of the attendance bonus if they were away from work or were late to clock on without prior approval. The bonus scheme, furthermore, gave foremen opportunities for blatant favouritism, incidents of which entered industry folklore.[29] Bullying foremen were a particular cause of worker dissatisfaction. According to one long-serving AEU tradesman at the Ford Broadmeadows plant, Sol Marks, the foremen could be divided into three categories: 'the bastards, the bastardised, and those who try and stay decent, with the last very much a minority'.[30]

The 1975 Jackson Committee Report into the manufacturing industry, commissioned by the Whitlam Government in response to a wave of strikes among migrant workers in the early 1970s, described the social organisation of the average factory as 'stratified, authoritarian and undemocratic'.[31] It reported that many workers were dissatisfied with jobs that offered them little personal satisfaction or achievement.[32] Workers who complained usually received little sympathy from managers.

A further factor that created grievances was the oppression that faced workers from non-English-speaking backgrounds, who arrived in large numbers in response to the shortage of labour. Between 1947 and 1972, 2.3 million migrants arrived in Australia.[33] Forty-four per cent, just shy of one million, were from British or Irish backgrounds, but over time the proportion from non-English-speaking backgrounds began to rise significantly.[34] Initially the main source of the latter was northern and central Europe, but this changed in the 1960s with the rapid influx of migrants from southern Europe and the Middle East. By 1970, 10 per cent of the population were first-generation migrants from 'other European' backgrounds, equal to the share born in the UK and Ireland.[35]

One contemporary described the migrant workforce as a 'super-exploited section of the proletariat'[36] and the Jackson Committee Report painted a grim picture of the lives of migrant workers.[37] Most male migrants worked in the most dangerous and dirty jobs in heavy manufacturing, on construction sites, the railways and road gangs, in the abattoirs, cement factories and power stations, and down the mines. Many females worked in light industry, in the clothing, textile and boot industries and in food processing. In 1966 one-half of all female workers from southern Europe were employed in process work, compared to only 9 per cent of Australian-born women.[38]

Migrant workers also received little help from their unions. Few union officials had any competency in a second language and unions failed to provide translations of their written materials.[39] Migrants were also significantly under-represented in steward positions. In 1958 the Victorian branch of the VBEF, for example, had 14 000 members, of whom 2240 were Italian and 1960 Greek, but there were only one Italian and five Greeks in shop steward positions.[40]

The rapidly growing white-collar workforce was experiencing its own problems. White-collar workers were increasingly subject to mechanisation, routinisation of the job, a more fragmented division of labour and deskilling, the loss of job autonomy, and a reduction of wages relative to those of blue-collar workers. Furthermore, white-collar and blue-collar employees did not live in separate universes: many in the new generation of white-collar workers came from blue-collar families.

A pick-up in strikes

The booming economy did not just help to restructure the Australian working class and subject it to increasingly alienated working conditions; it also enhanced the capacity of workers to resist. By the early 1960s a new generation had emerged who had not known mass unemployment, wartime austerity or industrial defeats and who were determined to win more of the benefits of the boom. They took full employment and labour shortages as a given. Wages were rising but workers' expectations were rising still faster. In the new economic circumstances, short strikes, or even just the threat of one, were often enough to win a pay rise from employers who were in most cases keen to keep production going.

The year 1959 marked the nadir of strike activity in the postwar years. Thereafter the strike rate began to pick up, albeit slowly and hesitantly at first as workers took direct action to demand wage rises, with the metal trades to the fore. If wages were often the catalyst for strikes, they were not the only factor. One of the most significant struggles in the early 1960s concerned the demand for three weeks' paid annual leave.[41] A claim was lodged by the ACTU with the Arbitration Commission but the left unions were not prepared to leave it at that – they understood that their claim was far more likely to be successful if the Commission was put under pressure by strikes. Four thousand New South Wales union delegates from manufacturing unions met in Sydney in late 1962 and called for a 24-hour strike. When hearings began before the Arbitration Commission in February 1963, the Melbourne Trades Hall organised a mass meeting of 3000 delegates from worksites across the city. Several more were to follow over the next 15 months. In winter 1963 there were mass rallies of building industry workers. Two thousand building workers met at the Melbourne Town Hall in February 1964 and three thousand delegates met at the Sydney Town Hall a month later. Melbourne saw a further sizeable rally in April 1964. The result was a resounding victory: bending to the wave of strikes, the Commission handed down an extra week's leave, starting in November 1964.

Alarmed employers increasingly sought to invoke the bans clause to stem the rising tide of strikes and the Industrial Court imposed fines with ever-increasing regularity. In 1962, the Industrial Court imposed fines of £9150, increasing to £12 550 in 1963 and £22 450 in 1964.[42] The left-wing union leaders became increasingly agitated and in April 1964 were only narrowly defeated by the more conservative unions when they tabled a motion at a Federal Unions Conference to strike for 24 hours against the penal powers.

The role of shop committees

Emerging shop committees, comprising delegates from one or several unions, frequently called strikes without first going through the 'proper channels' to resolve disputes. At the Borg Warner plant in Sydney three CPA members of the AEU forged a shop committee of approximately 25 shop stewards, which met weekly in working time and published a regular factory bulletin, *Gear Talk*.[43] The shop committee organised regular strikes, controlled the allocation of bonuses, and monitored staffing levels. The company responded by frequent recourse to the Industrial Court, which was effective in the short term at halting disputes but did not prevent them from constantly recurring.

Shop committees such as those at Borg Warner aroused trenchant opposition from the moderate and right-wing union leaders. In 1961 the right used its majority on the ACTU executive and the floor of the ACTU Congress to push through measures to curb them, including a Charter for Shop Committees that sought to sharply circumscribe their operations. In March 1962, and again in December 1963, the ACTU executive complained that shop committees were usurping the role of the ACTU and the labor councils.[44]

The union leaders were joined in their concerns by employers and the tribunals. In November 1962, the Australian Metal Industries Association (AMIA) complained that 'Shop committees have, in a high proportion of cases, been responsible for creating unrest and extending disputes beyond the area to which they might properly be confined.'[45] The AMIA advised its members that shop committees were not recognised by law and played no part in the arbitration system. They exercised power without responsibility, trespassed into award matters that were properly the business of the tribunals, and were 'an open invitation for the skilled agitator'.[46] Shop committees should on no account be given official recognition or on-site facilities.[47]

Likewise, Commissioner Winter described the situation in which area committees organised strikes in defiance of union leaders as 'industrial anarchy'. The Commissioner, himself a former union secretary, lamented 'the efforts of trade unions which are actively struggling in the interests of their members being aborted by the action of irresponsible and inflammatory members.'[48]

The constraints on the shop committees appeared to have little immediate effect. In 1964 the number of unauthorised strikes began to increase, spearheaded in many cases by shop committees. In February 1964 the Victorian branch leadership of the VBEF noted 'the persistent refusal of sections of members at the Ford Broadmeadows plant to acknowledge the authority and constitution of our organisation' and warned that 'further activities of this nature will be dealt with in accordance with the disciplinary authority vested in this executive.'[49] A strike in April 1964 by postal workers over rosters at the Sydney Mail Exchange also challenged the authority of the branch officials, requiring ACTU president Albert Monk's personal intervention to bring the strike to an end.[50]

In winter 1964, pressure continued to build. Metal trades shop committees led strikes over wages and annual leave at Commonwealth Defence plants at Maribyrnong and Williamstown in Melbourne and at the Garden Island naval dockyards in Sydney. In August, workers at the Government Aircraft Factory walked off the job in pursuit of greater rights for job delegates.[51] The ACTU executive again weighed in, demanding adherence to the Charter of Shop Committees.[52] The problem that the ACTU faced was explained by Kevin Hince:

> The steward and in particular the committees represent alternative centres of allegiance and alternative centres of power and authority. This power is derived from a close contact with the worker at the workshop level, and committees are in strong positions to assess the feelings and opinions of the rank and file, and they are also in a strong position to influence and shape these opinions.[53]

In contrast to the right-wing leaders, the left-wing union leaders were broadly supportive of the shop committees. They frequently criticised the ACTU's attempts to rein in the committees and argued that the committees were a natural response by workers to the restraints of arbitration and the tight job market. Metal trades union organisers encouraged their formation and assisted them where they could.

Nonetheless, at the same time, the left-wing union leaders were anxious lest the activities of the shop committees should lead to escalating fines on the unions, and they were keen not to encourage outright defiance of the ACTU.[54] In the name of 'the general unity of the trade union movement', the strategy of the left-wing leaders was to avoid a direct confrontation with the Government and the Industrial Court over the penal powers until the right-wing union leaders could be persuaded to agree to action.[55] They held back the militant minority of unions that were prepared to fight and that had the strategic power to win. This strategy undermined action by rank-and-file workers that could have broken the stranglehold of the right-wing unions. This was demonstrated in two important disputes in late 1964, at GMH in Melbourne and at the Mount Isa copper mines.

The contradictory role of the left-wing leaders

The four-week strike at GMH in October 1964 was a landmark in postwar Australian unionism, partly because of its size but also because it represented a trial of strength between the emerging shop committees and the ACTU.[56] The background to the strike was a growing combativeness among production workers in the vehicle industry, evident in strikes at GMH Pagewood and Ford Broadmeadows in 1962 and 1963.

In July 1964 the VBEF submitted a claim on behalf of the 600 foundry workers at Fisherman's Bend in Melbourne for a £3 increase. The company refused, and the Arbitration Commission was notified of a dispute on 18 September. The five unions covering GMH workers responded to management intransigence by extending the claim for a £3 increase to cover all GMH employees. In the last week of September, workers at Fisherman's Bend walked out and before long the dispute spread to other plants. The ACTU convened a disputes committee in Melbourne with 34 representatives from the five unions and the ACTU took charge.

On 5 October a tumultuous mass meeting of 5000 GMH workers in Melbourne voted to strike indefinitely. They were joined shortly afterwards by GMH workers in South Australia, 5000 of whom voted to strike at the biggest industrial meeting ever held in that state. The strike lasted until 30 October and involved 16 000 workers from Melbourne and Adelaide.

Not trusting the leaders of the VBEF and the ACTU, the workers, with the assistance of the Victorian branch of the AEU, established a large-scale combined unions strike committee for the first time in the history of the vehicle industry. The strike committee became the focus for activism around Melbourne and drew dozens of enthusiastic workers into union activity for the first time. Meetings of the strike committee attracted up to 200 workers, many of them Greek and Italian. A core of 30 volunteered their services for committee work.

The GMH strike was a rallying point for left unions. In Victoria they helped raise funds by levying their members and by the end of the strike £86 500 had been collected.[57] The left unions also organised action in support of the GMH workers, with the Melbourne branch of the WWF and the South Australian branch of the ARU (both led by the CPA) organising black bans of GMH goods.

The company quickly appealed to the Commission to invoke the bans clause in the award. On 9 October the Industrial Court ordered the five unions to end the strike. They refused and on 16 October each of them was fined £500 for contempt of court. Further fines were levied a few days later. Management stood down 1800 workers at GMH plants in Brisbane and Sydney. On 20 October mass meetings voted to continue the strike, no concessions having been made by management.

Faced with mass enthusiasm for the strike and anxious to impress upon management the power that they could bring to bear, the ACTU and VBEF executives at first publicly supported the strike. Privately they were dismayed at the turn of events, in particular the activities of the strike committee. They quarantined the strike to Melbourne and Adelaide, prevented the formation of a strike committee in Adelaide, and sought to bring the dispute to an end at the earliest opportunity. In late October, the ACTU disputes committee called on GMH workers to return to work on what were essentially the company's terms. In making this call, however, it had to contend with the Melbourne strike committee, which was adamantly opposed to the company's offer. Such was the strike committee's authority among the Melbourne GMH workers that the ACTU would almost certainly have been defeated in an open vote. The ACTU therefore organised a combined unions mass meeting in Melbourne at which ACTU president Albert Monk was the only speaker. Monk urged the workers to return to work and await further negotiations. The workers were warned that if they rejected the ACTU's recommendation they would be abandoned by the peak council. The workforce was then directed to participate in a secret ballot to decide on the ACTU's recommendation.

Although they had opposed the recommendation to return to work and were against secret ballots in principle, the left-wing union leaders buckled in the name of 'unity' with the right. They failed to support the strike committee in defiance of the ACTU, fearing a breach among the union leaders. The GMH activists were isolated. Fearful of the consequences of continuing the strike, and abandoned by the leaders that they trusted, the GMH workers voted to return to work, albeit with one-third of the Melbourne workforce registering its opposition.

The return to work and resumption of negotiations took the pressure off GMH management and the Arbitration Commission. The company agreed to pay 600 foundry workers at the centre of the dispute wage increases ranging from 10 to 30 shillings, but the rest of the GMH work-force had to wait as their claim was taken to the Commission. Eighteen months of hearings followed, ending in complete rejection of the claim in 1966.

The defeat was a major setback for rank-and-file trade unionism. Thousands of workers had struck for four weeks with no reward, and GMH had secured large fines against the five unions involved. The confidence of the militants was shattered. Theo Zianas, an AEU tradesman active on the strike committee, said later:

> The defeat was serious . . . We lost faith in our power until 1967–68 . . . We didn't have the guts to make any big claims on the company because of our big loss in '64.[58]

The defeat had national consequences for union activism more generally. Strike days in the metal industry had peaked at 376 500 in 1964. In 1965, the rate fell by two-thirds to only 122 600.[59] Nonetheless, although it was a clear defeat, the militancy of the GMH workers and the preparedness of migrant workers to strike, even in the face of every obstacle put in their way by the ACTU and the tribunals, was a sign of things to come.

The other significant episode of worker activism in 1964 occurred thousands of miles away in Queensland at the Mount Isa copper mines. Starting in February, Mount Isa Mines (MIM) workers, members of the AWU, had been in frequent dispute with the company over everything from conditions of work to wages, supervisory harassment and the state of the amenities block.[60] In August the MIM workers, who had been working on a system of piece rates, demanded a pay rise, which the company refused. The workers then opted to revert to award conditions, which resulted in a big drop in pay but an even larger drop in production – effectively a form of go-slow. This went on for several weeks, at which point the company simply locked the 2700 workers out and sacked their elected representative, Pat Mackie. The workers adopted a six-point list of demands, including increases in pay and the reinstatement of Mackie.

The Nicklin Country Party State Government gave MIM every assistance, including the despatch of hundreds of police, the declaration of a state of emergency in December, and regular attempts to portray the dispute as a communist plot. This much might have been expected from a conservative government. In addition, however, the leadership of the workers' own union sought to undermine it from the first day. The AWU leaders joined the mass media in red-baiting the leading activists, expelled Mackie from the union and made it plain that they would not accept him back under any circumstances. The State Labor Opposition was totally ineffectual.

Betrayed by their own leaders, Mackie and his comrades formed the Mount Isa branch of the Council for Membership Control of the AWU (CMC), which served as the local organising body. The AWU refused to allow any of the CMC members to represent the union in discussions with the management. Undeterred, the Council quickly set to work, organis-ing relief for miners and their families, a Women's Auxiliary, and – when the company reopened the gates in February inviting workers to return on the company's terms – picket rosters. As at GMH, the organisation brought workers together across dozens of different nationalities. Regular mass meetings of 1000 to 1500 workers made the decisions and the Council organised a public meeting that attracted 3500 townsfolk. After a month the company gave ground on the pay demand and offered workers a £3 pay increase on Christmas Eve. However, this was not enough. The issue in dispute had now moved on from the initial demand for a pay rise. The workers now demanded as a condition of a return to work the reinstatement of Pat Mackie and a total overhaul of the AWU – including the right to select their own leaders. It was now a fight for democracy within the union.

The action of the MIM workers inspired support from around the coun-try, with Broken Hill workers levying themselves two pounds a week to help relieve hardship. The left unions, in particular the WWF, the Seamen's Union, the building and metal trades unions and, eventually, the ACTU took up the cause and donated thousands of pounds over the course of the dispute. When the Nicklin Government threatened a state of emergency, the

Queensland Labor Council (led by the CPA's Alex McDonald) announced plans for a one-day state-wide general strike, leading the Government to drop its threat after only five days.

Despite the enormous courage of the MIM workers, they were isolated by the AWU hierarchy. As the weeks wore on, the number of miners trickling back to work increased and new legislation and heavy policing prevented effective picketing at the mine site. Only one thing could have saved the Mount Isa workers – bans on the transportation of copper by the waterside workers and the railway workers. Mackie sent telegrams to leaders of the AEU, the WWF and the NSW South Coast Labor Council seeking concrete solidarity.

At this point, the limits of the left-wing union leaders became apparent. They had organised substantial financial relief and a speaking tour for Mackie in Melbourne and Sydney. They had sent protest letters galore to the Queensland State Government, but when it came to banning the movement of copper, and thereby elevating the dispute to a national level, the left-wing union leaders went to water. The Queensland Labor Council advised against a ban on the grounds that it meant a confrontation with the Menzies Government and the ACTU could not be expected to lead such a fight. Instead, it proposed only that the Mount Isa workers seek satisfaction from a compulsory conference with the Industrial Commission. Initial plans for a state-wide strike against Nicklin's new picketing provisions were allowed to die. To his telegrams Mackie received only one reply. The Victorian secretary of the WWF had passed on the request to the union's national secretary, Charlie Fitzgibbon, who advised the Mount Isa workers that he was not willing to take any action unless endorsed by the leaders of the Queensland Labor Council.

The strikers could not continue the strike on their own and reluctantly accepted the company's terms – an offer of work for all tradesmen who had been locked out, but work only for those AWU members whom the company selected. Neither Mackie nor any of the other 96 AWU militants blacklisted by the company would find work in the mine again. Nonetheless, the strike forced a change of practice by the company management towards the workers. It was not just higher wages but also a more respectful treatment of the workforce. The workers won the right to negotiate locally over wages and the CMC was able to continue functioning.

The strike upswing continues despite defeats

GMH and Mount Isa were both needless defeats, given the way that the tide was beginning to flow in the working class. If the left union officials had been prepared to organise strike action in support of the workers, both of the disputes could have been won. However, the leaders of the left-wing unions were only prepared to offer the workers support up to a point and shied away from the kind of fight that was necessary if they were to win. At this stage they were not prepared to lead a struggle against the penal powers or directly challenge the authority of the ACTU. They therefore put off for several more years the ultimate destruction of the penal powers.

Nonetheless, these defeats did not halt the slow pick-up in union militancy in the mid 1960s. No upswing in strikes is likely to proceed evenly and without setbacks. Some groups of workers are always ready to move forward and challenge employers before the majority of workers are prepared to act, but this is part of the process of a general advance. Moreover, defeats, by teaching workers important lessons about the need for more determined action and by testing leaders, can actually pave the way for a resumption of the upswing in the near future.

Strike *days* dropped after 1964, but the *number* of strikes remained around 1300 each year, the highest level for a decade. What is more, strikers were increasingly taking action without waiting for their leaders. Employers complained:

> There have been situations where industrial agitation generated solely by shop stewards has reached a point where the union organisers when called in found a situation that they were unable to control.[61]

Most strikes were over in a day or two with a quick wage rise, but in an increasing number of cases strikes were being met by employer recourse to the bans clauses.

The ACTU made it clear that, while it decried the excessive use of the bans clauses, it had no intention of challenging them. It sought instead to prevent workers from organising strikes. The 1965 ACTU Congress demanded that any strike likely to attract fines be brought under the control of the ACTU and the federal executive of the union concerned.[62] In 1966 the Melbourne Trades Hall took charge of a strike by State Electricity Commission workers in the Latrobe Valley against the wishes of the workers. George Wragg, secretary of the Gippsland Labor Council, complained that the Melbourne Trades Hall's action was 'a betrayal of the very fundamentals upon which trade unionism was built'.[63] More and more, the use of the bans clauses was raising the question not just of judicial and government repression but also of democracy and worker control within the unions themselves.

The Cold War political environment that had suffocated left-wing political action on the part of unions in the 1950s was beginning to wane by the mid 1960s. Waterside workers were taking action to protest against apartheid in South Africa, but the crucial issue that fired up workers' interest in politics was the issue of conscription and Vietnam. The decision in November 1964 by the Menzies Government to introduce conscription and in April 1965 to send a battalion of combat troops to fight in Vietnam was a watershed in Australian politics.[64] Maritime unions in particular took up the challenge. In 1965 the Sydney branch of the WWF held up 37 ships in Sydney Harbour with a 24-hour strike in protest against military intervention in Vietnam. Two thousand five hundred wharfies also walked off the job in Melbourne. In May 1965, 500 seamen, waterside workers and ships' painters picketed the US Consulate in Brisbane.

The maritime unions then sought to directly impede the movement of munitions. In May 1966, the Federal Government chartered the merchant ship *Boonaroo* to carry stores and equipment to Vietnam. The SUA refused to crew it or any other ship carrying supplies to aid the war effort. However, the union faced a wall of hostility from other waterfront unions and the ACTU. Albert Monk had ruled in 1965 that the ACTU would not support any action that jeopardised the flow of goods or troops to Vietnam. The SUA was forced to back down.

In November 1966, Labor went to the federal election campaigning against conscription and Australian involvement in the war but was heavily defeated. The union campaign against the war would now focus on direct action in the workplace and on the streets. In February 1967, when Melbourne seamen walked off the *Boonaroo*, which was again laden with war supplies, they resisted pressure from the ACTU to lift their action and the Government was forced to use the Navy to crew it. The seamen imposed bans on the *Jeparit* in the following month for the same reasons. At successive stop-work meetings SUA members expressed overwhelming support for the black-banning of merchant ships carrying munitions to Vietnam.

In September 1967 the seamen were joined by 2600 waterside workers, who walked off ships in Sydney in support of a worker suspended for refusing to load bombs on the *Jeparit*. Action by the maritime unions emboldened others. In January 1967 six Queensland unions imposed bans on aircraft used by visiting South Vietnamese premier Air Vice-Marshal Ky. This also meshed with an increasingly radical anti-war movement on the campuses.

The Victorian rebel unions

If left union leaders were not prepared for an industrial confrontation with the ACTU in the early 1960s, they came under increasing pressure to take a stand by 1967. They were under pressure from two directions – from workers prepared to strike for wage increases and from employers ever more eager to invoke the penal powers. The battle between left and right in Victoria came to a climax with a split in the Melbourne Trades Hall. Following the death of Vic Stout in 1964, the Trades Hall leadership had become more right-wing. Secretary Mick Jordan and his assistant Ken Stone maintained control through a voting system heavily weighted towards the smaller, usually more industrially passive, unions. The larger industrial unions complained bitterly that the small unions were the tail wagging the dog and demanded fairer representation and the election of an executive on the basis of industry groups of unions.

The issue came to a head in 1967 around the question of financing the activities of the Council. Faced with escalating debts, the Trades Hall executive doubled per capita affiliation fees.[65] The larger unions refused to pay the higher levy, arguing that, since voting power on the Council was not determined on a per capita basis, neither should the levy be. The executive suspended four left-wing metal unions from the Council, but these suspensions were followed by the suspension of a further 23.

The result was the emergence of the 27 'rebel unions' as an alternative coordinating bloc in the Victorian trade union movement. While these unions had not sought exclusion, they were now able to pursue militant industrial and political strategies without the dead weight of the multiple smaller unions. The 27 rebel unions went on to play a critical role during the union offensive of the late 1960s and early 1970s. They also promoted greater autonomy for the predominantly left-wing regional labor councils, most notably in the Latrobe Valley, the site of major disputes in the following decade.

On the verge of a breakthrough

By the late 1960s, unions were on the cusp of the first major upturn in struggle since the late 1940s. Major changes had taken place in the union movement between the two high points. Nearly two decades of conservative government had created an atmosphere of stultifying conservatism, from which the Labor Party and trade union leaders were not immune. The moderate and right-wing union leaders who dominated the union movement acted as an effective brake on militancy and political action. The CPA, a key player in the immediate postwar period, no longer enjoyed the high level of support and influence it had had during the big strikes of the late 1940s.

At the same time union membership was growing, and the changing composition of the working class meant that militancy and organisation were spreading beyond the traditional industries associated with union action and particularly into white-collar areas. Organisation at the shopfloor level, which would prove crucial in the coming upturn, had been steadily built, and in the context of relatively full employment gains could be made and living standards steadily improved. This contributed to a sense of confidence and preparedness to fight on the part of workers in spite of the conservative political climate.

These contradictory developments were struggling to be contained by the late 1960s and the stage was set for a revival of militancy. And while wage rises were the crucial issue around which workers fought during the last upsurge in the 1940s, defeating anti-union laws and mobilising around political issues would underpin many of the battles of the late 1960s and early 1970s. The Menzies era thus gave way to a period of radicalism and rank-and-file activity that even the union leaders proved powerless to control.

Part I

THE FLOOD TIDE, 1968–74

Chapter Two

THE UNION UPSURGE, 1968–74

The breakthrough, 1968–69

By the end of 1967 the situation was ripe for a breakthrough. The employers were using the penal powers to prevent workers from striking to take advantage of the labour shortages and a booming economy. The ACTU had lobbied the Coalition Government for years to amend the penal powers in some way, but to no avail. The penal powers would have to be broken by a full-scale confrontation. The Transport Workers' Union had shown the way when in 1963 it had threatened a national strike by its 60 000 members, resulting in the removal of the bans clause from its award.[1] The so-called 'absorption decision' of the Arbitration Commission started a series of events that were to culminate in such a confrontation on a national scale.[2]

In December 1967, the Full Bench of the Arbitration Commission granted metal tradesmen a $7.40 wage increase following a 'work value' inquiry. However, it also advised employers that they were free to offset ('absorb') this increase against existing over-award payments that were almost exactly equivalent to the work value increase. Further, there was to be no increase for tradesmen's assistants. The work value case had resulted in precisely nothing for the workforce. The metal trades unions did not take this lying down. Strikes in the metal and engineering industry were already on the increase and in 1967 the sector accounted for more than one-third of all strike days. The workers were already primed for action and the Full Bench decision was the spark.

The first six weeks of 1968 witnessed an explosion of 400 strikes in the metal industry. The high point was a 24-hour stoppage on 6 February 1968, involving 180 000 workers. On 23 February, 1300 New South Wales union delegates vented their anger at a mass meeting in Sydney Town Hall. Arbitration Judge Dunphy called it an 'unprecedented situation':

> Never before in my memory have employers more reason to fear industrial disruption on a grand scale than is now in evidence before us in NSW.[3]

Some companies acceded immediately to union pressure and paid the $7.40 on top of existing over-awards. Others stood firm and invoked the bans clause. Through the course of 1967, 50 fines had been imposed on unions. In the first quarter of 1968, the number jumped to 122. The metal unions were fined $58 000 plus $15 000 in costs.[4]

Shop committees were the engine for the campaign. Short rolling stoppages involved first one group of workers, then another, in an attempt to both disrupt production and foil employers' ability to make use of the bans clause. Those workers not taking action raised funds to compensate those who lost pay, and metalworkers toured worksites raising funds at factory gate meetings.[5] Within 12 months, every major workshop in New South Wales had taken strike action. According to Jim Baird from the Boilermakers' union, metalworkers were ringing their organisers complaining: 'It's our bloody turn, why aren't we getting a turn?'[6] No leader in the metal unions could be seen to oppose the strikes. Jim Baird commented: 'The union leaders were placed in a position where elections were taking place and they had to be on side, otherwise they wouldn't have got elected again.'[7] Faced with this tide of defiance, the Arbitration Commission capitulated. It withdrew absorption and ordered that 70 per cent of the work value increase be paid immediately and the remainder in August.[8]

Other unions, including building and construction, the railways and wharfies, took confidence from the metal trades victory and struck for similar pay rises.[9] A new-found preparedness to strike to force concessions from the Commission engulfed unions. Employers took fright at the situation, with the Metal Trades Employers' Association commenting in March 1969 that:

> People can be forgiven for gaining the impression that the Commission considers strike action to be no longer inconsistent with compulsory arbitration, and that it may even be acceptable conduct.[10]

Perhaps the most important effect of the metalworkers' victory, however, was that it heightened working-class anger at the penal powers and hastened their destruction. For some years there had been increasing demands that the ACTU fight the penal powers by action rather than just by resolutions and deputations. Nonetheless these calls went unheeded and the 1967 ACTU Congress avoided discussing the issue altogether. The ACTU's objection to the escalation of the penal clauses in the 1960s was not an *in principle* objection to the penalties but to the employers' 'capricious use' of them. The ACTU was certainly not organising to break the powers by direct action.

Nor were the left-wing unions, initially. As can be seen in Chapter 1, they were prepared to fight up to a point but backed off rather than defy the ACTU. At the 1964 federal unions conference the left-wing unions had unsuccessfully moved that the ACTU mount a 24-hour general strike against the penal powers. Their motion defeated, the left-wing unions continued to pay the fines even as they escalated dramatically.

With the breakthrough in the absorption fight, however, and under pressure from members, the left-wing union leaders began to shift ground. By late 1968 the AEU, the Boilermakers and the Sheet Metal Workers had resolved to pay no more fines. In January 1969 the CPA national committee urged a 'bolder confrontation with the penal powers'. The situation came to a head with the O'Shea dispute of May 1969. Diane Fieldes remarks:

> If the absorption battle opened the door to eliminating the penal powers and reasserting the right to strike, the events surrounding the jailing of Clarrie O'Shea tore it from its hinges.[11]

The Victorian branch of the Australian Council of Tramways Unions, led by the CPA(M-L)'s Clarrie O'Shea, had been subject to increasing fines for taking action in opposition to 'one man operation' of buses. By 1966 the fines were so large that the union decided to pay them off in instalments of $100 per month. For 18 months it was allowed to do this, but the arrival of a new Industrial Registrar, Dr Ian Sharp, put an end to this. Sharp demanded that $3000 of the remaining $9000 be paid as a lump sum. The union offered to raise its payments to $200 per month. In response, the Federal Government issued a writ aimed at collecting the entire $9000. On 30 November 1967, the Registrar confiscated the union's bank account and recovered $3741. Early in 1969, the Registrar announced his intention to collect a further $8100. O'Shea was ordered to appear before the Industrial

Court on 18 February to produce the union's books. He refused. In March, the Australian Council of Tramways Unions stated that, if there was any attempt to collect fines from any state branch, all branches must stop work.

O'Shea was then summonsed a second time, to appear on 15 May. The issue was now at a crisis point and the militant union delegates rallied behind O'Shea. Five thousand Melbourne union delegates met at 8.30 a.m. prior to the court hearing and resolved:

> We determine that any attempt to take direct punitive action . . . will be met with an immediate 24-hour stoppage of work by all workers represented at this meeting, and call upon all other workers to stand and defend Unions and what they mean to Australian workers.

The workers marched to the Industrial Court. O'Shea appeared, but refused to produce the union's accounts and was charged with contempt. Justice John Kerr found him guilty and committed him to Pentridge Jail.

The fuse had been lit. The left unions, under pressure from members, had finally cast aside their policy of not taking action unless endorsed by the ACTU. The Victorian rebel unions, in defiance of the Trades Hall which denounced the strike, took action. On 16 May, Victorian unions organised a 24-hour strike. Power was cut for four hours, and all public transport stopped, along with gas and most television. On 20 May a second state-wide 24-hour stoppage took place, with 40 Victorian unions joining in.

The determined response in Victoria sparked stoppages around the country. Hundreds of thousands walked off the job. Workers from unions not endorsing action turned up independently at mass meetings. White-collar unions not then affiliated to the ACTU endorsed the movement to free O'Shea. For the first time in history, all public transport in Sydney stopped. Six thousand waterside workers in New South Wales struck, as did actors, musicians, architects and engineers. The Queensland Trades and Labor Council called a state-wide strike and hundreds rallied up and down coastal industrial towns. In total, one million workers struck or took part in stop-work meetings in the week following the jailing of O'Shea.

The Federal Government was in a jam. There was a real possibility of a national general strike to free O'Shea. Right-wing union leaders were split. Mick Jordan from the Victorian Trades Hall urged workers to take no part in it.[12] The NSW Labor Council and the ACTU simply tailed behind events, powerless to stop the flood of activity. The Government was only saved from a further escalation of the struggle when an anonymous donor, described in the press as Mr Dudley McDougall, a Sydney lottery winner, stepped forward to pay the fines, allowing the release of O'Shea. O'Shea declared defiantly: 'I didn't pay the fine and neither did the Tramways Union. We will never pay the fine.'[13]

Following O'Shea's release, the ACTU executive, which had done nothing in an official capacity during the crisis, met on 21–22 May and determined that, pending discussions with the Federal Government, trade unions were 'advised not to meet any outstanding fines imposed under the Penal Clauses'.[14] The ACTU now endorsed direct bargaining:

> When the unions take action in the field of over-award payments, they are doing no more than to exercise their right to secure what they regard as a fair price for what they have to sell – their labour. This is precisely the right which is allowed to be used by the employers in this country in fixing the prices they consider appropriate for what they have to sell.[15]

Unions maintained the pressure with further strikes. On 26 August 1969, the Federal Government asked employers not to use the penal powers until an alternative could be organised. The impotence of the penal powers was officially recognised when in June 1970 the relevant sections of the Act were amended.[16] Fines were still levied, but no unions paid them, more anonymous donors stepped forward, and the penal powers became a dead letter. The significance of this was made clear by A.E. Woodward QC, chairman of the Stevedoring Commission, who lamented that:

> When the organised trade union movement defies 'the might of the state', and is supported by the alternative government and at least a significant section of public opinion, law and order necessarily take a back seat.[17]

The flood tide gathers force, 1969–74

The defeat of absorption and the penal powers signalled a reinvigoration of union mobilisation. Arbitration was discredited among hundreds of thousands of blue-collar workers and not a few white-collar ones too. Workers had not only won back the right to strike; they had gained the confidence to use it. Arbitration Commission president Richard Kirby stated in his annual report for 1969 that 'The balance of power "in the field" has swung more than ever one way'[18] and one commentator observed that workers had become 'aggressive in their approach and in their demeanour'.[19] Figure 1.1 illustrates the sharp jump in strikes that continued almost uninterrupted for seven years. In 1971, 30 per cent of workers were involved in strike action, compared to an annual average of just 13 per cent in the period 1952–68.[20]

Workers flexed their muscles on a wide range of issues. Strikes over wages reached their highest levels since the war and accounted for three-quarters of all strike days in this period. High inflation internationally fed through to Australia, and workers used direct action to ensure that their standard of living did not suffer. If one group of workers won an increase, others struck to keep up. Workers used direct action to win shorter working hours, with workers in coal mining, the post, and the waterfront winning the 35-hour week by the simple method of working it and demanding full pay.[21] The limitations of arbitration as a method for winning such gains were demonstrated graphically by the contrary experience of the AWU, which applied to the Arbitration Commission for a reduction in the working week for station hands. Its application was bluntly rejected.

In assembly line industries workers took a stand against their appalling working conditions, forcing health and safety onto the union agenda. Workers also struck as a way of asserting their authority over long-resented supervisors and managers. Workers were not afraid to challenge management authority by using dramatic means. In one metal industry plant in 1971, 450 workers formed a human wedge to forcibly 'reinstate' a sacked worker onto the premises.[22]

Ideas of worker control began to win a hearing. Builders' labourers working on the revolving stage section of the Sydney Opera House construction site effectively removed foremen and supervisors from operational control. When ECCUDO, the organisation of shop committees in the NSW power industry, took action in pursuit of a 35-hour week in 1973, delegates elected two of their number to ensure that sufficient power was generated to keep basic industry running to prevent the need for large-scale stand-downs.[23] The Askin Liberal Government responded by choking off supply to industry, thereby bringing about the stand-downs that ECCUDO had sought to avoid. In response, ECCUDO placed advertisements in the newspapers advising workers affected by stand-downs on how to restore the power supply and restart operations. A range of workplaces complied, prompting the state Government to lift power restrictions. The power workers' aim was not to stop the energy supply but to place control over power generation in the hands of the workers.

Other episodes of 'worker control' were more defensive and involved campaigns against redundancies or closures. 'Work-ins' involved employees remaining at the workplace and refusing to accept dismissal. Two of these took place in the coal industry, at South Clifton on the New South Wales south coast in May 1972 and at Nymboida in northern New South Wales in March 1975. The latter action resulted in the mine being bought out by the Miners' Federation.[24] The third work-in took place at Harco Steel in western Sydney in November 1971. The Harco workers occupied and ran their plant for several weeks. They elected their own foremen, worked a 35-hour week and planned their own work schedules.[25]

Rank-and-file workers were driving the agenda, and union leaders who did not keep up were simply bypassed. In August 1969, the Brisbane *Courier-Mail* reported on a strike at the Evans Deakin shipyards that was so tightly organised by the rank and file that one unnamed union official commented:

> The real trouble is rank and file control . . . The campaign is being run by a bunch of stirrers . . . Every time the Metal Trades Federation makes a decision, the rank and file knock it over . . . the matter is getting out of hand.[26]

Latrobe Valley power workers used strong workplace organisation to drive strikes, defying calls for 'discipline' by the Victorian Trades Hall. Their fellow power unionists in New South Wales denounced the leaders of the NSW Labor Council and the ETU, which sought to control their activities, and demanded that ECCUDO delegates be involved in all negotiations with the State Electricity Commission.[27] Plumbers at Sydney's Cockatoo Island naval dockyards kept their strike going for six weeks in 1972, even after disendorsement of the action by their union leaders. VBEF leaders who tried to pacify angry production line workers on strike at GMH Elizabeth in South Australia in 1970 were faced with 'a barrage of grapes, bread, salami, tomatoes and anything else the men could throw'.[28]

Rank-and-file organisation did not worry too much about union demarcations. Shopfloor meetings were often attended by all employees regardless of union affiliation. Plant delegates were elected on a cross-union basis. The result was that workers' loyalty often lay with the work group rather than the official union apparatus. This resulted in a high level of plant solidarity. In some cases, as in the New South Wales power industry, this solidarity extended across many workplaces, creating a strong structure able to withstand ferocious 'red baiting' by both the New South Wales Government and the NSW Labor Council.

The building industry was probably the most radical union arena at this time, especially in Sydney, where the BLF was particularly notable for on-the-job organising and lively participation by members in union affairs. In the 1950s the BLF had been led by right-wing anti-communist union leaders who stifled any hint of militancy. The CPA, which already held the leadership of the BWIU and the Federated Engine Drivers and Firemen's Association (FEDFA), now took on the BLF.[29] Members of the CPA and other non-party militants began to organise on the job for permanency, better amenities, and the right to stop work in wet weather. Their efforts to build a layer of militant site delegates culminated in a successful challenge to the BLF leadership in 1961 by a reform ticket led by Mick McNamara. McNamara was succeeded in 1968 by CPA member Jack Mundey who, together with Joe Owens and Bob Pringle, put together a formidable team.

The time was ripe for change on Sydney's building sites in the early 1970s. Workers were in a strong position to take advantage of the building boom in the CBD. Workers used a series of militant tactics to fight for their demands, including stopping concrete pours and using flying pickets to drive scabs off building sites and knocking down the work that they had erected.[30] By these methods the BLF won some major breakthroughs: big pay rises, employment permanency, the right to elect their own foremen, and some respect at last for labourers who had traditionally been treated as the 'lowest of the low'. The BLF had an admirable record of supporting Aboriginal workers. The New South Wales BLF also challenged sexism in the industry and forced companies to employ women on jobs. The Victorian branch of the union, led by the CPA(M-L)'s Norm Gallagher, was less socially radical but also took a very militant industrial stance.

The New South Wales Builders' Labourers felt that they now had power, and they used this new confidence to further democratise their union. The leadership ensured that members had a real say in the union by organising worksite meetings that discussed not just industrial demands but also ways of opening up the union. Strikes were run by elected committees, with organisers working for strike pay, rather than their union salary, for the duration. The union also adopted a system whereby rank-and-file members came on as full-time officials for periods of three months to a year and then returned to the job. Between 1971 and 1973, 39 workers took up this opportunity.[31]

The industrial authorities were flummoxed by the turn to mass action. A.E. Woodward QC complained in 1970 about the breakdown of what he called 'firm leadership' in the unions, writing that 'One of the biggest dangers in union affairs today is the spread of so-called "participatory democracy" which means, in effect, rule by mass meetings.'[32]

Employers also were alarmed and demanded government action to curb strikes. In 1970 the newly formed Metal Trades Industry Association of Australia (MTIA) announced its determination to take on the unions. It would make blacklists of strikers and seek deregistration of the metal unions. Metal industry employers in Sydney's western suburbs resolved to resist 'all unreasonable demands'. These included those for four weeks' annual leave, sick leave in excess of five days per year, and severance pay.[33] The employers also resolved to cancel the employment continuity of strikers, which jeopardised seniority and annual leave entitlements; to refuse to hire strikers or workers who had been stood down; and to ensure that strikers did not gain admittance to factories for the purpose of collecting funds.[34]

This was the formal policy. The reality was more as described by Chris Burns, industrial relations manager at the Hoover washing machine factory in Ryde, Sydney:

> Senior management said no to everything . . . the men went on the grass . . . we were hit by a two day strike, and then we gave in on every point.[35]

Similarly, the industrial relations manager at GMH Elizabeth, Mike Holland, recalled:

> We had the attitude then that we would do all in our power to keep production going. This gave [AMWU plant convenor] Teddy [Gnatenko] an environment to take up a whole range of issues. It was better to give in to union demands in this situation than to have production disrupted.[36]

Just as the employers had had the upper hand in the 1950s, now the workers were setting the agenda.

A shift to the left

The new union confidence was reflected in and reinforced by political developments. The Vietnam War was central and Melbourne was the storm front. It was not accidental that Melbourne was both the home of the most militant section of the Australian union movement and the site of the largest and most effective section of the anti-war movement. Having seen off the penal powers, Victorian trade unions were now more confident to take political action on other fronts. By early 1969 the broad campaign against the war had gathered pace. There had been violent demonstrations outside the US Consulate in Melbourne in July 1968, university students at Monash were collecting funds for the Vietnamese National Liberation Front, and public opinion was steadily shifting against the war.

Two issues now came to dominate the rebel unions' political agenda: draft resistance and a national Moratorium against the war.[37] Draft resistance was increasingly taken up by the anti-war movement in preference to the more passive tactic of conscientious objection. The latter involved working inside the law; the former was a frontal challenge. Through the course of 1969 the rebel unions campaigned on behalf of John Zarb, a young postal worker who had been jailed for two years for resisting the draft. The Postal Workers' Union held stop-work meetings, other unions mounted protests, and Zarb was released after only 10 months on 'compassionate grounds'.

The rebel unions also supported Laurie Carmichael Jr, another draft resister and son of the AEU branch secretary. In September 1969, following the arrest of Carmichael Sr at a protest outside the Williamstown Court House where his son's case was being heard, 500 workers from the Williamstown Naval Dockyard and 700 meatworkers from Newport stopped work and marched to the court in support of father and son.[38] In the following month, the Boilermakers' union threatened a national strike if its officers were jailed for signing a statement urging draft resistance.[39] In December, a meeting of 300 Melbourne union representatives from 32 unions passed a motion that called on:

> all young workers to refuse to register and refuse to comply with the National Service Act. We encourage those young men already conscripted to refuse to accept orders against their conscience and those in Vietnam to lay down their arms in mutiny against the heinous barbarism perpetrated in our name upon the innocent, aged, men, and women and children.[40]

This call to mutiny aroused widespread outrage in the media and condemnation, not just from the conservative Gorton Government but also from Gough Whitlam, the Labor opposition leader.[41] By encouraging the troops to mutiny, members of the rebel unions were risking life imprisonment. However, the conservative Government was on the defensive and dared not act.

Over the summer of 1970 the rebel unions and some important left unions interstate backed calls by the CPA and radical students for an anti-war Moratorium on 8 May around the slogan 'Stop Work to Stop the War.' The maritime, construction and metal trades unions led the way in the union movement.[42] The establishment reaction was hysterical, with Liberal Minister for Labour and National Service Billy Snedden labelling the organisers 'political bikies pack-raping democracy'. The dire threats of chaos and bloodshed did not deter the demonstrators: 80 000–100 000 people, predominantly students, but also including many blue-collar workers who had stopped work, gathered in Melbourne for the march and joined in a sit-down in Bourke Street.[43] In cities interstate 80 000 protested. Two further Moratorium marches were held over the following 13 months.[44]

It was no coincidence that the flood tide in unionism in Australia gathered force after 1968. This was a period of political radicalisation around the world.[45] A new generation of students and young workers had adopted what one observer called 'a more enquiring and challenging attitude towards the practices and institutions of society'.[46] The Vietnam War was important, not just because of its barbarism but because of what it indicated about the priorities of Australia's conservative business, military and political establishment. Increasing numbers of students and young workers were demanding wholesale change to 'the system' and a growing minority were open to socialism and revolutionary politics. The Liberal Party think-tank, the Institute of Public Affairs, noted 'an alarming amount of anti-business sentiment in the community and public criticism of the free enterprise system',[47] while Sydney University Law professor C.P. Mills wrote in 1971 that:

> Frankly, I think that there are now so many people who are convinced that the rules and conventions under which we live do not secure justice and fairness as between different groups that the strict enforcement of those rules and conventions is no longer a practical proposition, and all this boils down to a question of the morality of our law.[48]

In Sydney, coalitions united radical students and BLF activists in areas of common struggle, such as the planned tour in 1971 by the all-white Springboks rugby team from South Africa. When draft resisters sought refuge in the Sydney University student union, BLF members built barricades to keep the police out.[49] Wharfies and coal miners on the New South Wales South Coast also established links with political activists from outside the labour movement. Brisbane boilermaker Jim Craig expressed the sentiment of many militants at this time:

> The sooner the trade union movement takes a leaf from the students and youth in their actions for civil liberties and anti-draft actions, the better – if it's a bad law, defy it; and the sooner we start publicly burning [anti-strike] Court Orders, as the kids burn their draft cards, the better.[50]

Just as radical students were inspired by student revolts in Paris, Berlin, Berkeley and Mexico City in the late 1960s so militant unionists, especially those from migrant backgrounds, were inspired by workers' struggle overseas. European and Latin American workers were launching massive general strikes and factory occupations. In the United States a working-class upsurge pushed strikes to record heights. In the case of the British unions, with which many Australian workers had personal or family connections, a strike by coal miners brought down the right-wing Heath Government in 1974. Conservative governments all over the world were in retreat and the conservative Government in Australia likewise appeared increasingly ineffectual. One conservative response blamed the union upturn and campus unrest on communist agitators (or even on the new ACTU president Bob Hawke). More astute sections of the ruling class knew their problem went deeper. Ian McPhee, later the Minister for Industrial Relations in the Fraser Government, understood that:

> Current affluence, universal unrest, increased and increasing social and material aspirations, adjustment to technical change, the generation and education gaps and the vicissitudes of union politics are the real causes of industrial turmoil in Australia today. For employers to see Mr Hawke as a bogeyman would have been an exercise in self-delusion.[51]

The upsurge in radicalism in Australia in the late 1960s and early 1970s aroused furious condemnation from the right-wing unions and labor councils, who did their utmost to sabotage the Moratorium marches.[52] They were successful in ensuring that the Vietnam War was virtually ignored by the 1969 and 1971 ACTU Congresses.[53] Nonetheless, they were fighting a rearguard action. Although the right-wing unions enjoyed a boost in the ACTU with the affiliation of the AWU (with its 140 000 members) in 1967, the grip of the right-wing union leaders was under attack. Serious resistance to the Groupers and their right-wing allies was being mounted in some of their strongholds. In the FIA, Laurie Short lost control of the crucial New South Wales South Coast branch to a more progressive ticket. The AWU, despite its size, was not the force that it once had been, due to a steady population shift away from country areas to the big cities and consequent loss of jobs in the primary sector.

Even so, the CPA was not able to rebuild its membership and influence. It had already been hurt by the 1963 split, which had led to the formation of the CPA(M-L). In 1971 the CPA lost further ground as a significant number of union leaders from the BWIU, the Miners Federation, the WWF, the Railways Union, the Sheet Metal Workers' Union and the SUA broke away and formed the Socialist Party of Australia (SPA) in protest at the CPA's jag to the left and its increasing criticisms of the USSR.[54]

The role played by leaders of the three communist parties varied. Those hailing from the SPA were, for the most part, dismissive of the radicalisation then sweeping the working class and youth of Australia. They continued to promote the line followed by the CPA in the 1950s and early 1960s, according to which 'unity with the broad labour movement' prohibited what they called 'adventurist' actions. Its leaders had opposed the CPA's 1969 decision to mount an industrial challenge to the penal powers. They regarded talk of 'workers' control' as a threat to the structures of trade unionism and they were the most evidently conservative of the three parties.

The CPA retained important leading positions in a host of unions.[55] Sections of the party swung to the left in response to the widespread ongoing radicalisation. The New South Wales branch took up the issue of workers' control, encouraged shop committee activity in the power industry and in metals, and played an important role in the BLF in Sydney in the early 1970s. Nonetheless, with the exception of the New South Wales BLF, the practice of most CPA union leaders, most notably in Victoria, was still very much circumscribed by their fear that spontaneous action by workers might loosen their grip, and most CPA officials still subscribed to the idea that 'unity' with ALP union leaders was of paramount importance. The CPA failed to attract significant numbers of new members at this time.

The smaller CPA(M-L) pursued vigorous industrial action where it had a foothold, for example on the Melbourne waterfront and construction sites. It sought to relate to the most radical elements of the anti-war movement and sponsored the formation of Worker–Student Alliances on campuses. Seeking to break out of its confinement to Victoria, the CPA(M-L) also tried to win a following in the Adelaide car factories. Starting at the GMH Elizabeth assembly plant in 1972, a group of members led by Les Bowling drew around them a network of worker militants who organised guerrilla stoppages at the plant, including a short sit-in at the administration block, to force management to improve conditions. In 1973 activists from the Worker–Student Alliance at Flinders University took jobs at Chrysler's Tonsley Park plant in order to pursue political work at this plant as well. Setting up the Rank and File Group, they quickly attracted other workers fed up with the 'do-nothing' passivity of their union, the VBEF. They campaigned against sackings and victimisation, and fought for better work conditions. The Chrysler Rank and File Group also established an in-plant newsletter and within two years had produced 100 editions of this publication, which skewered the company management and the union leaders in equal measure.

From the late 1960s to the mid 1970s the CPA(M-L), most obviously in unions where it did not hold leading positions, advanced the most militant rhetoric of the three parties and its practice reflected that of the CPA itself in its sectarian turn – the 'Third Period' – in the late 1920s and early 1930s.[56] In the VBEF, CPA(M-L) militants tended to dismiss work within the established union structures, a strategy that laid them open to victimisation later in the decade. The party was also bureaucratic, secretive and conspiratorial, which hindered its ability to grow. Further, its uncritical tailing of Mao Zedong, its ferocious attacks on 'Soviet social imperialism' as the chief danger to world peace, and its striving for 'Australian independence' led it to move considerably to the right and into a theoretical impasse by 1976, followed soon afterwards by serious splits.

As well as those from the three communist parties, it is necessary to consider the role of union leaders from the Victorian branch of the ALP who were a significant component of the left in the labour movement during this period. Since the ALP Split of 1955, the Victorian branch had formed the basis of the left wing of the ALP nationally and stood in sharp contrast to the New South Wales branch, where the traditional Catholic Right dominated the party and the NSW Labor Council. An intervention by the ALP federal office in 1970 broke left-wing control of the Victorian branch but did not undermine the authority of the left industrially. Key left-wing union leaders, including George Crawford from the Plumbers, Bill Brown and Ken Carr from the Furnishing Trades, Tom Ryan from the Food Preservers, and Percy Johnson from the Boilermakers played an important role in the Vietnam Moratorium campaigns and other radical activity in and around Melbourne, frequently outflanking the CPA to the left.

The main beneficiary of the decline of the CPA and the hard right was the centre left. At the 1969 ACTU Congress, the centre left and the left-wing unions banded together to elect ACTU research officer Bob Hawke as president, replacing Albert Monk who retired after 35 years. The election of Hawke, shortly after the defeat of the penal powers, saw the peak council become more open to the mood of the times. Hawke used his casting vote on the ACTU executive to endorse the 1970 Moratorium, to the anger of the right.[57] He made it clear that the ACTU was now prepared to address a broader agenda, noting that:

> ... there has been a tendency to draw a dividing line in unionism. On one side have been placed things that are traditionally union matters – wages, working conditions – but on the other side are placed issues that are not touched by unions. My reasoning is that there should be no dividing line. Anything that constitutes discrimination or hardship against our people – then in we go.[58]

In August 1970, the ACTU organised a three-hour national strike by 750 000 workers against the federal budget, the first such strike in the history of the peak body. In the same year the ACTU placed black bans on Dunlop sporting goods, which had refused to supply goods to Bourke's discount department stores because the latter sold goods below Dunlop's 'recommended retail price'. Within 24 hours Dunlop backed down and shortly afterwards the Federal Government brought in a law to stamp out resale price maintenance.[59]

The ACTU also took up issues outside basic 'hip pocket' questions. The left-wing unions had long campaigned against racism. They had supported Aboriginal struggles in the 1940s; they supported the Wave Hill land rights dispute of 1966; and they mobilised for a 'yes' vote in the 1967 referendum giving the Commonwealth Government power to legislate for Aboriginal people. With the announcement of a tour by South Africa's Springboks in 1971, the ACTU urged unions to 'take whatever action is necessary as an act of conscience' to obstruct the tour.[60] Airline, brewery and transport workers placed bans on any work or services connected with the Springbok tour, and unionists played a leading role in the protests. In Melbourne, George Crawford from the Plumbers was in the front row of the largest demonstration. Unions made the connections between racism overseas and at home. Bob Anderson, an Aboriginal organiser for the BWIU, described how he persuaded building workers not to build facilities for the tour in Brisbane:

> There was a big team of plumbers working, installing temporary urinals, wash troughs and things like that. So I had a discussion with them, and said 'The union policy is that we're against apartheid, we're not supporting the playing of this game here,' and I explained what it is to be black in your own country, and the workers said 'Well, if that's the case, let them piss on the ground,' and walked off.[61]

The Green Bans campaign by the BLF is well known.[62] In Sydney the union banned development in areas of parklands and affordable inner-city housing. It banned construction of new buildings at Macquarie University in protest at the victimisation of a gay student in one of the colleges, and stopped work at Sydney University in protest at the university vetoing a women's studies course. In Melbourne the union imposed Green Bans to prevent the demolition of the Regent Theatre and the Queen Victoria Market.

Union concern for the environment was also demonstrated by their involvement in the campaign to prevent the construction of a power station in the working-class suburb of Newport in Melbourne.[63] In 1972, following lobbying by community groups, several unions in Melbourne announced a ban on all work associated with the project and in 1974, following the reincorporation of the rebel unions into the Victorian Trades Hall, the ban on the Newport power station was extended to all Trades Hall affiliates.[64]

White-collar workers

White-collar unions also began to reflect the mood of change. They were affected by the influx of young workers from blue-collar families with union traditions and many had been exposed to radicalism on the campuses.[65] White-collar unions increasingly jettisoned reservations about striking and 'inconveniencing' the public.[66] In October 1968, the NSW Teachers' Federation held its first state-wide strike. In December 1968 the Australian Bank Officials' Association (ABOA) staged its first stop-work[67] and in 1970 a wide range of white-collar workers took action, including pharmacists, nurses and ancillary staff in hospitals, New South Wales and Victorian teachers, and bank officers.[68] In 1972 thousands of insurance clerks marched down Melbourne's Collins Street singing 'Solidarity Forever' as part of their campaign for higher pay.[69] White-collar unionists soon learned that strikes were the most effective weapon against Government restrictions. In 1971, the Victorian Government threatened to withdraw teachers' long service entitlements if they attended stop-work meetings. The teachers went ahead anyway and the Government backed down.[70]

The new white-collar militancy had organisational ramifications. From its inception the ACTU had been an overwhelmingly blue-collar union federation, reflecting the division between 'salaried' workers on staff conditions, and 'wage' workers on hourly pay.[71] With the deterioration in the relative conditions and salaries enjoyed by white-collar workers and their growing propensity to strike, the issue of affiliation to the ACTU came to the fore. The Australian Council of Salaried and Professional Associations (ACSPA) had become increasingly active and was now liaising with the ACTU. The two bodies merged in 1976, with ACSPA bringing in 37 affiliated unions with 350 000 members.[72] Similar trends explain the growing closeness of the ACTU and the Council of Australian Government Employees Organisations (CAGEO), which was also rapidly expanding at this time – from 16 affiliates and 84 000 members in 1969 to 22 affiliates with 173 000 members by 1975.[73] It too was eventually to merge with the ACTU.

Migrant workers

Migrant workers played an increasingly significant role during the flood tide. The very oppression that made migrant workers more timid and apparently apathetic much of the time, and their very alienation from the conservative structures of most mass production unions, could also make them more explosive in their methods of struggle. Migrants suffered disproportionately from unemployment and from harsh conditions in unskilled and semi-skilled jobs. However, at the same time they became increasingly conscious of the leverage that they exercised as workers in mass production. Alongside the church- and business-dominated migrant organisations there were significant left-wing migrant groups active in working-class communities. Many Greek and Italian workers had supported communist parties in their homelands and the Italian CP maintained an organised presence in Australia. They were joined by Spanish, Turkish and Latin American workers fleeing repression.

Resistance to dehumanising conditions, agitation by radical unionists, and the failure of the unions to deal with migrant worker grievances gave rise to a nine-week strike at Ford Broadmeadows in 1973 that became a national *cause celebre*.[74] A sharp increase in the demand for cars in 1972–73 had led Ford to introduce new shifts, transfer workers and increase the pace of the Broadmeadows assembly line. Absenteeism, labour turnover and the number of faulty cars produced all rose quite substantially as a result. An atmosphere of 'incipient revolt' began to develop.

In a break from previous practice, the federal leaders of the AMWU and the VBEF announced in mid May that short strikes had been planned at GMH plants in four different states to force the company to make an acceptable pay offer. The plan was to use gains won at GMH as a lever for improving rates and conditions throughout the industry. The union leaders addressed lunchtime mass meetings to explain their strategy without any objection until at one such forum, at Ford Broadmeadows on 18 May, the workers told their leaders that they were not prepared to await developments at GMH. They walked off the job and commenced an immediate and indefinite strike.

After three weeks Ford offered its workforce an increase of 5 per cent, at a time when inflation was running in double digits. The unions held a mass meeting at Broadmeadows Town Hall on 11 June at which the leaders urged workers to accept the offer. They called for a show of hands, did a count and declared the motion carried. Outraged militants suspected a deliberate miscount by the AMWU's Laurie Carmichael. They stormed the stage and jostled Carmichael, forcing him to retreat out the back of the hall, tearing his jacket in the process.

On 13 June, when the return to work was supposed to occur, 1000 workers picketed the plant. When they realised that work had already started they surged forward, pushing over a wall, turned a fire hose on to the company offices, smashed windows and then entered the plant. Ford was forced to close and the strike continued for several more weeks.

The Broadmeadows 'riot' turned a national spotlight on the strike. The media, the company and the Victorian state Government attacked what they called 'mob rule' at Ford. However, the workers saw their stand as an act of liberation. The weight of years of harsh working conditions and racist abuse was lifted for a moment, and the incident was seen by migrant factory workers around the country as a revolt against the oppression that they all faced.

The Furnishing Trades Union placed a ban on the supply of windscreens and repair of windows at the plant after the riot and the WWF banned the handling of Ford parts at Port Melbourne. Workers on the Westgate Bridge and at Williamstown Naval Dockyard contributed five dollars per week to support the strikers, and students at three Victorian universities also donated funds. Altogether students and workers from other unions raised $47 000 to finance relief for the Ford workers.

The strike ended after nine weeks with an important victory. Ford's pay offer was lifted slightly, but the workers won a significant improvement in relief and tea breaks as well as an agreement on Ford's part to slow the assembly line, hire more workers, take on women, and repair leaking roofs. The strike also changed management attitudes. Abuse and name-calling were replaced by more respectful treatment. As one worker put it:

> We showed the company that we were not slaves . . . they started being very
> afraid of the workers and the union. They speak to workers with respect. They
> don't address us like you would a dog, as they used to.

Most importantly, the strike lifted the workers' confidence that by their own actions they could bring about change.

Following the Ford strike, unions began to slowly change their internal practices. Literature began to appear in languages other than English. The number of migrant officials employed by Victorian unions rose from nine in 1971 to 16 in 1975.[75] In 1973 and 1974, the left unions sponsored Migrant Workers' Conferences and in 1975, the ACTU congress for the first time debated the specific grievances of migrants.[76]

Women workers

Female employment had been on the rise for decades but in the early 1970s it increased dramatically. Between 1971 and 1975 the number of women in public administration and defence rose by 30 per cent, in banking by 27 per cent and in community services by 24 per cent.[77] Even in 'non-traditional' areas female employment was on the rise, with the number of women working in mass production industries rising sharply.

As women entered paid work in increasing numbers, demands for equal pay grew louder.[78] Nurses, teachers, insurance clerks, bar staff and production workers all struck and demonstrated over the issue. In 1969 the Arbitration Commission announced the introduction of equal pay in all awards, to take effect over the following three years. A further decision in 1972 extended this provision to cover 'work of equal value', which gave the Arbitration Court the power to compare work undertaken by women to work in other industries.

While these were an important victory, the Commission decisions alone did not guarantee equal pay. Indeed, by the time of the second equal pay case in 1972, benefits from the 1969 decision had been felt by only 18 per cent of women workers. The extent to which pay equality became a reality depended in large part on the commitment of individual unions to pursue it industrially at the workplace level. Not surprisingly, metal trades unions were some of the most successful in this regard, despite women in the industry constituting just 2 per cent of the workforce in 1969. Shortly after the 1969 equal pay ruling, the metal trades unions lodged an application in the Industrial Court to remove all reference to the female rate in their award in order to bring women's pay rates into line with those of men. Following a vigorous campaign by the unions, the application was successful. When in the following March the employers lodged an appeal, the unions threatened industrial action to defend their victory, resulting in the employers' objections being immediately dismissed.

The fortunes of women workers in less militant unions were not as good, often despite a greater concentration of women workers in these industries. In the banking and insurance industries, where initially a purely legal strategy was pursued over the question of equal pay, very little progress was made and the achievement of equal pay was delayed by some years.

In addition to the battle to have equal pay recognised on the shop floor, union activists also had to combat employers' attempts to reclassify female workers downwards to frustrate the intent of the equal pay decisions. According to a survey taken following the 1972 decision, 60 per cent of employers had attempted to reclassify women's jobs in this way to avoid the consequences of this ruling. In 1975, this was the issue that led to the first national strike by clerical workers in Australia, led by the Insurance Workers' union.

These campaigns had a significant impact on the level of female participation in the union movement. The metal trades unions organised the first state conference of women workers in Victoria in September 1969, and at the 1971 conference of the AEU women were represented for the first time in proportion to their participation in the industry. In 1968 the Victorian branch of the Insurance Workers' Union elected the first female secretary of a white-collar union, and in January 1970 the first full-time female organiser in the metal trades unions' history was appointed. In 1970 women unionists had established a Women's Action Committee to lobby the ACTU on a range of issues concerning the rights of women at work. In 1971 women's caucuses were established within the ACTU and CAGEO and in 1973 a Women's Alternative Trade Union Conference was held. In 1975 white-collar unions funded a Working Women's Centre in Melbourne and a Women's Trade Union Commission in Sydney.

The struggle by women for equality had to overcome resistance in some unions. On the Melbourne trams women were barred from drivers' jobs, on the basis of a 1956 union mass meeting resolution that reflected traditional attitudes about men's role as breadwinners and fears of 'dilution' by female labour.[79] Over many years, female conductors had continued to agitate in the union to overturn the ban. They began to make progress in the early 1970s as the social climate changed, and as the issue began opening the union to outside pressure and criticism from quarters such as the women's movement and the ALP. A mass meeting in 1974 narrowly upheld the ban, but the next mass meeting in 1975 voted 267 to 181 to overturn it. On 5 December 1975, Joyce Barry became the first classified female tram driver in Melbourne.

The equal pay campaign in the insurance industry also led to a dramatic increase in membership, with 1700 new members recruited in 1972 and a further 1100 in 1973.[80] Given the domination of women in the industry, this undoubtedly represented an important influx of women workers into unions. More generally, female membership of all unions rose by two-thirds between 1969 and 1975, at a time when male membership rose by 'only' one-quarter. The proportion of women in unions rose from 36 per cent to 48 per cent.[81]

These developments in turn transformed attitudes towards women workers. Whereas before the equal pay struggles it would not have been uncommon to find sexist cartoons or sexist material in union journals and newsletters, these occurrences were greatly reduced or entirely eliminated by the mid 1970s. The insurance industry union journal *Premium*, for example, contained no sexist content from 1972 onwards.[82] The Engineers' *Monthly Journal* carried thirteen editorials or articles about equal pay between 1969 and 1972 and began to regularly include women in photographs of mass meetings and union events. The experience of male workers taking industrial action alongside women co-workers, and the sense of solidarity this engendered, also contributed to a sense of camaraderie that had a lasting impact on many workers. It changed the attitudes of many women to their working lives, establishing in their minds their right to be in paid work regardless of marital status, and their right to enjoy equal rights in this pursuit to those of the men they worked alongside.

Gains from the flood tide

The first and most obvious benefit of the flood tide was a sharp lift in real wages. Between 1968 and 1974 both average weekly earnings and award wages for male workers rose in *real terms* by 30 per cent (Table 2.1). Award rates for women rose by an astonishing 21.2 per cent in real terms in 1974 as a result of the struggle for equal pay.[83] The rise in wages lifted the wages share of national income to a record high (Figure 2.1).

A range of industries won the 35-hour week. Public servants won four weeks' paid annual leave, while metalworkers made more gains by direct bargaining between 1971 and 1974 than they had through arbitration in the whole period since 1952.[84] These included four weeks' annual leave with leave loading, full pay for employees on workers' compensation for a limited period, equal pay for women, and substantial gains for apprentices and juniors.

Table 2.1 Increases in real wages 1968–69 to 1973–74

Period	Male minimum weekly wage rates (federal awards) (% increase, real terms)	Average weekly earnings (% increase, real terms)
1968–69	4.8	4.7
1969–70	1.7	5.1
1970–71	3.4	6.0
1971–72	4.1	3.0
1972–73	5.0	3.5
1973–74	11.9	7.2

Source: Australian Conciliation and Arbitration Commission, National Wage Case April 1975, Reasons for Decision, 30 April 1975, p. 44

Strikes proved an excellent recruiting tool. Union coverage had declined in the 1950s and 1960s, falling from 60 per cent in 1951 to 49 per cent in 1970. In 1970, the AEU recorded that:

> Wide comment about the future of the trade unions, with a tendency towards giving them a declining importance in Australian society, has become a popular pastime for many politicians and journalist observers.[85]

By 1975, all talk of union decline was silenced. Union coverage recovered to 56 per cent. Some important blue-collar unions nearly doubled their membership between 1969 and 1975, including the BLF, the Storemen and Packers and the TWU.[86] Those blue-collar unions with a more passive industrial record lagged behind, notably the FIA (5.2% growth) and the AWU (5.5%).[87] Union coverage among white-collar workers rose from 30 per cent in 1964 to 41 per cent in 1971.[88] In several cases, including those where growth was most rapid such as in the Storemen and Packers, unions imposed closed shop or union preference arrangements on employers.

Membership of the public service associations was also on the rise. The state public service associations increased membership by 51 per cent between 1969 and 1975 and those in the Commonwealth by 98 per cent. Major contributors were growth in employment and the establishment of payroll deduction of union dues in 1970 and union preference in 1973.[89] The introduction of union preference in the Commonwealth public service

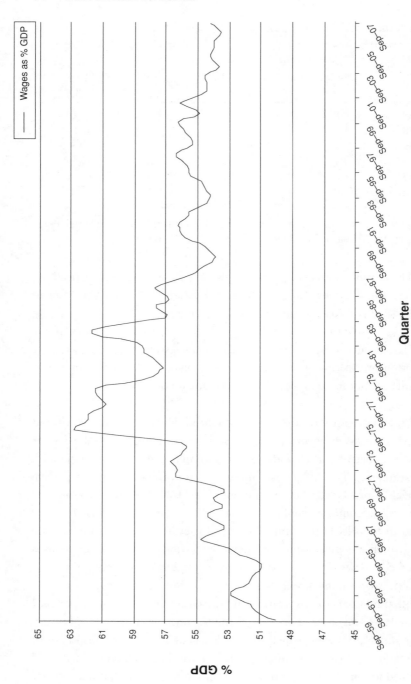

Figure 2.1 Wages share of national income (GDP) 1959–2007
Source: ABS Australian National Accounts: National Income, Expenditure and Product, September 2007, cat. no. 5206.0

was the direct result of pressure by the union movement on the Whitlam Government (see below).

Closed shop arrangements did not help just the more powerful unions. They also contributed to the rapid rise of the industrially weak. In 1972, the High Court allowed a union preference arrangement between the FCU and the oil companies, a sector where the Clerks' Union was quite a powerful force. This decision created a precedent for deals in other industries where the union was much weaker. These included closed shop agreements with the big retail employers, where it split membership with the Shop, Distributive and Allied Employees' Association (SDA) and the major drug companies. The FCU grew by 48 per cent between 1969 and 1975 to 86 000 members and the Shop Assistants by an enormous 343 per cent, to the point where they became one of the country's largest unions with 105 000 members.[90] The same was broadly true of the ABOA, which secured an agreement with the private banks in 1973 to require all new entrants to join the union. The Association grew quickly to more than 60 000 by the mid 1970s.[91] Growth on this basis was a mixed blessing for the union movement, as these were passive unions with large numbers of 'paper' members signed up by employers when they were hired. Their large membership boosted their voting power within the labor councils and the ACTU, which helped counter the more militant unions.

The flood tide of unionism pulled the ALP to the left. Senior Labor figures asserted the right to strike, even over political issues. At the time of the O'Shea dispute in 1969, Labor's industrial relations spokesman Clyde Cameron declared in parliament that the right to strike was 'the one thing that distinguishes the free man from the slave' and that the strike was 'the only weapon with which organised labour can defend itself against greedy employers and the biased industrial commissioners'.[92] Labor politicians called for a redistribution of wealth to the workers and contrasted the 'free market' for employers, when it came to determining the price of their goods, with the coercion and fines confronting workers seeking to maximise the return on their labour through strikes.[93]

Gough Whitlam was elected leader of the ALP in the aftermath of the party's devastating 1966 election defeat. His reputation is that of a progressive reformer, but at the time of his election as leader he was a noted right-winger. He was distrusted by the left of the ALP – one of his first acts as leader in 1967 was to scrap the party's commitment to pull conscripts out of Vietnam and in 1970 he led the federal intervention that purged the left in the Victorian branch. Whitlam supported state aid to private schools, opposed union action on political issues, and strongly backed the US alliance. Nonetheless, under the impact of the general shift leftwards in mass consciousness and the struggles of the unions and social movements, the party's platform also moved steadily to the left. By the time of his election as Prime Minister in December 1972, Whitlam was espousing political positions that would have been anathema to him five years previously.

The resurgent unions prevented Whitlam's shadow Cabinet from reintroducing a version of the penal powers into party policy. The party as a whole had played no role in destroying the penal powers. The 1965 and 1967 ALP conferences had barely touched on the question. It was only when the penal powers were defeated by workers that the 1969 conference directed Whitlam to include a commitment to repeal the penal powers in his policy speech for the forthcoming election. Whitlam refused to abide by the decision, committing only 'to put conciliation back into arbitration'.[94]

With the penal powers dead, Labor offered a new policy that would supposedly satisfy both the employers and unions. The credibility of the arbitration system was significantly diminished and the president of the NSW Industrial Commission argued for 'some fundamental re-thinking about the adequacy of our system of conciliation and arbitration for present and future needs'.[95] Clyde Cameron told parliament on 1 April 1971:

> A Labor Government would bring to the industrial arena an expertise which has been lacking for more than a generation. Labor could, and would, secure the support of organised labour in hammering out a new approach that would eliminate avoidable stoppages, develop better understanding between labour and capital, and lift production to the level that will be necessary if we are to compete with the rest of the world.[96]

Labor's use of Clyde Cameron as industrial relations spokesperson was significant – he was from the party's left and, as secretary of the South Australian branch of the AWU, had proved his credentials by taking on the national AWU machine. On the other hand, he was not 'unreliable'; he was a crucial figure in engineering the federal intervention in the Victorian branch in 1970. Cameron, unlike Whitlam who had no background in the labour movement, was a man many union leaders believed they could trust.

In 1970 Cameron, together with ACTU president Bob Hawke, established an ALP Industrial Relations Committee to develop arrangements for a forthcoming Labor government.[97] The committee recommended that the Arbitration Commission set only wage minima, to be topped up by over-award payments. Unlike the existing system, however, such over-award payments were to be set out in collective bargaining contracts enforceable by the Commission. Shop stewards would receive extensive new rights to be involved in negotiating these contracts. The idea was to incorporate union delegates into formal processes of industrial relations so as to prevent wildcat strikes. Most union leaders were happy with these plans, but the Committee's proposal to empower the Industrial Court to impose fines on unions in breach of the contracts raised their ire; this was only too reminiscent of the penal powers. They protested that they should not be held responsible for the acts of a minority they could not, or did not desire to, control.[98] Within days Cameron was forced to abandon the plan.[99] This indicated the balance of forces within the ALP at the time: when the interests of the union leaders and those of the parliamentary leaders came into conflict, the former had the power to pull the latter into line.

The Labor ascendancy, 1972–74

The union leaders had great hopes for the 1972 election and sought to assist Whitlam's progress by ending strikes. The WWF signed a new agreement with the employers in 1972 without a strike, the metal unions withdrew their demand for a 35-hour week, and the NSW Labor Council ended stoppages by Sydney bus workers, plumbers and oil industry workers in the months leading up to the December election.[100] Despite this temporary ceasefire, the upsurge in working-class struggle, in the context of a booming economy, ensured that when Labor took power it introduced some important reforms. In many cases these reflected the gains being won by direct action on the job.

Within a year, the Whitlam Government granted large pace-setting wage rises, the 36-and-a-quarter-hour week, four weeks' paid annual leave, and paid maternity leave for all federal public servants. Union preference was generalised throughout the public service. The Government backed the ACTU submission to the Arbitration Commission for 'equal pay for work of equal value', laying the basis for higher wages in female-dominated industries. The Government also supported ACTU claims at national wage case hearings, backed the 35-hour week in the oil and electricity supply industries, and offered verbal support during significant strikes. Whitlam also introduced measures that improved conditions for the working class in general. These included single parents' pensions, Medibank and free tertiary education. Health outlays rose by 20 per cent, education spending doubled and spending on housing quadrupled. National land rights laws recognising Indigenous claims were drafted and subsequently passed under the Fraser Government.

Although the Whitlam Government rode to power on the back of a wave of working-class militancy, sections of big business were initially positive towards it.[101] Press magnate Rupert Murdoch supported Whitlam, as did known conservative figures such as mining chief Lang Hancock. Many business leaders saw Whitlam as a figure who could give direction to the Australian economy. Whitlam was eager to reassure them of his Government's credentials:

> The program of social reform embarked upon by the present Government cannot be achieved without a strong and growing private sector. Nothing could be further from the truth than that we are anti-business or hostile to business.[102]

Labor's industrial relations program made some important concessions to the unions but it was thwarted by a hostile Senate. In April 1973, Industrial Relations Minister Clyde Cameron tabled a new Conciliation and Arbitration Bill. This proposed to abolish the penal powers *in toto* and to provide unions and their officials with immunity from tort liability for acts associated with an 'industrial matter' or an industrial dispute. The Bill extended legal protection to shop stewards and union members participating in union activities, and required the Commission to certify a collective agreement unless it would result in a 'major detriment to the public interest'. The Bill also removed some of the restrictions introduced in 1972 by the Liberal Government to halt the amalgamations of the left-wing metal trades unions.[103]

The Labor Government's Bill drew enormous hostility from the Opposition. The conservative parties saw the arbitration system as a reliable and trusted means of controlling union activity. Collective bargaining as proposed by the Bill was an unwanted intrusion into the industrial framework and would only give more voice to shop stewards, who were 'unwanted imports from Europe' and 'the playthings of the Communist Party'.[104]

The Bill was obstructed in the upper house. Only in November 1973 did the Senate pass a much diluted version. The main features of the new Act were protection against victimisation, right of entry for union officials to workplaces, a limitation on the awarding of costs in proceedings under the Arbitration Act, and a requirement that all full-time officials be elected directly by the membership and not by collegial voting systems. The Act also provided $3 million to establish a Trade Union Training Authority (TUTA) in Albury. However, immunity from tort actions and the abolition of strike penalties were dropped.

If the conservatives in parliament looked to arbitration as the antidote to union militancy, employers at industry level largely accepted the shift towards collective bargaining then in progress. They had no alternative, given the prevailing conditions. National wage cases were becoming increasingly irrelevant. Most wage rises were now coming from two sources. One was over-award bargaining – by 1974 over-award payments accounted for nearly 30 per cent of award wages for the metal trades. The other was industry-specific consent awards. These were agreements negotiated between unions and employers on an annual basis and then simply ratified by the Commission.[105] Such awards involved significant pay increases and became common in the metal trades, transport, motor vehicles, the building industry and the waterfront.

Some employers hoped that by negotiating directly with unions they could win important concessions in working practices and 'no-strike' agreements. They had no chance. In the metal industry, those unions that rarely struck, the ASE and the FIA, were happy to commit to a no-strike arrangement, but unions that struck on a regular basis, such as the AMWU, were not going to give up their most effective weapon. The Commission (or Government) might grant some improvements, but it was the struggle on the job that made the breakthroughs and laid the basis for flow-ons through the award system or legislation. A mass meeting of AMWU delegates in Victoria declared:

> We are firmly opposed to any agreement or consent award which precludes
> metal workers from exercising their inherent right to struggle on an individual
> shop or group basis for improvements in wage rates or working conditions.[106]

It was not just wages and working conditions that were at stake but the
purpose and character of the unions themselves. AMWU organiser Frank
Cherry explained:

> Without the local struggle for wage growth, the shopfloor movement would
> grow very weak. In many cases people would lose their desire to fight for their
> rights on the job. They'd say 'What's the point? So and so at the federal level,
> they'll nut all that out.' I think that the whole democratic base of the union
> would be at stake.[107]

Conclusion

The metalworkers' rejection of the employer's 'no-strike' proposals in 1973
was but one indication of the industrial confidence of hundreds of thousands
of unionised workers during the flood tide. The old pattern of industrial
relations, premised on centralised arbitration, union passivity and a relatively docile workforce, had been broken. In its place came the rush to
over-award bargaining, a break-down in the authority of the Arbitration
Commission and the Industrial Court, an increased readiness by workers to
demand improvements in their wages and conditions of work, and a crisis
of confidence in the ranks of employers. The advent of a Labor Government brought employers no relief. Strike days trebled from two million in
1972 to more than six million in 1974, and strikes continued to build trade
unionism. Union membership, which had risen by 300 000 between 1969
and 1972, rose by a further 300 000 between 1972 and 1975, with union
coverage increasing to its highest rate in more than a decade.

The story of this period of militancy and radicalisation in the Australian
union movement and broader working class is overwhelmingly positive.
Nonetheless, there were two important limitations. First, although there
were cases of coordinated action involving workers from a range of workplaces, industries and occupations, these were the exception rather than the
rule: most struggles were sectional and restricted to individual workplaces or

individual industries. While these were sufficient to win significant improvements in a period of economic expansion, the generally sectional nature of the struggle limited workers' capacity to mount a defensive when the economic climate shifted. Second, while militant workers were willing to take action over Vietnam, racism in South Africa and environmental protection, they by and large accepted that political reform required the election of a Labor government. Very few saw the need to go beyond Labor, to construct a political alternative based on the industrial power of the working class. This was less of an obstacle when Labor was being pushed to the left by the wave of struggle, but when the situation changed and Labor began to pursue a more conservative agenda, the Australian working class was ill-prepared for the turn of events.

Part 2

THE STAND-OFF, 1974–83

Chapter Three

ECONOMIC CRISIS AND THE HALTING OF THE FLOOD TIDE, 1974–75

The years 1974–75 mark an important turning point in this account of trade unionism. Up until this point unions operated in relatively buoyant economic circumstances. When they began to press seriously for reform in the late 1960s, the capitalist class had sufficient profitability to concede higher wages and an upgraded welfare state. From 1974–75 onwards, as the postwar economic boom subsided into a period of stagflation, the relationship between capital and labour became more fraught. Specifically, employers were driven by the deterioration in the rate of profit to attack the conditions of the working class, to resist reforms and, indeed, to seek to wind them back. Employers switched from a relatively accommodating to a more aggressive stance with regard to workers' jobs, wages and conditions of employment. The response of the working class to this offensive was not predetermined but was dependent on the politics of the labour movement, its leadership, the role of the activist layers and the moods of the broader working class. This chapter will explore the onset of the economic crisis, the response of employers, the actions of the Whitlam Government, the Governor-General's coup, and the reaction of the working class and its leaders to these developments.

The onset of economic crisis

The end of the postwar boom in Australia had its origins in a crisis of profitability in the world economy.[1] The rate of return on investment in

US manufacturing fell from 22.2 per cent in the 1960s to 16.8 per cent in the 1970s. As the rate of profit declined, so business confidence to invest deteriorated, sending the US economy into recession. US multinationals pulled capital out of overseas operations in order to prop up investments in their home base. The slow-down in the world's largest economy had knock-on effects throughout the world system, resulting in company fail-ures, cancelled investments, takeovers and acquisitions, and a slowing of international trade. Furthermore, inflation became endemic in the face of the collapse of the Bretton Woods system of fixed exchange rates, the flooding of the world economy with US dollars resulting from the Nixon administration's spending on the Vietnam War, and the quadrupling of oil prices in 1974.

If a decline in the rate of profit was the underlying *cause* of the great slowdown in the world economy in 1974, the most obvious *manifestation* of the crisis was excess capacity. While at any point in the development of the capitalist economy there is a gap between output and the purchasing power of the working class, it is at times when the incentive for capital to fill this gap disappears (when the profit rate is too low to justify new productive investments) that problems of excess capacity appear. And so the emerging crisis in the world system saw unsold goods stockpiled in large quantities in the warehouses and dockyards of North America, Western Europe and Japan. To reduce these stockpiles and to begin restoring the rate of profit, employers slashed jobs, thereby reducing the market for consumer goods. Mass unemployment returned to the West for the first time since the 1930s.

Australian capitalism was not and could not be isolated from these trends. The rate of profit in Australia, in common with that in the United States, had been in decline since the mid 1960s (see Figure 3.1). In the early 1970s the pace of decline began to accelerate. The profit share of national income also fell sharply (see Figure 3.2).

In late 1974, nine months later than the rest of the OECD, the Australian economy also moved into recession. Growth slumped from more than 4 per cent in 1974 to 1 per cent in 1975. Industrial production fell at an annual rate of 13 per cent in mid 1975.[2] Inflation surged to more than 20 per cent.

Business goes on the attack

The capitalist class responded in several ways to the economic crisis. One was by large-scale sackings. Every sector of blue-collar industry, from textiles

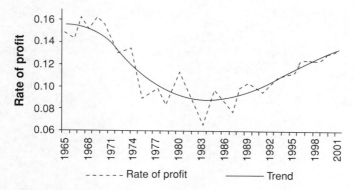

Figure 3.1 Rate of profit 1965–2001
Source: S. Mohun, 'The Australian rate of profit, 1965–2001', *Journal of Australian Political Economy*, 52, 2003, p. 88

and clothing, to building and construction, the electrical trades and motor vehicles, laid off thousands of staff, causing a steep rise in unemployment (see Figure 3.3).

Employers took advantage of the recession to turn the tables on militant unionists. In his 1976 study of 20 large metal industry plants, Milton Derber observed:

> Some companies reported that they were able to eliminate extra-militant or troublesome employees in the course of retrenchment. While the retrenchment process was often difficult, creating anxieties for employees, uncertainties for management, and work stoppages in a number of plants, it was ordinarily followed by a period of quieter relations in the plant, including fewer grievances and less absenteeism.[3]

Ted Gnatenko, founder of the AMWU shop committee at the GMH Elizabeth plant and editor of the union's factory newsletter, *Elizabeth Engineer*, became one such victim of this process when he was sacked in November 1974. In the construction industry, the big employers collaborated with BLF federal secretary Norm Gallagher to destroy the New South Wales branch of the BLF by employing only those with federal office union tickets in circumstances where jobs were becoming increasingly scarce.[4]

Accompanying these direct measures was a sharp ideological offensive by business that sheeted home responsibility for the crisis to the demands of trade unions and the working class more generally. Much was made of the increase in real wages between 1969 and 1974, which had created

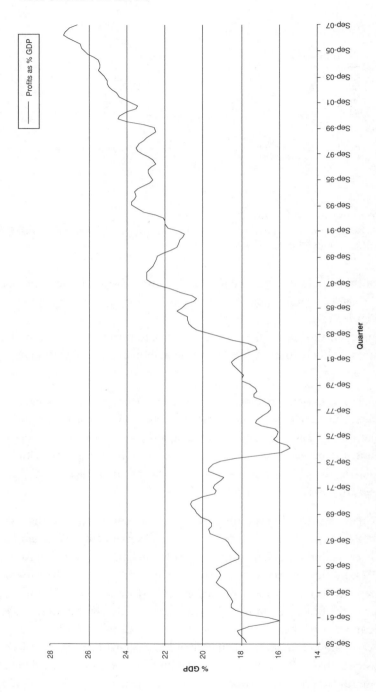

Figure 3.2 Profit share of national income 1959–2007
Source: ABS *Australian National Accounts: National Income, Expenditure and Product*, September 2007, cat. no. 5206.0

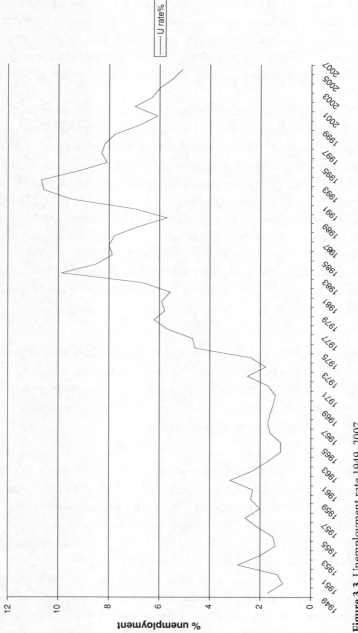

Figure 3.3 Unemployment rate 1949–2007
Source: ABS Labour Force Australia, cat. no. 6202.0

a so-called 'real wage overhang', whereby wages growth had outstripped productivity. Newspaper headlines and editorials became increasingly and virulently right-wing, alleging industrial chaos, communist conspiracies, rampant overstaffing in the public service and widespread welfare cheating.[5] The only solution, they argued, was to cut wages, jobs and the welfare state.

The Whitlam Government responded by taking up the anti-union crusade. Ministers accused unions of irresponsible strikes and wage demands, and complained about inefficiencies in the postal services and on the waterfront.[6] The first attempt by the Government to gain control over wages took place even before the onset of the crisis. In December 1973 the Government held a referendum to give the Commonwealth the constitutional power to control wages and prices. Trade unions urged workers to reject control over wages but to support price control. The referendum failed ignominiously, as workers understood that the focus of the Government's restraint would be on wages, not prices. The Government now sought other means to rein in the unions. Clyde Cameron slammed militant unionism early in 1974:

> The general public – including that section of the public that consists of trade unionists themselves – are sick and tired of the near anarchy that pervades the industrial scene. It is this bloody-mindedness on the part of a small section of the trade union movement that is slowly, but surely, pricing thousands of Australian workers out of employment.[7]

In the latter half of 1974, Government attacks on militant unionism increased. The Whitlam Government used the RAAF to break two strikes, intervened to prevent a wages deal between Qantas and the airline pilots, and established a Royal Commission to investigate the Seamen's Union.[8] Angered by a strike of New South Wales South Coast miners, the Government made strikers ineligible for unemployment benefits.

On the other side of the ledger, the Government cut business taxes and granted subsidies to companies that were threatening to sack workers. The Government's Prices Justification Tribunal authorised a 14 per cent price rise by BHP, while blaming unions for rising unemployment and inflation. On 25 January 1975, Whitlam told the Young Labor Conference:

You have to place the blame for inflation in Australia on wage claims. Wage claims in the past 12 months have so greatly reduced the profitability of employers that they have ceased to employ. As long as wage demands continue to cut profits, there is going to be unemployment.[9]

In February the ALP Conference at Terrigal on the New South Wales Central Coast, which Labor economist Barry Hughes would later call 'a pro-business orgy', witnessed the final interment of the Government's reform agenda. Whitlam repeated his message that profitability had to be lifted. The private sector had to be boosted and public spending got short shrift. Labor's left wrung its hands but went along with it all. Treasurer Jim Cairns told delegates:

I know that the capitalist system is exploitative and leaves many genuine desires of many people unfulfilled. I also know that the jobs of most of our people depend on private industry – much of it part of the multinational system. I know, therefore, that we must follow policies generally in the interests of the private sector.[10]

The Government now began to cut public-sector jobs in earnest, eliminating 1500 civilian jobs in the Department of Defence and freezing recruitment to the public service.

Union responses to the crisis

Wage indexation

Although denying direct responsibility for the economic crisis, the large majority of union leaders agreed with the Whitlam Government that restraint was now in order. In the last week of August 1974, the ACTU executive resolved to accept

. . . a responsibility to the industrial movement and the community generally to cooperate with Government in an attempt to bring greater stability, security and improved living standards for our members, their dependants and for the community generally.[11]

Specifically, the executive endorsed wage indexation, whereby the Arbitration Commission would assume responsibility for pegging wages to the consumer price index. The right-wing union leaders welcomed indexation because it provided wage increases without any need for strikes or action on their part. It was the left-wing unions, whose members retained some capacity to wreck indexation by striking for higher wages, that were crucial to determining its fate. Even if unemployment had weakened some of their strongholds, militants were still capable of mounting stiff resistance to any attempt to force down wages.

The ACTU executive took its recommendation to a two-day Federal Unions Conference in September 1974. The left unions, led on the floor by the AMWU, urged rejection of the executive's motion, arguing that 'legitimate wage claims' should not be restricted. However, as it turned out, this opposition was mostly for show. On the second day of the conference, after an intervention by ACTU president Bob Hawke, the executive's recommendations were unanimously endorsed, including by the leaders of the AMWU and every other left union present. The left union leaders had now demonstrated that they would not rock the boat, and the decision by the AMWU to support indexation had important consequences not just for the AMWU but for the entire union movement. Hawke's role at this conference was telling. As well as holding the presidency of the ACTU, Hawke was also president of the federal ALP, and throughout the economic and political crises that were to unfold over the course of 1974–75 he played a critical role in ensuring cooperation with the Government by union leaders from left to right.

Indexation could only restrain wages if it was accompanied by a union commitment not to pursue higher wages 'in the field' by direct negotiation with employers. The Full Bench of the Arbitration Commission made this clear when it demanded at the autumn 1975 National Wage Case that the ACTU agree to 'substantial compliance' to the core principle of indexation – 'negligible wage increases' outside indexation. The ACTU representative at the National Wage Case hearings obliged. Satisfied with the ACTU's response, the Commission introduced quarterly wage indexation on 30 April 1975, warning that:

> Violation of this condition ['substantial compliance'], even by a small section of industry, whether in the award or non-award, would put at risk the future of indexation for all.[12]

The ACTU executive welcomed the Commission's decision. It responded to criticisms on its left that it had now accepted a wages freeze by pointing out that wages were indexed to the rate of inflation and that unions were still free to make claims to the Commission on the basis of rising productivity and changes to work value. In addition, unions whose wage claims were cut short by the introduction of indexation could lodge 'catch-up' claims with the Commission.[13]

The AMWU leaders were in a bind – they were committed to wage indexation but they were also under pressure from militants unhappy about the new set-up. Apart from anything else the new system did not index over-award payments, which accounted for 25–30 per cent of wages in some workshops. For such workers, indexation represented an immediate wage cut unless they were free to fight for higher wages on the job. The AMWU leaders' solution was to mount an over-award campaign on a shop-by-shop basis, taking advantage of the fact that the Commission and the ACTU accepted that 'substantial compliance' might take some time to be enforced in every union. Nonetheless, the AMWU leaders' hearts were not in the campaign and they led it into a dead end. They were lambasted by militants who complained that:

> The present Federal union leadership is no longer competent to lead a national campaign. They have wasted our time with long drawn-out negotiations, Arbitration Court hearings, short and worthless stoppages, deals with the Labor Government and mass meetings where weaker and weaker recommendations were made.[14]

Without a national industrial campaign by the metal trades unions, even larger employers were inclined to hold out. The employers' resolve was stiffened by the dumping of Clyde Cameron as Industrial Relations Minister and his replacement by Jim McClelland, who immediately attacked the AMWU's wages campaign. Widespread redundancies through winter 1975 also weakened the confidence of many workers to pursue an aggressive wages campaign. As the weeks progressed without a substantial breakthrough, the AMWU over-award campaign fizzled out.

There were profound consequences of the unions' decision to accept a shifting of wage-fixing from shopfloor struggle to the bureaucratic process of arbitration. According to Tom O'Lincoln:

Once the unions had committed themselves to trading industrial peace for periodic pay increases, their officials were required to police the agreement and pressure increased on shop stewards to do likewise.[15]

Starting in the middle of 1975, the strike rate fell sharply across the board.

The emphasis on union 'discipline' was evident at the September 1975 ACTU Congress, which aroused 'more intense public interest than probably any other in the ACTU's history' according to seasoned Congress observer, Ross Martin.[16] Business, the media and the Whitlam Government applied intense pressure to Congress delegates, demanding that they show 'responsibility': in other words, their preparedness to accept wage restraint. They were supported in this by the ACTU executive. Hawke set the scene on the first day of the Congress, declaring that 'We meet at a time of the gravest crisis for the labour movement and the whole Australian community since the end of the Second World War'.[17] While asserting the right to free collective bargaining and denying union responsibility for the economic crisis – a nod to the militants – Hawke went on to assert that restraint was now in order. The growth in wages was untenable, unemployment could only be fixed if the profit share recovered, and any attempt by unions to pursue claims outside indexation would be irresponsible.[18]

Two motions attracted attention at the 1975 Congress. The first, on economic policy, gave the ACTU a 'left cover' – an impression that it was resisting the Government's broadly conservative economic program (on which more below). It advocated a more expansionary fiscal and monetary policy, a range of labour market support measures, a comprehensive policy of price restrictions, and the 'gradual nationalisation of monopolies and essential industries'.[19] This motion, however, amounted to little more than a wish-list, with no practical intent, and was passed unanimously.

The crucial test for the left unions lay in the executive's second motion, which committed affiliates to accepting the system of wage indexation. Very significantly, this motion was moved by AMWU national secretary Jack Devereux.[20] The motion welcomed indexation but demanded that the Commission allow wage increases on the grounds of productivity and work value, and that the Government index income tax scales to inflation. The motion also reaffirmed the right to engage in collective bargaining, allowing the ACTU some room to manoeuvre. Nonetheless, the overall thrust of ACTU strategy at this time was clear from the overwhelming defeat of a BWIU amendment, which rejected all forms of compulsory wage control and any responsibility for the crisis. The executive's motion was then endorsed unanimously, including by the BWIU leaders. The left officials had now endorsed the ACTU executive's message to business and the Government – that the union movement was prepared to accept sacrifice and that the union leaders would discipline union militants to ensure that this sacrifice was effectively enforced.

Protectionism and corporate handouts

The acceptance of wage restraint was one indication of the commitment by the union leaders to cooperate with government and business. Another was their response to the large-scale lay-offs. Instead of campaigning for shorter working hours on full pay to share the work around, union leaders for the most part joined forces with employers in their attempts to resolve the crisis by demanding greater industry protection and financial assistance from the Government.[21] In the name of saving 'our' industry, union leaders covering textiles, electronics, motor vehicles, sporting goods, whitegoods and the food industries all joined their respective employers in lobbying the Federal Government for action against import competition.[22]

This strategy undermined any conception of workers' solidarity and instead sought to persuade workers that their jobs might be saved by allying themselves with their own employers in competition with workers in other companies both at home and overseas. Protectionism was also being pursued by union leaders elsewhere, and the result of the strategy was to reinforce sectional divisions among workers rather than overcome them. In addition, if restoring profitability was now an important union goal, it laid the unions open to employers' arguments for wage cuts and speed-ups. It also led unions to place their faith in even the most unlikely allies. A VBEF demonstration in Geelong in October 1975 cheered Liberal leader Malcolm Fraser and hoisted him aloft after he promised to reverse the Whitlam Government's tariff cuts.[23]

The left union leaders' response to the mass sackings was posed in much more radical phraseology but was constrained by the same nationalist politics. In August 1975 the AMWU issued a General Statement on the Economic Crisis in which it argued:

> The system of capitalism is in its final stages. Completely new attitudes, financial concepts and formulas must be adopted. The Labor Party and the Australian Labor Government have a special responsibility in such circumstances. There is no short term solution to the growing and deep malaise of our capitalist system. There is no long term solution under outmoded capitalist economic thought. Only a socialist solution is possible.[24]

However this did not, despite appearances, actually entail a challenge to capitalism. The statement very much bore the stamp of the CPA, whose analysis of the crisis reached back to a long tradition of foreign conspiracy theories in the Australian labour movement.[25] The CPA (and the AMWU leaders) attributed the crisis not to factors inherent in the capitalist mode of production – its dependence on a 'healthy' rate of profit which over the long term was unsustainable because of the contradictions arising from processes of capital accumulation – but to the 'manipulation of the Australian economy' by multinational companies.[26] The CPA and AMWU's solution was for Government to nationalise multinational companies, and to introduce a 35-hour week with no loss of pay, an increase in company tax, and full wage indexation.[27] These demands were certainly radical, but they did not engage with the fundamental causes of the economic crisis. The CPA and AMWU's essentially *nationalist* analysis of the causes of the crisis, whereby solutions to the crisis could be found by protection of 'our' industry, led it in coming years to demands that, far from being radical, actually ended up derailing another powerful tradition in the Australian working class movement: that of *struggle*.

The response of the militants

The economic crisis highlighted some political limits of the militants who had been at the forefront of the flood tide. Under conditions of full employment and full order books, the readiness of workers to stop work was usually sufficient to force concessions from employers fearful of losing production. Although there were examples of some long and tenacious struggles during the flood tide, in most cases short stoppages were enough to get results. Militant unionists did not need an analysis of capitalism to make major gains. Their consciousness was, for the most part, anti-boss, anti-tribunal and anti-Liberal. It was not anti-capitalist in any meaningful sense.

When the postwar boom gave way to the slump of 1975 and the ALP tacked to the right, the union movement was not equipped to meet the challenge. The tougher economic circumstances meant that employers were more prepared to resist demands for higher wages and shorter hours. Indeed, they now went on the offensive to roll back the improvements that workers had won in previous years – through retrenchments, cuts to wages and work intensification. Snap strikes were no longer enough for workers to make gains. Militants also encountered resistance from union leaders who were increasingly prepared to argue the case for restraint in the face of rising unemployment and, indeed, from fellow workers, many of whom were won over by the new 'common sense' being trumpeted by the media – that strikes could only worsen the crisis.[28]

It was not that the militants were crushed by the turn of events. Many rejected the Government's and employers' argument that union militancy was the cause of the crisis. They were angry that 'their' Government had turned on the unions and appeared intent on cosseting business. Further, the economic downturn was still a relatively new phenomenon and was dismissed by some militants as simply an aberration. Next year, perhaps, the crisis would recede and it would be back to business as usual.

The problem was not the destruction of the militants but their *disorientation*: they lacked a strategy to go forward. The parties that held sway among the militants – the CPA and the Socialist Left of the ALP – positioned themselves, not as resolute opponents of the increasingly rightward drift of the Labor Government, but as in-house critics. An editorial in the AMWU *Monthly Journal* in March 1975 gives some indication of this, complaining in a pained tone that:

> Mr Whitlam's continued blaming of the wage campaigns of unions as being the cause of unemployment, certainly stretches the bonds of friendship with the trade unions . . . The Government's leading figures apparently fail to see the need to have very close relations with the trade union movement and not to lend themselves to the employers' attacks blaming wages for all our economic ills.[29]

This positioning of the left unions as loyal critics of the Labor Government had important consequences. In April 1974 a CPA union official persuaded power industry militants in ECCUDO to lift the bans that they had imposed in pursuit of a 35-hour week, for fear of damaging Labor's election campaign.[30] His rationale was: 'Neither the workers' struggle nor the Labor Government are expendable.' But clearly, to call off the action *was* to make the struggle expendable – winning the election came first. Nine months later, in January 1975, it was the CPA leadership of ECCUDO that again persuaded power industry workers to call off their bans campaign for a 35-hour week under pressure from the NSW Labor Council.[31] The claim was referred to the NSW Industrial Commission, where it was promptly rejected.[32] Leading union figures in the CPA were prepared to fight, but only up to a point and, as in the 1960s when an open breach with the ALP and moderate union leaders appeared possible, they shrank from the confrontation.

The limitations were self-imposed – it was not that workers could no longer win gains. In June 1975 a 10-week strike by workers at Containers Limited at Footscray in Melbourne won a $10 wage rise and the reinstatement of sacked workers. In July, mine workers in Queensland and New South Wales took action.[33] In August, meatworkers struck for higher wages, while printers at Fairfax in Melbourne struck for two weeks to resist employer attempts to break the closed shop. In September, the Clydemaster railway carriage works at Bayswater in Melbourne struck for five weeks for higher pay.[34] The struggle continued to draw in fresh forces to union activism. In March 1975, Ansett flight attendants won significant pay rises for new staff, a rise in the compulsory retirement age to 45, and six weeks' annual leave. Company owner Reg Ansett was forced to apologise after referring to them as 'glorified waitresses' and 'a bunch of old boilers'.[35] Also in March, four thousand Victorian nurses rallied outside the Victorian parliament in pursuit of a 50 per cent pay rise.[36] Workers were taking a beating from the lay-offs but they were by no means defeated. Events that were to unfold in the last quarter of 1975 only gave them even more reason to fight.

Unions and the Kerr Coup

The sacking of the Whitlam Government on 11 November 1975 led to one of the most intense periods of mass working-class radicalisation in Australian history. Hundreds of thousands of workers, long-standing Labor loyalists for the most part, concluded that the rich and the well-connected had engaged in a conspiracy to bring down 'their' Government. Memories of the Chilean military coup of September 1973, which had brought down a social democratic government in that country and led to the killing of thousands of working-class militants, were fresh in people's minds. There was a real questioning of parliamentary democracy, and those arguing that the Kerr Coup proved that a revolution in Australia was both necessary and desirable could find an audience. The residue of the Kerr Coup was a deep-seated and profound hatred for the successor Liberal Government that was to mark it throughout its seven years in office.

The Whitlam Government was not brought down because of its excessive zeal for reform. Far from it. From early in 1975, as was made clear at the ALP conference in Terrigal, the Government began to pursue a distinctly rightward trajectory under intense media and business pressure.[37] In June Whitlam purged his Cabinet, replacing left-wing ministers Cairns and Cameron with right-wingers Bill Hayden and Jim McClelland. The new Treasurer, Hayden, obliged business by delivering a budget in August that was straight out of the monetarist textbooks. Workers became increasingly jaundiced by the Government's performance; this was brought home to Labor at the Bass by-election in Tasmania in late June, when its candidate suffered defeat and a swing of 14 per cent. Among blue-collar workers support for Labor at this election fell from 67 per cent to 41 per cent.[38]

Nonetheless, try as he might, Whitlam could not move fast enough to keep business happy. The working-class offensive was too recent, and the pressure by the unions inside the party too great, for Whitlam to mount an all-out attack against the gains made in the previous decade. In the view of business, Whitlam had to make way for a government that could do just this. However, the process was fraught with danger and at several points the strategy threatened to come unstuck.

There were several elements in the mounting challenge to the Whitlam Government. From early in the year the Opposition, with the direct assistance of Treasury Secretary Sir Fred Wheeler, began to make great play of the so-called 'loans scandal'. This 'scandal' comprised an attempt by the Minister for Minerals and Energy Rex Connor to borrow funds from oil-rich Middle Eastern states to develop the mineral resources of the North West Shelf. In the end no funds were borrowed and no financial impropriety was uncovered, but the Liberals and the media confected a scandal around this issue that rolled throughout the year and did much to associate the Whitlam Government with the stigma of corruption and incompetence.

In February, the Liberal–Country Government in New South Wales appointed a conservative independent to fill a vacancy in the Senate caused by the appointment of Labor Senator Lionel Murphy to the High Court, breaching the convention that the replacement should come from the same party. In March, the ineffectual Liberal leader Billy Snedden was dumped in favour of the Victorian grazier Malcolm Fraser, who promised a more strident attack on the Whitlam Government. In April, right-wing economist Milton Friedman, fresh from advising the Chilean dictator Augusto Pinochet, addressed meetings around the country on measures to restore business confidence in Australia. Big business did its bit, withdrawing investments from the country, and capital inflow dried up.

In September, the conservative Bjelke-Petersen Government in Queensland appointed another conservative to the Senate to replace Labor's Senator Bert Milliner, who had died in office. The Coalition now had a majority in the upper house and its leaders, Liberal Malcolm Fraser and the Country Party's Doug Anthony, barnstormed the country demanding that Whitlam call an early election. On 15 October, the Senate, citing the 'loans affair' as a pretext, blocked Supply (budget funding) in an attempt to bring down the Government.

The situation was now intensely polarised. Although workers had become increasingly cool towards the Whitlam Government, they understood the significance of the right-wing offensive against it – a conservative victory would usher in a Liberal government, which might destroy all the gains that they had won over the previous period. Workers responded vigorously. In the nine days following the blocking of Supply, 50 000 workers attended rallies and a further 100 000 struck in defence of the Whitlam Government.[39] Workplaces in every corner of the country took action, from meatworkers in Townsville to brewery workers in Perth.[40] Every state labor council passed strong resolutions condemning the Opposition for withholding Supply.[41]

Working-class resistance to the Coalition's attempt to choke finance to the Government produced a sharp lift in Labor's popularity, particularly among blue-collar workers. Labor's Gallup Poll support rose by 6 per cent in late October.[42] It was no coincidence that Labor support was strongest in Victoria and most especially Melbourne, the centre of the rallies and strikes.[43] The union mobilisation threatened to derail the Liberal attack. The Melbourne *Age* and Brisbane *Courier-Mail* took fright at Fraser's high-stakes tactics and urged the Senate to pass Supply. There were rumblings inside the Liberal Party and a real possibility that one Liberal senator would cross the floor to pass Supply. With the situation on a knife edge, the Governor-General, Sir John Kerr, who had previously earned notoriety as the judge responsible for jailing Clarrie O'Shea, dismissed Whitlam on 11 November and appointed Fraser in his place as interim Prime Minister.

Led by the militants, workers poured out on strike and in mass demonstrations against what quickly became known as the 'Kerr Coup'. The Communist newspaper *Tribune* interviewed Mike Jackson, secretary of the Combined Unions Committee, at the Garden Island Dockyard in Sydney:

> Announcement of the Kerr business hit like a bombshell. There was spontaneous hostility and amazement . . . people wanted action. The call went up straight away for a nation-wide stoppage. It was not *whether* we were going to take action, but *how quickly*. The Shop Committee called an emergency meeting next morning . . . and contacted other waterfront shops. Though some Shop Committee members were uncertain about how far people were prepared to go, the mass meeting decisions were unanimous . . . As we marched into Pitt Street we caught sight of the workers from Cockatoo Dock, who had also stopped work. You could hear the roar that went up from both groups all over town! The two marches joined . . . together with seamen and office workers who swelled our ranks as we went. At Liberal Headquarters, officials refused to see a deputation from the march, so workers decided to march on the citadel of Australian high finance and power, the Sydney Stock Exchange.[44]

The overwhelming call on the streets and from the leaders of all the key left wing unions was for a general strike. At the rally in Melbourne on the afternoon of 11 November, AMWU and CPA leader John Halfpenny (the figure to whom many militants looked to give a fighting lead) told the crowd of 5000:

> The trade union movement must destroy Kerr and restore democracy in this country. Now is the time for people to rise in anger and intervene in events. The demand must be for the people of this nation to respond in the streets and in the workshops so the elected representatives will be allowed to govern. People must be prepared to take to the streets time and again in the next four weeks. Let us destroy Fraser and Kerr and the forces of reaction in this country.[45]

The call for a general strike was backed by resolutions from labor councils and worksite meetings. A general strike, however, was just what Bob Hawke wanted to avoid. Indeed, Hawke's initial reaction was to advise that Whitlam had 'no alternative but to accept this amazing decision'.[46] Warning of 'violence in the streets' and 'anarchy' if a strike went ahead, Hawke, with the backing of the just-deposed PM and his deputy and the country's senior union leaders, directed the resistance off the streets towards a conventional electoral campaign.[47] If Labor were to retain office it was not to be off the back of a general strike; this would have made any continuation of its conservative economic policies all the more difficult. Hawke stuck to his guns throughout the constitutional crisis, despite workers flooding union offices with phone calls and telegrams demanding a general strike. Many years later Hawke explained his reasoning as follows:

> The level of emotion among Labor parliamentarians and supporters was beyond measure, but I felt in my dual capacities as president of the party and the ACTU, that this was very much a time for rational calculation . . . Pressure was being exerted on me by many to call a national strike in protest against the events of that infamous day, but I thought it would be stupidly counterproductive to succumb. My position was that the terrible trio [Fraser, Kerr and High Court Judge Garfield Barwick, who had offered legal advice to Kerr] had acted improperly and unconstitutionally, and that we should take the high ground.[48]

'Stupidly counterproductive' was Hawke's assessment of the call for a national strike, and yet that was the demand that rang around the country. Melbourne was central to the campaign against the Coup and, if a breakthrough was going to be made, it was likely to happen there. On the morning of 12 November, the leaders of 30 left-wing Victorian unions called a half-day general strike and mass rally in the city centre for Friday 14 November. However, having made the call, they almost immediately began to retreat. This was to become clear on the Friday, when more than 400 000 workers struck and 50 000 attended a rally in Melbourne's City Square. Union militants were boiling with anger against the Coup and were only waiting for the call from their leaders for a general strike.

The rally started with a speech by Hawke at which he condemned the conspiracy against the Whitlam Government but called on workers to 'cool it' and to direct their energy (and a day's pay) to Labor's election campaign. The demonstrators were then led away from the city centre and finished up at the Old Treasury Building on Spring Street, where they heard further speeches urging them to campaign for the ALP from the just-sacked Deputy Prime Minister Frank Crean and Victorian ALP branch secretary Clyde Holding. The militants waited on John Halfpenny to provide the leadership that the movement needed if it was to go forward. Far from calling for more action, however, Halfpenny simply repeated Hawke's advice and told the assembled crowd to go home.

The left union leaders had put themselves at the head of the demand for action only in order to head it off. The potential for so much more was evident in the fact that tiny far-left groups were able to lead 10 000 demonstrators off on a march to the Stock Exchange, to reinforce the point that Kerr's Coup was underwritten by big business and that, if the Coup were to be stopped, business had to be hit hard. However, while the revolutionary left could lead a break-away march, it was far too small to wrest the leadership of the labour movement from the reformists, left and right, who had decades of established influence and material resources to draw from. In particular, the CPA at this crucial juncture refused to mobilise its networks of worker militants for a general strike, preferring to tail the ALP leadership.

The momentum for a general strike having been broken, the campaign switched to electoral mode. The ALP organised mass rallies to pull support behind the Government, and workers stopped work in large numbers to attend them, including Labor's campaign opening at the Sydney Domain, which attracted 40 000. Eight thousand attended an election rally at Festival Hall in Melbourne, and meatworkers, seamen and wharfies walked off the job to join a crowd of 7000 to hear Whitlam speak in Perth. Union members donated a day's pay for the election campaign and the AMWU donated $35 000, saying 'We regard this as the most important single event which has occurred in the Australian political life in the last 30 years.'[49]

As the movement on the streets was diverted to a campaign dominated by orthodox electioneering, the focus of the campaign shifted. Labor's campaign initially emphasised its defence of 'democracy and the Constitution'. However, under assault from the Liberals on questions of economic policy, Labor's leaders switched over to selling their fiscal conservatism. Labor used its most right-wing ministers, Hayden and McClelland, to promote its platform of 'sound' economic management, its commitment to wage restraint, and its ability to control the unions. To the extent that Labor campaigned on economic 'responsibility', it gave credence to the Liberals' argument that the problem was excessive wages, rampant strikes and out-of-control Government spending. In that sense, the ALP only legitimised the main thrust of the Liberals' campaign. Labor's early poll lead ebbed away. Four weeks after the Government's dismissal, Labor was swept away by a national swing of 6.5 per cent. The new Government won 91 seats out of 127 in the House of Representatives and took control of the Senate with a six-seat majority.

The essential contradiction embedded in Labor's reform project was exposed: in order to stay in power, the Whitlam Government had to placate business, a process that so alienated its base that it lost office at the elections. This process had become clear at the Bass by-election, where even right-wing loyalists such as the New South Wales secretary of the AWU, Barry Egan, complained that 'The traditional Labor voter has deserted them [Labor] in herds because they have lost touch with realities and with their own supporters'.[50]

The success of the Kerr Coup was a serious setback for the Australian working class. However, it was only the first skirmish in what was to become a protracted war between employers and workers. In a highly charged and polarised political situation, many workers expected a series of big confrontations to unfold. The new government was not going to have an easy time.

Chapter Four

UNIONISM IN THE FRASER YEARS

Two factors shaped the character of class struggle in the Fraser years. The first was the economic crisis that destroyed Gough Whitlam and dogged his successor through seven years in office. The rate of profit continued to fall and slow economic growth alongside high inflation and unemployment appeared to have become permanently entrenched (see Table 4.1). The second factor was the continued resistance by workers to the Government and business agenda. The success of the Kerr Coup had radicalised a significant minority of workers who loathed the Fraser Government and who saw every union or working-class victory as one step towards bringing it down.

Faced with these two apparently intractable problems, the Fraser Government's actual achievements fell short of its ambitions. It disappointed employers who had looked to it with such enthusiasm on its taking power in 1975 and who had seen it as a vehicle for achieving substantial advances at the expense of the working class. The working class, although battered by the Kerr Coup, high unemployment and a series of important industrial defeats in 1976–77, managed to regroup by late 1978. Over the course of the following three years the strike rate soared, destroying business hopes that the Fraser Government could rein in the unions. The strike wave was followed shortly afterwards by a serious recession, and the two combined to seal the Government's fate.

Table 4.1 Australian economic performance pre- and post-1974

	Pre-1974 (annual average)	1974–83 (annual average)
GDP growth (%)	5.2	1.8
Inflation (%)	3.3	11.4
Unemployment (%)	1.3	5.6

GDP calculated from 1960
Inflation and unemployment calculated from 1953
Source: S. Bell, *Ungoverning the Economy: The Political Economy of Australian Economic Policy*, OUP, 1997, p. 88

A period of retreat, 1976–78[1]

Medibank and the ALP retreat

In the first two years of the Fraser Government unions suffered some serious defeats. The first took place when Fraser succeeded in stripping back Medibank, one of the Whitlam Government's historic reforms. In early 1976 the new Government announced a 2.5 per cent tax levy to finance Medibank, but with an exemption for those who took out private health coverage.[2] Its aim was to reduce Medibank to a threadbare public health insurance system for the low-paid.

Given the significance of Medibank to working-class families, the unions had to defend the scheme.[3] Many workers were more than ready to do battle with the new Government. The first area to move was the New South Wales South Coast, where militants had strong influence within key unions, including the Miners' Federation, the FIA and the WWF. On 26 May, a mass meeting of South Coast delegates called for a 24-hour stoppage and rally. On 7 June, 40 000 South Coast workers struck. Thousands marched and attended a mass meeting at the Showgrounds, where they voted for further action.

On 9 June, workers in Victoria entered the fray when 1500 union delegates voted for a 24-hour strike, rejecting Trades Hall's proposal for a limited four-hour stoppage. Trades Hall then sought to overturn the decision, creating uproar. Militants flooded union offices with demands for a full-day strike. This pressure led the left officials to break ranks with the right wing on the Trades Hall executive, and at the next mass meeting they backed demands for a 24-hour stoppage. The strike pulled out workers from public transport, manufacturing and power generation.

Faced with significant strikes taking place without its endorsement, the ACTU executive shifted ground. At a special unions conference on 5 July, it moved for a 24-hour stoppage on 12 July. The white-collar federation ACSPA immediately endorsed the call. The resulting strike was the single biggest stoppage in Australian history, involving 1.6 million workers. Nonetheless, the public impact of the strike was more limited than this figure would suggest: with the exception of the labor councils in the ACT, the New South Wales South Coast and Newcastle, the unions refused to call rallies on the day of the strike. ACTU president Bob Hawke ostentatiously played tennis to convey the impression that the stoppage was merely a holiday. In Sydney and Melbourne it fell to the far left to call demonstrations on the day, in the case of Melbourne attracting several thousand. Sizeable meetings and demonstrations in support of Medibank were held in the ensuing months, but with no follow-up action called by the ACTU the campaign fizzled out. The left unions resorted, where they could, to demanding that employers pay the levy for their employees.

The failure of the union struggle over Medibank demonstrated that, if militants were keen to take up the struggle against Fraser, the same could not be said of Hawke. The ACTU president made a series of overtures to Fraser for a truce. In May 1976 he told the Government that the ACTU would reconsider its call for higher wages if the Government could demonstrate that wage demands were 'a significant impediment to economic recovery'.[4] In December 1976 Hawke proposed a wage freeze in return for tax cuts. Hawke's proposal was quickly repudiated by the rest of the ACTU executive, but at the 1977 ACTU Congress he announced that unions were 'prepared to sit down with the Government' and would support 'constructive, mean-ingful consultations' on the economy.[5] Hawke had always occupied a quite unusual position for a union official; he enjoyed a remarkable national pro-file and favourable media treatment, and from very early on was hailed as a likely prime minister. However, whereas in the early 1970s he had been known to make speeches full of militant bluster, he now had the reputation of an industrial 'firefighter', hosing down union action and decrying strikes over political causes.[6] After being elected on a support base of the left, his supporters on the ACTU executive by 1976–77 were to be found among the right-wing unions, which now controlled the executive.

But it was not just Hawke. The great majority of established leaders of the ALP drew conservative conclusions from the economic crisis of 1975 and the Kerr Coup. Labor politicians quickly forged a new consensus that social and political reform had to be suspended until business profitability was restored. Regardless of the personalities involved, this has been the bedrock belief of the Labor Party since that time, whether in power or in opposition. The rightward drift in the party was further accentuated by the sharp decline in the strike rate in 1976–77 and the disappearance or rightward shift of the social movements, which reduced pressure on the party from its left. At the 1977 election, Whitlam campaigned on a quite conservative platform. The *Sydney Morning Herald* praised Whitlam's speech at the campaign launch:

> The tone, compared with 1972 and 1974, is muted. There is no crusading fervour, nothing about the redistribution of wealth and the restructuring of society.[7]

Labor suffered further losses at the 1977 election. Whitlam stood down and was replaced by Bill Hayden, a noted Labor conservative. Keynesianism was formally buried and the Labor opposition became converted to the nostrums of monetarism: tight budgets, wage restraint and a firm grip on monetary growth. Hayden told Labor's supporters: 'Much and all as we may regret it, now is not the time for the visionary reform programs of earlier years.'[8] Senior Labor figures were outspoken in their condemnation of strikes.[9]

Given that Labor was now positioning itself as something of a carbon copy of the Fraser Government, the ALP became virtually irrelevant as a significant source of opposition to the Fraser Government between December 1975 and November 1980. The main opposition in this period came from the trade unions.

On the industrial front

The first major industrial clash took place in the printing industry, at Fairfax Newspapers in Sydney.[10] In February 1976, Fairfax announced its intention to introduce computers to allow journalists to enter copy directly, thereby eliminating the jobs of compositors. The objective was partly to cut costs by eliminating 300 jobs but, more importantly, to weaken the printing trades union, which retained significant job control.

The Fairfax workers established a Combined Unions Committee, and on 21 October 1400 Fairfax print workers went on indefinite strike.[11] They demanded a guarantee of no forced redundancies resulting from technological change, a 35-hour week, payment of the Medibank levy and a $20 pay rise.[12]

The strike was bitter, all the more so for the fact that journalists continued to work throughout the dispute. The Combined Unions Committee organised large-scale picketing and appealed for solidarity from other workers.[13] The strikers also produced their own paper, *The Fair Facts*, to put their side of the story in the face of the hostile commercial media. At one point postal workers refused to deliver mail to the Fairfax newspapers, which had a significant effect. When the Federal Government ordered the Postal Commission to suspend employees who were black-banning Fairfax mail, it looked as if a national postal stoppage was imminent, but this was averted when the postal union backed down.

As the strike dragged on without a breakthrough, demoralisation set in. The former head of the chapel (union branch) organised a 'back to work' movement among the printers; the secretary of the NSW Labor Council, John Ducker, seized control of the dispute from the Combined Unions Committee; and when a vote was taken after eight weeks, the decision to return to work was overwhelming. The journalists' failure to support the printers was repaid in 1980 when a majority of print workers ran the presses during a long strike by journalists.[14] The result of these two defeats was the severe weakening of union power at what had been one of its strongholds, the Fairfax newspaper chain.

The second major industrial defeat in the first two years of the Fraser Government took place in Victoria's Latrobe Valley, where 2300 State Electricity Commission (SEC) maintenance workers struck in August 1977 for a $40 pay rise and a 35-hour week.[15] In common with their New South Wales comrades, power industry workers in Victoria had built strong workplace organisation over the years and they now sought to use it to win their pay claim. A pay breakthrough for the Latrobe Valley workers would clearly have threatened indexation and so the stakes were high. After four weeks, power shortages hit industry in Melbourne. Half a million employees were stood down and severe restrictions were placed on public transport and domestic heating and lighting.[16]

Despite the resulting hardship, there was widespread support for the power workers. Liberal Premier Dick Hamer threatened to invoke emergency powers but retreated, fearing that this would only inflame the situation. The SEC's attempts to recruit a scab labour force failed dismally, while financial donations flooded in for the strikers. The strike committee announced plans for anti-eviction and anti-repossession squads to prevent unionists from being turned out of their homes. Small businesses lent support to the power workers and their families, and the strike became something of a *cause celebre* for the Latrobe Valley community.

Strong though the power workers were, however, they were organisationally isolated. They needed industrial support from Melbourne but did not have the networks to organise this themselves. The AMWU office in Melbourne of course did have the necessary connections, but the union leadership was committed to working within the indexation system and did not want to be held responsible for its breakdown. Victorian AMWU secretary John Halfpenny therefore urged the strike committee to call off the strike and sought to divert the pay claim into a 'work value' case in the Commission. In order to succeed in this endeavour, the AMWU leadership sought to demoralise the strikers by creating the impression that they were isolated. Halfpenny encouraged the strike leaders to come to Melbourne, not to tour worksites to make collections and seek support, but to attend lengthy Commission hearings that consisted of hours of tedium and stonewalling by the SEC management. The AMWU leaders tried to convince the strikers that they had no support and that their action was jeopardising Labor's election chances at the forthcoming federal election.[17] The CPA newspaper *Tribune* warned the power workers against 'playing right into Fraser's election plans'.[18]

By these means the strike leaders were eventually induced to recommend a return to work after 11 weeks on strike, with a promise by Halfpenny that the union would vigorously pursue a 'work value' case in the Commission. As with the GMH dispute 13 years previously, the eventual outcome was a severe defeat. The 'work value' case dragged on for months, with the Commission eventually handing down a pay rise of between two and five dollars. Thirty per cent of the workforce won nothing.[19] The Latrobe Valley workers' defeat reverberated throughout the State over the following 12 months; while strike days in New South Wales rose by 80 per cent in 1978, they fell in Victoria by 20 per cent.[20]

The strikes by the Fairfax and Latrobe Valley workers, although defeated, showed a gritty determination to fight and resist on the part of the Australian working class. They also demonstrated the great capacity for initiative and organisation on the part of militants at this time. These were long strikes and in both cases they were organised by local strike committees comprising the militants and other rank-and-file activists. The leading Latrobe Valley militants continued to enjoy strong support in the industry even after their defeat. Nonetheless, their struggles were sold short by their union leaders and the militants lacked the wider networks that could organise industrial solidarity outside their own ranks in defiance of their officials. In this sense these strikes demonstrated both the strengths and the weaknesses of the militants in the union movement at this time.

Other workers took action in 1977. Oil workers, air traffic controllers, petrol tanker drivers and building workers all staged strikes for higher pay.[21] However, with unions on the defensive and strike days falling sharply – from 3.5 million strike days in 1975 to 1.7 million strike days in 1977 – the Arbitration Commission refused to concede the workers' demands and the strikes ended in defeat. The working-class retreat of these years was reflected on the electoral front as well. At the 1977 federal election, Labor's primary vote, which had fallen by 6.5 percentage points in 1975, fell by a further 3.2 percentage points to less than 40 per cent, its lowest figure since 1906.

Militants were being pushed back on a range of fronts. Activists from the old New South Wales branch of the BLF regrouped after the 1974 federal intervention to form Builders' Labourers for Democratic Control (BLDC) to fight for change within the union. This new group won a following on some important Sydney CBD construction sites, as it organised workers on the job to strike for better wages and conditions. In 1978 BLDC mounted an election challenge to the Gallagher-imposed leadership of Steve Black in a court-imposed ballot. However, despite their support on CBD sites, the challengers did not have the apparatus to get the vote out on a State-wide basis, while the incumbents drew on the full resources of the union to despatch organisers around the State to denounce the oppositionists as dis-loyal wreckers. The result of the ballot was a resounding victory for the Gal-lagher forces. The defeat in itself need not have been terminal for the BLDC but, as it had placed all its hopes on a successful outcome in the ballot and had overestimated the extent of its support, morale collapsed and it folded soon afterwards.[22]

In the South Australian vehicle industry, militant shopfloor organisation was eliminated in 1977–78 by joint action involving the employers and the VBEF branch leadership. Until 1976 shopfloor organisation in the industry had been on the upswing: at GMH Elizabeth the number of shop stewards had risen from 23 in 1972 to 50 in 1976, and at Chrysler's plant in Tonsley Park from 18 to 42. At Chrysler the Rank and File Group had been able to sustain militant activity for several years. Guerrilla stoppages ran management ragged.[23] Management were forced to improve conditions; compulsory overtime was abolished, sacked workers were re-employed, management began to consult the union over line speed, the excesses of the more ruthless foremen were curbed and workplace safety was improved.

Management and the VBEF leaders sought ways to rid themselves of the troublesome militants and their opportunity came in the winter of 1977. With a downturn in orders, Chrysler management stood down hundreds of staff and instituted a four-day working week.[24] The VBEF leadership offered no resistance. The militants in the Rank and File Group, however, were determined to fight. At the mass meeting held to consider a union response, they demanded the right to put their motion outlining their proposal for an industrial campaign to the meeting. The officials refused to let them speak. Dozens of outraged workers rushed the stage and the meeting ended in uproar, with the leaders beating a hasty retreat. Immediately after the meeting, the VBEF officials approached management with a list of its adversaries and urged the company to sack them all. Two days later, when the company announced 700 redundancies, the names of all 28 militants associated with the Group were included.

In August 1978 similar treatment was meted out to the militants at the GMH Elizabeth assembly plant. After a national wages campaign involving work bans, extensive stand-downs and a brief worker occupation of the administration block, GMH management sacked Les Bowling, the leader of the shopfloor militants, and 23 of his comrades. The result of these initiatives was that, at both Chrysler and GMH, the employers with the full support of the VBEF leadership had succeeded in beheading the militant rank-and-file opposition in the South Australian car industry.

Union resistance

The defeats of 1976–78 were significant but they do not tell the whole story. The union movement was in retreat but it was by no means routed. The traditions of struggle and the hatred of the Fraser Government ensured that, even though some union strongholds were set back, there were still plenty of workers prepared to resist.

White-collar unions in the federal and state public services were shaken up by the Fraser offensive.[25] These unions experienced a rather different trajectory from that of the blue-collar unions. For the most part they had not participated significantly in the strike wave of the late 1960s and early 1970s. The traditions of professionalism and 'common interests' with the employers weighed heavily on them. In the Administrative and Clerical Officers' Association (ACOA) senior staff played a disproportionate role in the union, particularly in Melbourne and Canberra where the head offices of the public services were located. Groupers ran the Victorian branch, mainstream Labor officials ran the New South Wales branch, and the ACT branch alternated between the two. Neither the ALP nor the Grouper leaders were prepared to rock the boat with ministers by engaging in militant action. In 1970 there was a brief surge of activity when the ACOA organised its first nationally coordinated campaign of stop-works over a pay claim. However, the surge proved short-lived. Between 1972 and 1975 any tendency towards militancy was forestalled by the rapid expansion of the service and improvements to conditions of employment by the Whitlam Government.

The situation began to change with the election of the Fraser Government. Cuts to public service staff and staff freezes were regularly imposed between 1976 and 1980. 'Joint management reviews' (a form of time and motion study) and efficiency audits were used to trim staff, and managers were encouraged to focus on operational 'efficiency'. The advent of computer terminals and word processors led to an enormous potential increase in productivity and with it the opportunity for cuts to staff. The Fraser Government also sought to directly weaken traditional conditions of employment. Specific legislation – the *Commonwealth Employees (Employment Provisions) Act 1977* (CEEP) and the *Commonwealth Employees (Redeployment and Retirement) Act 1977* (CERR)) – was passed to cover the public service. These Acts streamlined redundancies, threatened the traditional notion of 'career service' and gave managers much greater power to stand down workers during strikes.

Over time these trends contributed to a greater openness on the part of public servants to the use of traditional 'blue-collar' methods such as strikes and work bans. The ACOA leaders were already under fire from a new generation of young public servants who had been affected by radicalism on the campuses where many of them had studied. The leadership had done nothing in response to the Kerr Coup. The Fraser Government's attacks were a further test and in every case the leaders failed to meet the challenge, offering limp resistance at best. Given the gradual change in consciousness among public servants, an opening now developed for a change of leadership, most obviously in Victoria where the Groupers held sway. The formation of the ACOA Reform Group in Melbourne in 1976 was the first step. The Reform Group championed a greater preparedness to use industrial action to resist government attacks. It met regularly, had democratic procedures, issued publications and held open meetings, all features that distinguished it from the organisational methods of its Grouper rivals. It sought to combine the building of strong local workplace structures with a push to defeat the Groupers in branch elections. In 1979 it was successful in the latter aim, and the Groupers were also thrown out in elections in Tasmania. The election results both reflected and contributed to a process of greater militancy on the part of public servants, which was demonstrated in 1979 when the ACOA and the Public Service Association (representing lower-classification public servants) organised a coordinated campaign of work bans and strikes in response to the CERR Act.

Similar processes were under way among school teachers, who were being hit hard by reduced pay and conditions relative to other white-collar workers as a result of budget cuts.[26] In the inner, western and northern suburbs of Melbourne, branches of the Victorian Secondary Teachers' Association challenged school principals' rights to manage staff, organised walk-outs once maximum teaching hours as set by the union were exceeded, and campaigned against staff victimisations. School representatives came together on a regular basis at delegate forums which attracted dozens, and sometimes up to 100, attendees. These forums gave delegates the opportunity to pressure the leadership of Peter Vaughan, who represented a more conservative layer of old-style teacher unionists. Over time, agitation at school level generated a momentum for change and in 1982 Vaughan was toppled by a new leadership comprising former student radicals with a base among the younger generation of teachers.

The inability of the Fraser Government to fully drive home its sweeping victories in the electoral sphere is clear on a range of other fronts. It was obvious with the failure of the Fraser Government's new union watchdog, the Industrial Relations Bureau (IRB). The Bureau was charged with stamping out closed shops, investigating breaches of industrial law and bringing offending parties before the Industrial Court, where penalties included deregistration, seizure of union funds and fines. Despite its extensive powers, the IRB was virtually stillborn. This became clear over the course of 1977 and 1978 when a string of individuals, using the new legal provisions, sought to assert their right not to belong to a trade union and to cross picket lines.[27] These included Sydney swimming instructor Kerry Ferguson, Broken Hill mechanic Noel Latham, Melbourne tramway workers Paul Krutulis and Barbara Biggs and Melbourne council maintenance worker Frank Kane. Their cases were taken up with gusto by the IRB, Fraser's Industrial Relations Minister Tony Street, and the news media, who championed them as popular heroes standing up to union bullies. While the IRB enjoyed mixed results when it took the cases of these individuals to the Industrial Court, the workers won no support from their workmates, who refused to work with them and, on several occasions, walked out on strike. The IRB was incapable of imposing its authority and was rendered a dead letter.

The Government also had little success with its 1977 'secondary boycott' provisions, which banned unions in one enterprise from striking in support of workers in dispute in another. The Federal Court was empowered by these provisions, which were inserted in the Trade Practices Act, to impose fines of up to $250 000 and the award of damages against offending unions. Such was the strength of unions at this time that no major employer sought to invoke these provisions.

Campaigning on the political front[28]

Unions also took action in the mid 1970s on two important political issues: uranium mining and the proposed Newport (Victoria) power station. Unions objected to uranium mining because of its contribution to the proliferation of nuclear weapons, its consequences for Aboriginal land rights, the health hazards for workers involved in the industry and the dangers of nuclear power stations, something that was brought forcefully home with the Three Mile Island radiation leak in Pennsylvania in 1979. In a rare rebuff to Hawke, the 1975 ACTU Congress had voted to ban the mining and transport of uranium, pending a full public inquiry. In May 1976, the Australian Railways Union struck nationally for 24 hours over the sacking of

Queensland unionist Jim Assenbruck, who had been dismissed for refusing to load material for uranium processing. Assenbruck got his job back. In the same year unionists black-banned the US nuclear warship *Truxton*.[29]

Early in 1976, the Fraser Government established the Ranger Inquiry, chaired by Justice Fox, to investigate the impact of uranium mining in the Northern Territory. In October the Inquiry handed down its first report, which contained ammunition for both anti-nuclear campaigners and the uranium producers. The second Fox report in May 1977 was equally inconclusive. The anti-nuclear campaign kept up the pressure. In July, hundreds of anti-uranium campaigners in Melbourne held a protest at Swanson Dock against the loading of yellowcake on the *Columbus Australia*. After the police arrived, the wharfies stopped work and the ship was forced to leave without its valuable cargo. On 25 August, the Fraser Government raised the political temperature when it approved unrestricted uranium mining and export. In October, the left-wing unions joined Friends of the Earth and the Movement Against Uranium Mining to organise large city rallies, with marches of between 15 000 and 20 000 in Melbourne and Sydney.

The unions were by no means united on the question of uranium. The right-wing unions implacably opposed the bans. The AWU in particular favoured the mining, enrichment and export of uranium and was keen to sign up new members in the industry. It was to the fore in trying to get the union bans lifted. In June 1976, after heavy lobbying by the AWU, the ACTU executive gave the green light to CRA's Mary Kathleen mine in Queensland. Uranium mining was hotly debated at the September 1977 ACTU Congress, where it took up the entire fourth day of proceedings. The ACTU executive, by now with a solid right-wing majority, rejected a motion by the left-wing unions, led by the ARU and AMWU, to ban work on existing contracts at Mary Kathleen. Instead, Hawke called on the Government to organise a referendum on the issue and threatened that, if this was not done within one month, unions would resume bans on the mining and transport of uranium.

With the stakes high, the Fraser Government drew up secret plans in October 1977 to use the defence forces, supplemented by heavy legal firepower, to break any union blockade of Mary Kathleen. One Cabinet paper explained the seriousness of the issue:

MKU [Mary Kathleen] must be maintained as an operating mine. If it fails as a result of union pressure, the effect on the domestic industrial relations scene and on the international front would be irreparable from the Government's standpoint.[30]

Possibly sensing a severe confrontation, the ACTU backed off, and operations at Mary Kathleen proceeded unmolested.

In February 1978, the ACTU executive widened its exemptions to allow *all* existing mining contracts to be honoured. However, under pressure from the big anti-uranium street marches, it also declared its opposition to the opening of any new mines until further safeguards were in place. This resolution was openly flouted by the major right-wing unions in the industry, which saw opportunities to recruit hundreds more members at new mines being opened up at Roxby Downs and Nabarlek. The 1979 ACTU Congress reaffirmed union policy on 'no new mines', and the AWU continued to disregard it with impunity.

Leaders of the left-wing unions were not themselves resolute in opposing uranium. The Miscellaneous Workers' Union, though formally opposed to the industry, was recruiting workers in the mines so as not to lose ground to the AWU. Members of the ARU were transporting supplies to Mary Kathleen, Nabarlek and Ranger. In September 1979 the national leadership of the WWF said it would ban all uranium cargoes, but only on condition that all 25 unions engaged in the industry do the same. Given that the right-wing unions had repeatedly emphasised their disinclination to do this, the resolution amounted to an empty gesture.

In 1981, on the grounds that they had become unenforceable, the ACTU executive lifted all bans on the industry.[31] Nonetheless, the campaign had not been entirely in vain. The 1982 ALP conference voted to limit the uranium industry to the three existing mines if the party won government at the forthcoming election.

The union and community campaign against the Newport power station, which had fired up in 1974, had gone into abeyance during the drama of 1975. However, it revived in 1976 and a similar line-up of forces presented itself. Victorian Trades Hall had imposed bans on any work involved in building the power station. The right-wing unions in Trades Hall, led by former secretary Ken Stone, sought ways to dilute the ban on construction work on the basis that it would provide work for union members. On two occasions in 1976, solid lobbying by left-wing unions and community campaign groups prevented Trades Hall from reversing the ban.

Frustrated by union opposition, the Liberal Hamer Government raised the stakes, suspending nearly 300 State government projects[32] and introducing a Vital State Projects Bill, which threatened fines of up to $50 000 for any organisation boycotting 'vital State projects'. Despite denouncing the Bill as 'fascist', the Trades Hall leadership was anxious for a compromise. The leadership, with the support of the AMWU, pushed through a resolution in November 1976 in favour of a State Government inquiry.[33] The inquiry found that a power station would cause immense damage to the area, yet recommended that construction go ahead. Seven right-wing unions broke ranks with Trades Hall and endorsed members working on the project.[34] By late June 1977, 150 workers were on the job. Sporadic efforts were made by the leaders of the left-wing unions to have the work stopped by direct appeals to the workers on the site and by black-banning supplies, but their efforts were not vigorously enforced. Serious mass picketing was needed, but this was not organised. By 1979 the bans had become a dead letter, and in 1980 they were lifted by Trades Hall.[35]

Both Newport and the uranium campaign demonstrated a crucial weakness among the left-wing union leaders. Although they fought, albeit at times inconsistently, against the right at the level of the ACTU and labor councils to secure policies that promoted progressive causes, they did not effectively mobilise to put these policies into practice. The result was that they might announce bans but, in circumstances of high unemployment, their members continued to work regardless. It was not that rank-and-file workers could not be persuaded to act on these issues. In some cases, in fact, they were well in advance of their officials. In 1980, AMWU members at Sargeants/ANI voted to ban work on 4000 tons of steel for the Ranger uranium mine.[36] When management decided to outsource the work to other companies, workers at Evans Deakin voted to follow the lead of Sargeants' workers and banned work on the contract themselves, even at the risk of losing 20 jobs. Nonetheless, without strong workplace organisation, actions such as these were episodic and insufficient.[37] And, without an orientation to building this organisation and mobilising workers around these issues, the left-wing union leaders found themselves defeated in practice even at times when they could win the vote.

Union recovery, 1978–81

The years 1976–78 were ones of overall retreat, but the situation was fluid. Workers had been knocked about by the retrenchments and high unemployment and by defeats in some key areas but they were still prepared to fight. The balance between capital and labour had swung towards capital, but from the second half of 1978 the balance started to swing back again as workers began to reassert themselves in a process that culminated in the smashing of wage indexation.

The first sign of a lift in confidence occurred in June 1978, when 1750 workers at Utah mines in central Queensland struck for six weeks for higher wages. The campaign was led by rank-and-file workers and directed by weekly mass meetings.[38] This rank-and-file involvement was a key to winning significant concessions from management, including payment of a $100 weekly bonus.[39]

As the Utah strike drew to a close, Telecom technicians took action in protest at plans to centralise and computerise the maintenance of telephone exchanges, which was forecast to cost hundreds of technicians' jobs.[40] Twenty-six thousand Telecom workers took part in a 24-hour strike and work bans. Management retaliated by standing down 4000 workers, but was forced to commit to consultation over the changes and to only introduce the system on a two-year trial basis.[41] The Telecom dispute helped to debunk employer claims about new technology promising a brighter future, and highlighted the impact that computerisation was having on jobs. It also helped to establish technological change as a union issue, and not the exclusive prerogative of management.

The Fraser Government won re-election in 1977, but the response by workers to its austerity Budget in August 1978 demonstrated once again that it had not won the war. Without waiting for a lead from their officials, rank-and-file unionists in all the major cities, including waterside workers in Port Adelaide and Melbourne and hundreds of Melbourne construction workers, spontaneously walked off the job in protest at the Budget. The ALP and union leaders ran to catch up. On 17 August they called marches in the capital cities, which drew in 5000–10 000 workers from the wharves, the metal industry, the dockyards, the print industry, the metal trades and the abattoirs.[42] Workers were angry. Following marches in Sydney and Melbourne, the far left led significant numbers of demonstrators in

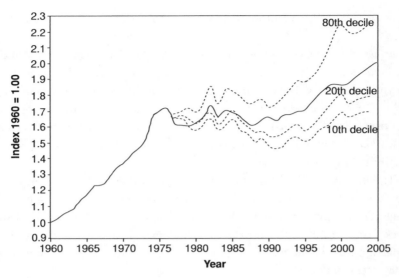

Figure 4.1 Trends in male earnings 1960–2005
Source: Paul Frijters & Bob Gregory, 'From golden age to golden age: Australia's "Great Leap Forward"?', *The Economic Record,* vol. 82, 2006, p. 20. Reproduced with the permission of Wiley-Blackwell Publishing.
Note: All adult male full-time weekly earnings indexed at 1.7 in 1976

breakaway marches on the stock exchanges. More than 120 were arrested at an anti-Budget rally in Brisbane.[43] At a meeting of 1000 shop stewards in Melbourne, workers called on the ACTU to organise weekly half-day stoppages in protest at the Budget.[44] Hawke, however, had no intention of doing such a thing and the campaign fizzled out for want of leadership.

The fight over wages re-emerged in early 1979. Following a series of national wage cases that resulted in only partial indexation, the share of wages in national income and real wages had fallen sharply (see Figures 2.1 and 4.1). Unemployment also fell slightly for the first time in years, putting unions in a stronger bargaining position. Workers were keen to make good their losses. The ACTU, however, was initially hesitant to challenge indexation. It supported individual unions pursuing wage rises outside the Commission to compensate for partial indexation, but it did little to help them concretely. It was more interested in using the threat of strike action as a tool to persuade the Commission to maintain full indexation than as a serious weapon to push up wages by action in the field.[45] When train drivers struck for higher wages in June 1978 their union earned a rebuke from the ACTU.[46]

Nonetheless, pressure from workers to break the indexation guidelines soon became unstoppable. In 1977 the Commission had sent the Latrobe Valley power workers away with nothing when the AMWU submitted a 'work value' claim on their behalf. Two years later the Commission was no longer in a position to simply dismiss wage claims, such was workers' preparedness to fight. In 1979 the Commission granted wharfies an $8.60 wage rise on the basis of work value improvements 'in the whole industry', rather than only on the exceptional and limited grounds for specific occupations that had been the pattern until this point. The wharfies were soon followed by every other strong union anxious to get its share of the work value bonanza. Eight dollars now became the standard claim. The gap was forced open wider still in March 1980, when the Commission awarded the Storemen and Packers Union in the wool industry rises of between $10.75 and $12.75.[47] Meanwhile, increasing numbers of strongly placed unions were winning wage rises by negotiating directly with employers.

The Federal Government vacillated, making a series of contradictory suggestions as to the future of indexation. In winter 1981 the situation came to a head. The TWU had lodged a claim for a $20 pay rise and imposed bans on deliveries to supermarkets. The ban had an immediate effect on supplies. The Victorian Liberal Government declared a state of emergency. Unwilling to escalate the confrontation, Fraser reached an agreement with ACTU president Cliff Dolan to settle the pay claim through arbitration as a special case. However, the Commission rejected this manoeuvre on the grounds that a centralised system of indexation could not coexist with a series of 'anomalies' for individual unions. Its ability to hold the line, however, was undermined by employers who were beginning to pay the increase anyway. Unions covering Telecom, road transport, the Melbourne waterfront and sectors of the Australian public service were also winning significant rises. Rather than try to prop up indexation when its foundations were crumbling, the Commission then simply abandoned it.

The end of indexation led to a strike wave unparalleled since 1974. In the context of a resources boom, storemen and packers won increases of up to $50 per week. Metalworkers signed a new 12-month Metal Industry Agreement with the MTIA in December 1981 that lifted the fitter's rate by $25 (11.9%), introduced a supplementary allowance of $9 and ushered in a 38-hour week. Average weekly earnings raced ahead by 16 per cent. A dispute in the vehicle industry demonstrated that there were still plenty of workers with a desire to fight.

The vehicle industry unions had lodged a pay claim of $30 in May 1981 when indexation was still in place. After four months of waiting, VBEF members at the Ford Broadmeadows plant were fed up with stalling. Indexation had been scrapped but the company would not pay, and their own leaders did not appear to have any intention of calling a strike to pressure the company. At a meeting on 18 September, Ford workers at Broadmeadows voted for an indefinite strike. VBEF federal secretary Len Townsend immediately disowned the strike, declaring it to be the work of 'a few rebel shop stewards',[48] while ACTU president Cliff Dolan urged the strikers to return to work 'in view of the possibility that divisions and perhaps violence may occur' on the picket line.[49]

Undeterred, the Ford stewards set to work and took charge of the dispute involving 5000 workers, the large majority of them migrants. The stewards held daily meetings, and all plants in the complex were picketed continuously for the first time in the history of Broadmeadows. Financial collections were made at the GMH and AMI plants at Fishermans Bend, and leaflets and press handouts were prepared, translated and circulated throughout the car industry and beyond. The strikers also collected funds at stop-work meetings of other unions. Behind the scenes the ACTU and VBEF leaders sought to engineer a return to work.

Ford was intransigent and refused to improve on its pay offer: it hoped to use the conflict as an opportunity to deal once and for all with the Broadmeadows militants. After several weeks of deadlock, Ford requested the Arbitration Commission to order a secret ballot of the workers on a return to work. Even though the union movement opposed secret ballots on the grounds that they prevented workers debating out questions and voting collectively as a body, the ACTU and VBEF leaders went along with the Commission's order and urged workers to participate in the ballot. The result was close, but by a margin of only 169 votes out of 4000 votes cast the Ford workers voted to return to work. The stewards then organised another mass meeting on the Friday morning, 30 October, at which they pointed to a series of irregularities in the ballot, including many workers not receiving ballot papers and others receiving two. The mass meeting determined to resist the manoeuvres by the Commission, the company and the VBEF leaders to stampede them back to work. Chief steward Frank

Argondizzo slammed the union's leaders as 'bureaucrats with big cigars in their mouths'.[50] Nonetheless, faced with a sustained 'back to work' campaign in the media over the following weekend and despairing at their isolation, the workers eventually accepted defeat and returned to work on 2 November. The stewards' committee had kept the strike going for six weeks but it was not capable of sustaining it beyond this point.

If migrant workers at Ford were making union leaders sit up and take notice, the same was true with many women workers.[51] Nurses and health workers were increasingly taking industrial action, shaking off decades of industrial passivity. They imposed bans, struck and marched on the streets in protest at planned hospital closures and cuts to health services. Women workers also played an important role in the rising militancy among clerical and administrative staff in the public service in the late 1970s and were increasingly elected to delegate positions. Action by workers forced employers to open up opportunities for women to work in non-traditional occupations – as bus drivers and airline pilots and in a variety of blue-collar trades. By 1980, women comprised 32 per cent of total union membership.[52]

Increasing membership and unrest among female members had an impact on the official structures of the unions. In August 1976 women's activists in the unions convened a Women's Trade Union Conference in Sydney that drew in 500 delegates, mostly white-collar, but some blue-collar as well.[53] In 1977 the ACTU adopted a Working Women's Charter, which abandoned the long-held commitment to the family wage, and in 1978 a special ACTU conference was convened to discuss demands for child care, equal pay and union training. Women were increasingly winning senior positions; notable among these were Jennie George, elected secretary of the NSW Teachers' Federation, and Jan Marsh, appointed industrial advocate for the ACTU. In 1981 an ACTU women's conference with 140 delegates was opened by Cliff Dolan, and the 1981 ACTU Congress passed a resolution endorsing 'free, safe, legal abortion', defeating stiff resistance by the right-wing unions. All in all, women were clearly playing a much more significant role in the union movement than they had ten years earlier.[54]

The strike wave of 1979–81 was certainly an impressive achievement; nearly 7400 disputes were notched up over this three-year period, involving more than four million workers and accounting for more than 11 million strike days. Like the earlier strike wave of the early 1970s, it led to increased wages and contributed to raising union membership (by 130 000 on this occasion). Nonetheless, the *character* of the two periods was rather different.

The earlier strike wave was part of a broader lift in social struggle and a shift to the left in the community at large. It was associated with a political radicalisation among a significant minority of the Australian population and was part of a broader international movement. The latter struggle lacked these elements – there were no Vietnam Moratoriams, Green Bans or workers' control campaigns. Although it did involve some political questions, as identified in this account, the demands were much more 'bread and butter' – chiefly involving wages and hours.

The second major difference was that the earlier strike wave was driven by workers in many cases acting independently of, and sometimes in conflict with, their union officials. There were certainly episodes where this occurred in the late 1970s and early 1980s – the Ford strike being one important example – but this was not the typical situation; strikes were for the most part led and directed by the union officials. Militants had been squeezed out or suffered defeats in construction, the vehicle industry and the Latrobe Valley. They were also defeated at Tooth's Brewery in Sydney, the Redfern Mail Exchange and the Newcastle shipyards. With the shut-down of GMH Pagewood in Sydney in 1979 another militant centre was closed. These setbacks were not reversed in the strike wave of the early 1980s. The upturn in struggle was simply too short to rebuild the kinds of shopfloor committees that were needed to take things forward.

With the decline in independent workplace activism, the left-wing union leaders in the AMWU, BWIU and elsewhere were under less pressure from their members and began to adopt notably more conservative industrial and political strategies. They increasingly sought to substitute struggle on the job with bureaucratic manoeuvres like work value cases (as in the Latrobe Valley dispute). The underlying weakening of the union movement that had resulted was disguised briefly by the strike wave of 1981. It was, however, about to be sharply exposed by the deep economic downturn of 1982.

The end of the Fraser Government and the emergence of the Accord

The wages push of 1980–81 had taken place during an economic boom centred on the resources sector. In 1982, this boom came to a sudden end as commodity prices collapsed in the context of the sharpest downturn in the world economy since the Great Depression. Profitability hit a new low (see Figure 3.1). Employers responded by shedding labour and unemployment soared from less than 6 per cent to more than 10 per cent, the highest level since the 1930s.

The economic crisis was the last straw for many in the ruling class. Their hopes that Fraser might be able to fix the economy had not been realised. Furthermore, Fraser had not clearly broken the power of the unions as he had promised in 1975. The strike wave of 1979–81 demonstrated this dramatically. The Industrial Relations Bureau had failed, there was resistance to the CEEP Act in the public service, and the reform appetite of the Fraser Government was constrained by an underlying sense of its own illegitimacy, the legacy of the 1975 coup.[55] Important sections of business now began to view the Fraser Government with scepticism and to look more favourably on the ALP. Labor offered an 'Accord' with the ACTU, effectively a national no-strike pledge, and employers saw an opportunity to cut wages with union consent.

The ALP–ACTU Accord had its origins in the response by the leaders of Australian unions and the ALP to the economic crisis of the mid-1970s. The experience of the Whitlam Government demonstrated that the ALP was more than ready to introduce measures that imposed the burden of the crisis on the working class. After its defeat in December 1975, the ALP leadership drew the conclusion that it had to become, if anything, still more committed to monetarist policies and budget austerity.

Given that they shared a common social-democratic, political framework and saw Labor's role as one of managing and sustaining capitalism, most union leaders were also prepared to play their part in helping to restore profit rates for Australian business. Hawke had been to the fore, with regular pleas to the Fraser Government to include the ACTU in some form of consensus economic management involving state governments, the federal government, unions and employer organisations.[56] The Fraser Government, just as regularly, rebuffed Hawke's advances and the idea was stillborn. Hawke now sought to promote the idea of a tripartite business–union–government arrangement to take effect when the ALP regained office, and discussions to this end began to feature regularly at Labor conferences. In 1980 Hawke at last fulfilled the future long predicted for him when he won the seat of Wills in the federal election. This election also saw a big swing to the ALP, which gave an added urgency to the debate about a pact. In 1981 the ACTU Congress endorsed a proposal to accept an incomes policy under Labor, under which unions would accept wage indexation and a pledge not to pursue further wage claims in the field, in return for improvements to the 'social wage' comprising health, education and social security.

The ACTU resolution to support an incomes policy and a 'no extra claims' commitment under a Labor Government was supported not just by the leaders of the right-wing unions, who for the most part did not lead strikes anyway and for whom indexation offered a means of winning wage rises without the work associated with strikes. It was also warmly endorsed by most left union leaders, including the AMWU and BWIU, whose members still retained the capacity to wreck it and whose support was vital to the entire project. This represented a radical change in policy on the part of the AMWU. In 1971 the union had rejected attempts by the MTIA to insert a no-strike clause in the first Metal Industry Award. When indexation was introduced four years later, with the support of the AMWU leadership, the union's leaders had nonetheless maintained the union's right to campaign for higher over-award wages. The union reasserted its stance at its 1976 national conference, declaring:

> All awards, whether arrived at by consent, negotiation or agreement, must always leave our members free to struggle around their economic and social demands, including over-award payment and conditions. We reject ... turning the union into its opposite by requiring its officers to instruct members not to engage in struggle.[57]

In 1981 the AMWU leadership now decisively rejected its earlier positions. It not only endorsed the resolution on incomes policy at the 1981 ACTU Congress, but in December it signed off on a Metal Industry Agreement with the MTIA that contained a 'no further claims' clause prohibiting the metal unions from making any further wages demands for 12 months – in effect a 'no-strike' agreement policed by the AMWU itself. The results were immediate. Within four months of the agreement taking effect, MTIA president Bert Evans told a journalist:

> There have been occasions where employees on the job have sought to raise the question of wages but very properly, without exception, the metal unions have been quick to point out to the members that they voted on the [metal industry] Agreement and are bound to honour it.[58]

What had changed? Why was the AMWU leadership now prepared to play the very role that only five years earlier it had totally rejected? Two factors help explain this shift. The first was the economic crisis and demands by employers and government that workers sacrifice. The AMWU leaders, as an intermediary layer between capital and labour and committed ultimately to the capitalist order despite their at times radical rhetoric, adapted to this pressure, insisting only that wage restraint be offset by various supportive measures. Further, national pacts and peak-level committees of the type flagged in the ACTU resolution fitted well into their generally bureaucratic conception of how class struggle should be managed. The second factor responsible for the change in AMWU strategy was the series of industrial defeats suffered by workers in the latter half of the 1970s, which led to a lessening of the pressure on the union leaders from below. Without any fire under them from rank-and-file militants, the AMWU leaders became increasingly reluctant to fight. During the latter half of the 1970s, Victorian secretary John Halfpenny consistently shied away from a fight with the right-wing unions on issues ranging from Medibank to Newport.[59] The transition was marked in formal terms in 1980, when Halfpenny quit the CPA to join the ALP.

The political shift of the AMWU leaders can be traced in successive AMWU publications on the economic crisis.[60] In 1976 the union produced its 'People's Budget' in response to the Fraser Government's austerity package. The People's Budget was informed by the kind of Keynesian policies that had underpinned economic policy in many European countries in the 1950s and 1960s, with calls for deficit spending, expanded social welfare payments and public works projects to soak up unemployment. The union urged the raising of taxes on the rich and the introduction of the 35-hour week.

The People's Budget was followed in 1977 by a 20-page pamphlet, *Australia Uprooted*. This provided a much more substantial analysis of the problems of Australian capitalism and the measures necessary to deal with them. It brought together two arguments: one, that the working class could advance its interests by class struggle; two, that the economic crisis was the result of a conspiracy and could be set right by parliamentary intervention.[61] The AMWU attributed the crisis of the world economy to manipulation by multinational companies, particularly those in the resources sector. The Fraser Government was boosting the interests of the mining multinationals and allowing the run-down of domestic manufacturing industry.

The union's solution was a 'People's Economic Program', which the union tabled at the 1977 conferences of the ACTU and ALP. The Program called for nationalisation of the big corporations and tight control over interest rates and foreign investment. Small- and medium-sized companies were to receive public financial assistance, and those sections of big business not nationalised could be restructured under government direction using public funds, tariffs and quotas. The AMWU put these proposals forward as part of a transition to socialism.

Australia Uprooted was mass-produced and, by the normal standards of union publications, was attractively presented. It garnered significant attention well beyond the AMWU itself and was the subject of sympathetic debate by academics and left-wing officials at a series of workshops in Sydney. The analysis and policy prescriptions of *Australia Uprooted* followed very closely those of the CPA, which had a long tradition of distinguishing between what it described as 'productive' sectors of Australian capitalism and 'parasitic', usually foreign-owned, sectors of business, and it appealed to the former to join with the labour movement in an alliance against the latter.

Although the CPA had lost much of its mass base by the late 1970s, it was still a force in the AMWU leadership. The CPA also provided much of the theoretical framework of the Labor Left. After its leftward shift in the early 1970s, the CPA had swung back to the right again after the Kerr Coup in the context of the downturn in struggle. Talk of 'revolution' that had rung briefly at party conferences in the early 1970s gave way to a much more conservative strategy.

With the Australian state patently uninterested in introducing central planning, the only *practical* consequence of the CPA's economic program was for the AMWU leaders to collaborate with so-called 'progressive' national industrial capitalists to save 'our industry' from the machinations of the multinationals and their puppet Fraser Government. They further called on the ALP to commit to some form of industry consultative mechanisms. The problem for members of the AMWU was that 'saving' manufacturing required first and foremost the re-establishment of the conditions under which profitability might be revived, and for the most part this came down to attacks on jobs and wages. Australian capital, whether allegedly 'productive' or 'parasitic', was not about to sign its own death warrant in the name of rhetoric about 'alternative economic strategies' or 'revolutionary reforms' that peppered debates involving the left unions and sympathetic academics at this time.

For a period the AMWU leaders could combine talk of parliamentary reform and class struggle. The union's 1979 publication *Australia Ripped Off* asserted that class struggle could drive the parliamentary agenda of an incoming Labor Government to the left and force it to pursue policies that its right wing might oppose. In theory this was quite feasible. However, class struggle inevitably ran smack up against the union leaders' concurrent attempts to establish cordial relations with 'productive' national capitalists to 'save manufacturing'.

In the context of the collapse in strikes during the deep recession of 1982 and the union leaders' own inclinations to collaborate with business, the contradiction embedded in union documents between a class struggle approach and a parliamentary reformist approach was resolved decisively in favour of the latter. And so, while *Australia Ripped Off* had envisaged some combination of parliamentary reform and 'day to day resistance in the workplaces and localities', its successor, *Australia on the Rack*, launched jointly by the CPA's Laurie Carmichael and Labor leader Bill Hayden in early 1982, was little more than electoral publicity for the ALP for the coming federal election.

The trends under way in the AMWU were replicated in other left unions. Pat Clancy, Stan Sharkey and Tom McDonald, leaders of the BWIU and also of the Socialist Party, endorsed the 1981 ACTU Congress incomes policy resolution, as did the BWIU's arch-rival, the BLF. Supporters of the Accord counterposed struggle by workers on the job, which was derided as defensive, sectional and counter-productive, to an 'interventionist' strategy by the union movement. Mark Burford argued:

> It is necessary to break out of the circle of mobilisation followed by containment and frustration. The Prices and Incomes agreement can help to do that by extending the role of workers' organisations beyond that of defence against the reaction to the employing class and giving them an expanded and creative economic and political role. It can, if carried out to the level of union/government/employer negotiations and discussions, bring unions into the economic policy planning areas as well. Unions would then have a much expanded responsibility and potentially creative role.[62]

With the left-wing unions locked in behind a pact, the ACTU and ALP announced their Prices and Incomes Policy in August 1982. This was followed in December by the final version of the Accord document, which was endorsed at a special unions conference on 22 February 1983. The ALP promised to support a return to wage indexation, an expansionary budget policy to reduce unemployment, the repeal of Fraser's anti-union laws, the introduction of Medicare, improved social security and the establishment of a series of joint committees to oversee industry restructuring. In exchange the ACTU gave a commitment not to make claims on employers for extra wage increases outside those resulting from indexation: in other words, a no-strike pledge. The Accord offered not automatic and fully-indexed quarterly cost-of-living adjustments but only 'the maintenance of real wages over time'.

Despite the fact that successive AMWU publications had promoted industry nationalisation, this notion vanished in the Accord. The left-wing union leaders were left only with fragmentary statements such as: 'consultative mechanisms of a widespread nature . . . will play a coordinated and ongoing role in assisting the success of the transition of the economy onto a planned framework.'

The Accord was, if not embraced, at least accepted by most union militants. They could console themselves that at least it appeared to guarantee wage increases in tough economic times, and the prospect of a managed economic recovery promised more jobs. The alternative appeared much worse. Without an Accord, Labor leader Bill Hayden told the 1982 ALP national conference, an incoming Labor Government would have only 'fiscal and monetary measures . . . quite brutal and severe in their impact'.[63]

The traditional bases of industrial militancy, so far advanced in the early 1970s, were already in decline by early 1982 when a CPA document suggested that 'shop floor organisation [in the metal industry] has not expanded during the decade . . . there are few if any effective self-acting shop committees.'[64] The recession landed a further blow as employers imposed mass redundancies, temporary shut-downs, extended leave without pay and early retirements.

In the absence of any sizeable and well-organised radical current in the labour movement, union militants lacked a sophisticated political analysis capable of resisting the emerging consensus that economic crisis required workers to sacrifice. In the early 1970s they had rejected the argument that wage rises caused unemployment. However, defeats and recessions had created exhaustion in their ranks. Furthermore, the fact that the surge in unemployment followed on directly from the big wages push of 1979–81 appeared to create an obvious connection between the two phenomena. Many militants now accepted the argument that wage rises *did* cause unemployment and that therefore wage restraint would allow for economic recovery and job creation.

The loss of organisational capacity and their ideological disorientation created a paralysis in the ranks of union militants. They lost the self-confidence that had carried them through the earlier strike wave of the early 1970s which followed their victories over absorption and the penal powers. They began to look for parliamentary solutions. Whereas in the early 1970s the parliamentary Labor Party leant on the unions for support, the unions now pinned their hopes on a Labor victory at the forthcoming federal election.[65]

The militants were also undercut by a collapse of confidence among the broad membership of the unions. The recession saw the emergence of 'under-award' bargaining, whereby workers accepted dilution of award conditions, hoping to stave off redundancies. In many workplaces union organisers were now trying to hold the line against significant cuts to award conditions. Facing possible plant closure, workers at Betts Electric Motors, a division of Kirby Engineering, in Western Sydney accepted a 5 per cent pay cut against the advice of their organiser. This breakthrough paved the way for large-scale concessions in work practices at Betts 'in a way that would have been unthinkable ten years previously', according to the company's industrial relations manager.[66] Likewise, coal miners at Clutha in New South Wales accepted drastically reduced conditions in exchange for a six-month freeze on sackings.[67]

Not all workers went down without a fight. In September 1982, Australian Iron and Steel and BHP announced plans to cut thousands of jobs on the New South Wales South Coast – nearly 400 from the coal mines and 3000 from the steel plants.[68] Six thousand coal miners struck for 24 hours in protest and seven busloads of mineworkers travelled to Sydney where they briefly occupied the offices of BHP. On 13 October, South Coast miners went underground to occupy the Kemira pit, where 206 job losses had been slated.[69] The action at Kemira was a powerful stimulus to union activism above ground. Four thousand miners rallied at the Showgrounds in protest against the redundancies, followed on 21 October by another rally of 10 000 South Coast workers, which voted overwhelmingly for snap strikes in the steelworks and mines. On 26 October, 2000 unionists went to Canberra to protest outside Parliament House, demanding federal intervention to save jobs. This rally ended with an impromptu invasion of the Parliament building, which placed the issue of mass redundancies in the national spotlight.[70] Nonetheless, heartening though the struggle of the South Coast workers was, it did not succeed in halting the redundancies. Furthermore, it was isolated – the vast majority of redundancies took place without organised resistance.

On 7 December 1982, Fraser called a meeting of state premiers and federal ministers, which agreed to make a joint submission for a wage freeze at the National Wage Case then in progress.[71] With the strike rate plummeting and the militants in disarray the Arbitration Commission was able to oblige, introducing a six-month wage freeze. The Federal Government froze the pay of federal public servants for 12 months. Union leaders complained about the loss of real wages but, other than in one or two sectors, took no action.[72] The ACTU executive complained but went along with the freeze.[73]

The pay freeze was clearly not a long-term solution for business; in fact it demonstrated that Fraser had no strategic plan for the Australian economy. Labor's Accord with the ACTU, by contrast, offered a way of keeping wages militancy suppressed on a long-term basis. Labor's agenda was based around a simple appeal. Fraser had brought divisiveness to Australian society, and his economic policies had led to a wage breakout followed by recession. Labor promised social consensus, arguing that unemployment could be reduced if unions moderated wage demands, and that only the ALP could convince unions to do so for more than six or twelve months. Furthermore, the Wran Government had been in power in New South Wales since 1976 and had proven to be a 'safe pair of hands' for business, and moderate Labor governments had been elected in Victoria and South Australia with no threatening consequences. In a last-minute switch, the more popular Hawke, who had proven his credentials as a man with whom business could do business, and who had more credibility in the eyes of union officials and workers, pushed aside Hayden for the Labor leadership. Some sections of business were won over by Labor's pitch. Others were neutralised. The conservative Melbourne *Herald* endorsed the ALP for the first time in its long history.

The result of widespread working-class disaffection with the Fraser Government and the withdrawal of business support was a sweeping Labor victory at the 5 March 1983 election, with a primary vote just shy of 50 per cent. The ALP and ACTU now had the opportunity to put their Accord into effect.

Part 3

THE EBB TIDE, 1983–2007

Chapter Five

THE ALP–ACTU ACCORD, 1983–90

Many senior union figures regard the ALP–ACTU Accord as a significant achievement.[1] They point to the introduction of Medicare and industry superannuation, and close working relations between the ACTU and the government. They argue that the Accord was responsible for the creation of hundreds of thousands of jobs. They suggest that the Accord held at bay for 13 years the offensive that was to follow under the Howard Government. The Accord, in this view, demonstrated what could be achieved by partnership between unions and government working to advance the interests of Australian business while safeguarding the rights of workers. This chapter and the next present a rather more critical view.

The Accord marked the onset of the ebb tide in union affairs, a period of retreat that is still in progress. Whether judged in terms of working-class living standards or the vitality of the union movement, the Accord was a backward step. The regressive measures that the Fraser Government had failed to carry through were realised under the Hawke and Keating governments. Real wages fell in the 1980s despite a period of sustained economic growth, and the wages share of GDP contracted sharply as the profit share bounced back. Even the much-vaunted job creation of the 1980s gave way to large-scale job destruction in the early 1990s as the world economy went into recession. More damaging than any of these, however, was the impact the Accord had on union organisation where it really mattered – at the grassroots. Despite significant growth in the workforce between 1983 and 1996, union membership fell by 350 000 and union coverage fell dramatically from nearly one-half of the workforce to less than one-third. In their role as 'responsible' Accord partners, Australia's union leaders spent the first seven years of the Accord curbing rank-and-file activism and preventing workers from taking action to halt the sustained decline in their wages. The ACTU led the way in victimising trade unions that *did* want to fight and openly supported efforts by employers and governments to crush such unions. By these means the union leaders only paved the way for a sharpening of employer and government attacks in the 1990s.

The early years of the Accord, 1983–86

The Accord is set in place

Wage restraint lay at the heart of the Accord. The crucial paragraph of the statement read:

> The maintenance of real wages is agreed to be a key objective. It is recognised that in a period of economic crisis as now applying that this will be an objective *over time* [emphasis added].[2]

Wages were to be indexed to the consumer price index by the Arbitration Commission on a six-monthly basis, with no extra claims to be allowed outside tightly defined exceptional circumstances. Supposedly, restraint would apply not just to workers but to all social classes. The Accord set out plans to establish a Prices Surveillance Authority and to monitor the fees set by professional bodies such as doctors' and lawyers' associations. Directors' salaries would be made public and measures taken to crack down on tax avoidance by the wealthy. There would be 'an equitable and clearly discernible redistribution of income' involving a 'substantial restructure' of the income tax scale, to 'ease the tax burden on low and middle income earners' and improved social security, including pensions and unemployment benefits.[3]

The ALP promised a 'rational and less confrontationist' approach to industrial relations and to work with the unions in a wide range of areas. The party committed to an industry policy geared towards restoring full employment. Left-wing unions were optimistic about the 'institution of a planning structure which will determine the way in which the national economy will generate growth'.[4] They were also pleased to see commitments to freeze tariffs 'for the foreseeable future', to spend more on vocational training and education, and to boost public sector employment. The jewel in the crown was a promise to introduce a national health scheme, specifically a single public insurance fund (Medicare), and to remove all means testing from access to public hospitals and community health services.

At the February 1983 ACTU conference that ratified the Accord, ALP leader Bob Hawke had told the unions that:

> We as a Government will certainly not be your handmaiden, and this historic document makes it clear that you do not expect that . . . There will be just as much opportunity for consultation with employers as with you.[5]

So it proved with the Economic Summit, which was convened six weeks after Labor took office on 5 March 1983. The Summit brought together the Prime Minister and his senior Cabinet colleagues, the State Premiers, the ACTU executive, big employers and employer group representatives, and a smattering of community groups and welfare agencies.[6] At the Summit it became clear that the proposed redistribution of income was, if anything, to be in favour of business and the wealthy, and that 'collective restraint' was to weigh disproportionately on workers. The joint communiqué published at the conclusion of the Summit reiterated that the maintenance of real wages would be an objective 'over time'.[7] Furthermore, to the extent that the Government increased spending on essential social services the communiqué noted 'the union movement will pay regard to such expenditure in determining any [wage] claims.'[8] Union representatives would agree to 'an offset in wage increases on account of the health insurance scheme',[9] and newly elected ACTU secretary Bill Kelty also accepted that 'the employed are likely to be required to pay increased real taxation so as to increase employment.'[10] While employers respected 'the legitimate expectation that incomes of the employed shall be increased in real terms through time in line with productivity', the nub of the Summit communiqué was acceptance by the unions that 'the preservation of the private sector as a profitable operating sector' was essential.[11]

While there was some grumbling over the maintenance of Fraser's wages freeze, which continued until September 1983, and some unions continued to hold out against the new system (more below), the leaders of most unions warmly endorsed the Accord and were happy to give a commitment to the Commission not to pursue any extra claims following the September 1983 National Wage Case. As noted in Chapter 4, support for the Accord was not restricted to the senior leadership. Several years of argument by leaders of the left unions, backed by the CPA, had had their effect on union militants. Ford stewards at the Broadmeadows plant endorsed the Accord in April 1983 and offered 'full support to the Prime Minister and the Federal Government in their effort to bring about economic recovery by consensus and through equal sharing across all groups of the community of economic responsibility'.[12] The broader political climate was shifting to the right and most workers were prepared to give the Accord a go – long-term loyalties to the ALP meant that few believed that Labor would attack its working-class base.

The practice of the Accord

Within a year, Labor acted on its Accord commitments in the arena of industry and economic policy. These steps included the establishment of the Economic Planning Advisory Council (EPAC), the Advisory Committee on Prices and Incomes (ACPI) to review the operation of the Accord, and the resumption of the Australian Labor Advisory Council (ALAC), bringing together Government ministers and ACTU representatives. EPAC was to provide a forum for consultation between business, government and unions, and to analyse the economic situation. An Australian Manufacturing Council (AMC) was set up comprising 26 representatives from unions, companies, employer associations and government departments. Beneath the AMC were 11 sectoral tripartite Industry Councils charged with drafting plans for investment, labour market policies, structural adjustment and technological change.

The Accord proved a bonanza for the union leaders. The ACTU, which had already become a prominent force in union affairs under Hawke in the 1970s, now occupied centre stage in national politics. ACTU secretary Bill Kelty, elected in February 1983 after six years as assistant secretary, was the lynchpin. His close personal relationship with Treasurer Paul Keating was crucial to the success of Labor's economic agenda, as it afforded what Fraser had lacked – union acceptance of the Government's economic framework. Keating was originally a sceptic who had described the Accord during the

1983 election campaign as 'for the election, nothing more' but, according to Ian Hampson, 'He soon recognised the Accord's potential to legitimise the Government's economic policy in the eyes of union members.'[13]

Like Hawke before him, Kelty very much represented the new breed of union official, coming to high ACTU office via a research position with the peak body following university graduation. Like Hawke, Kelty had never held elected office in a union, had never been an organiser and had never worked in industry. Also like Hawke, Kelty exercised enormous personal power within the ACTU, even if he did not enjoy the same high profile among the broader public. Although as secretary he was the more junior ACTU officer, Kelty overshadowed successive ACTU presidents Cliff Dolan and Simon Crean.

If the ACTU enjoyed unprecedented clout in the labour movement at this time, so too there was a centralisation of power within individual unions. The traditional industrial campaigns of the 1960s and 1970s had served as a regular focus for union activists at the local level and drew them into organising or participating in meetings and street marches, as well as strikes, bans and picket lines. The Accord, by contrast, was premised on minimising these forms of mobilisation, replacing them with consultation and deal-making involving senior union officials, government and employers. By 1985, more than three dozen union officials had been appointed to the AMC or the various industry councils. Union officials were also appointed in large numbers to government advisory bodies and statutory authorities. Similar processes were replicated at the state level, where Labor held office everywhere except in Queensland.

The education unions in Victoria provide a useful case study. The election of the Cain Labor Government in 1982 saw the establishment of Accord-style tripartite consultative committees at central and regional levels involving the Minister's office, the Education Department and the unions.[14] The operations of the Victorian Secondary Teachers' Association underwent a transformation. Secretary Brian Henderson, who had been elected to office in 1982 on the back of greater teacher militancy in the 1970s, explained that with Labor in office:

> ... there was a chance for consultation ... In the past, all you had to do was say you didn't like what the Government was putting up and then call your members out and go into negotiations about it. But now you were talking about implementing things in relation to system-wide change. We were involved in

discussions about budgets and budget targets that the Government wanted
to meet, and how we could meet those targets.[15]

In education departments across the country, union leaders became partners
in the administration of the system and in many cases quit their posts to
take up appointments in the public service or ministerial offices. These
processes led to an increasing marginalisation of rank-and-file members in
decision-making within the teacher unions. Graham Holt, a delegate with
the Technical Teachers' Union of Victoria explains:

> . . . decisions that affected people in schools were being made by people in
> the Education Department after they had agreement from the central union.
> So the teachers wouldn't actually have much input. The decision would be
> announced that this had been negotiated with the teacher unions. So it would
> be decided at the top.[16]

Tripartite processes in the metal and engineering industry had similar effects. Ted Gnatenko, formerly the convenor of the AEU at GMH
Elizabeth and now education officer in the AMWU's South Australian
branch, lamented 'a growing tendency for senior federal officials in many
unions (including the ACTU) to make up their minds about what is needed
and then tell the members what to do, rather than taking their guidance
from the members.'[17] The consequences were serious:

> The more ordinary members are excluded from decision making process,
> the more agreements that are made without consulting the membership,
> the more irrelevant the union will become in their eyes. Agreement without
> consultation will also mean that the shop steward system, upon which the
> strength of the union movement ultimately depends, will tend to wither away
> through simple lack of use.[18]

The centralisation of power within the union movement and the decline in
rank-and-file activity were some of the major benefits of the Accord from the
perspective of the Government. They ensured that the rapid jobs growth of
1984–85 was not accompanied by a wages explosion. As Industrial Relations
Minister Ralph Willis (like Hawke, another former ACTU research officer)
explained to the Sydney Chamber of Commerce in May 1984:

Since the peak associated with the wages explosion under the previous Government, the real unit labour cost index has declined from 109 in September
1982 to 101 in December 1983. By the end of this year, real unit labour costs
should be back to the level of the late '60s and early '70s.[19]

The share of profits in national income, which had dipped slightly in the
recession of 1982–83, surged to record heights (see Figure 3.2). Most importantly, the rate of profit, whose decline in the late 1960s had been responsible for the onset of economic crisis in the 1970s, began to recover (see
Figure 3.1).

The Accord commitment to 'no extra claims' brought a dramatic decline
in industrial disputes, with the strike rate falling to its lowest level since
1967. Rank-and-file workers were instructed by their union leaders not
to strike for higher wages; in 1984 the *Financial Review* suggested that
'The Hawke Government has become a jailer for unions which dare to
buck the Accord's consensus, and the ACTU has become "an industrial
police force".'[20] The industrial relations manager at the Betts Electric Motors
plant in Western Sydney explained how it worked. A group of AMWU
members had gone on strike in 1985 for a 20 per cent wage rise. The manager
told them that their claim breached the 'no extra claims' condition of the
Accord:

> They didn't believe us, so we told them to contact their union office and that
> 'Your union will be very embarrassed by what you've done.' They did this,
> and the organiser was down here in no time, and got them back to work
> pronto.[21]

Employer representatives had little incentive, therefore, to pursue the option
of enterprise-based bargaining raised by the Hancock Commission, a
Government-sponsored review of the arbitration system, in 1985.[22] The
Business Council of Australia, formed with the encouragement of Bob
Hawke in 1983 and comprising CEOs of the top 50 Australian companies,
argued in 1986 that: 'For the immediate term, there appears to be no viable
alternative to a continuation of the structured centralised approach to wage
fixation.'[23]

In order for the Accord to stick, the minority of unions that sought to buck
its wage restraint had to be reined in. The hard-left Victorian branches of the
Food Preservers' Union and the Furnishing Trades' Union, which attacked

the Accord and took action for higher pay in 1983–84, were condemned by the ACTU.[24] In the case of the Furnishing Trades, the union was actually obliged to surrender a pay rise of $12 that it had already won on behalf of glaziers, under threat of deregistration. The union condemned the Federal Government's new legislation that allowed it to directly deregister a union and the ACTU's 'complicity in the standover tactics which were used against this union'. It went on:

> We declare that the Hawke Government's legislation to wipe out unions to be the greatest threat to the integrity and independence of the union movement in recent years and an attempt to force all unions to become 'tame cat'.[25]

In the case of the Food Preservers, the ACTU and Government efforts to isolate them were less successful. The union had started a campaign for a $16 wage rise prior to the adoption of the Accord and continued with it into the term of the Hawke Government. The secretary of the union, Gail Cotton, defended the union's actions at the 1983 ACTU Congress and was roundly condemned by Bill Kelty and Laurie Carmichael, now ACTU assistant secretary. The union refused to give an undertaking to the Commission that it would not pursue further wage rises outside indexation. The Commission then disbarred members of the Food Preservers from receiving any increases resulting from national wage cases, and the union's awards thereby began to fall behind those of its rivals. The union was forced to concede and gave the undertaking sought by the Commission in September 1984.

In the following month, however, 160 members of the Food Preservers' Union at the Rosella-Lipton factory in Melbourne struck for the reinstatement of 14 workmates who had been sacked. During the course of the dispute the workers added to their list of demands a five per cent pay rise. The Victorian Chamber of Manufacturers applied on behalf of the company for deregistration of the union, and its application was supported by the Federal Government. Far from assisting the union, the ACTU acted in close cooperation with the Government and the company. The BLF and ETU, however, declared their support for the Food Preservers' Union, and the railway unions and the TWU agreed to impose a ban on the company and its parent, the Unilever group, if its assistance were sought. Under threat of a shut-down, the company buckled and in January 1985 the workers returned to work with a satisfactory settlement.

The experience of the Plumbers' Union demonstrated the new confidence of employers to take on unions that threatened the Accord, safe in the knowledge that they would be supported by the Government and the ACTU. The Plumbers' Union imposed bans on 14 New South Wales building sites in 1986 in pursuit of a $60 site allowance in defiance of the Accord guidelines. It was taken to court and fined $280 000 under the secondary boycotts legislation (s45D Trade Practices Act).[26] As part of its Accord commitments, the Government had promised to repeal this legislation but, using Democrat opposition in the Senate as an excuse, it refused to proceed with the necessary Bill. Despite its formal opposition to the legislation, the ACTU did nothing to assist the Plumbers' Union for fear that its wages campaign, if successful, would have wrecked wage restraint. With the exception of a small number of hard left unions, the Plumbers were cut adrift and forced to pay the fine.

The cooperation of the CPA was crucial to the success of the ACTU in ensuring tight control over the unions during the early Accord years. Despite a declining membership, down to about 1300 in the early 1980s, the CPA still retained significant influence in many unions. During the 1960s and into the 1970s the party had been prepared to lead militant strikes, and it had announced its intention to challenge the 'sacred rights of the capitalists' to control industry. During the Accord, however, CPA-aligned union leaders became industrial disciplinarians and lambasted militants who wanted to fight. The credibility that they had earned among union militants by leading earlier generations of struggle was now used to sell wage restraint and strike-breaking. Challenging the 'sacred rights' of the capitalists was buried; the CPA now sought ways to enhance capital accumulation.

The CPA set itself up as a loyal, if occasionally critical, camp follower of the Hawke Government, trumpeting every reform or Accord commitment as a step towards a planned economy, even socialism, and damning those who criticised the Accord as the 'sectarian-dogmatic left'.[27] The departure of the party's Victorian leadership in 1984 to form the Socialist Forum, a way station to joining the ALP, was simply the logical extension of its political trajectory.[28] Those who remained in the party sought allies for the launch of a 'new socialist party' that might attract those repelled by the traditions of the CPA. In both respects, the tendency was towards organisational liquidation into the political mainstream, a direction in which the party had been heading for many years.[29] With fewer than 1000 members, most of them inactive, the party finally dissolved in 1991.

To the extent that the left-wing union leaders criticised the Labor Government, it was on the grounds of its alleged failure to implement the Accord properly. In particular, they objected to the Government's economic liberalisation, which involved the floating of the currency, the elimination of controls on foreign capital, the issuing of licences for foreign banks, and tariff cuts. Union leaders began to grumble that economic policy was dominated by the Treasury and the Reserve Bank, not the Economic Planning Advisory Council. which turned out to be not an instrument for economic planning but a research body and talk-shop. And so the 1984 AMWU conference, while promoting the Accord as an instrument for 'reconstruction in line with socialist objectives', complained that in practice the Labor Government did not seem to be facilitating such a reconstruction.[30] The conference acknowledged 'the achievements of the Accord' but sought to change some aspects that 'do not measure up to general performance'.[31] The union's complaints, however, were not centred on the transfer of wealth, nor on the squashing of union activism, but on the failure of the Government to pursue an industry policy to favour manufacturing. Greater state intervention, not more free market economic rationalism, would put things right. On the crucial question of the *class bias* of the Accord, AMWU leader John Halfpenny continued to argue in early 1985 that:

> the Government will be required to adopt measures that will produce a substantially more equitable distribution and redistribution of wealth within our society. On balance, most Australians will finish better off as a result of the Accord than they would have without it.[32]

In the following year, Laurie Carmichael complained that:

> The continued existence of the Accord is hard to discover, it's hard to find, it's hard to perceive. The Government has virtually thrown it overboard and all that exists is simply the agreement in relation to wages.[33]

However, Carmichael's complaints ignore the fact that 90 per cent of the Accord was window-dressing and, it has to be said, self-serving. The kernel of the Accord was, as it always had been, a device to cut wages with the blessing of the ACTU. In this sense the Accord was working to plan. Had the left-wing union leaders been genuinely dissatisfied with the Accord after three years in operation they had the perfect opportunity to demonstrate their *bona fides* by supporting the BLF, which was the greatest threat to the Accord in the mid 1980s. Instead, they led the way in destroying it.

The BLF had an ambiguous approach to the Accord. It had opposed the Accord late in 1982 but at the special unions conference in February 1983 signed on to it, albeit with little obvious intention of abiding by its restrictions. Federal secretary Norm Gallagher prepared but did not deliver the union's anti-Accord statement at the April Economic Summit.[34] Outside the Summit building workers rallied for their latest wage claim, which represented a clear breach of Accord guidelines. Although the BLF supported other unions who defied the Accord's wage restraint, it did little to build an anti-Accord campaign. Indeed, Gallagher denounced calls for the unions to break with the Accord as 'empty sloganeering'. Nonetheless, if the BLF refused to fight the Accord *politically*, it was willing to strike for higher wages in defiance of the Accord's 'no extra claims' commitment.

With CBD construction undergoing a boom in the period 1984–85, the BLF's actions were costing the big construction companies millions of dollars and threatening the framework of 'consensus' industrial relations. The BLF therefore came under increasing pressure to back off from the ACTU, the Federal Government and Labor state and territory governments in Victoria, New South Wales and the ACT.[35] These governments had already prepared the ground for an offensive on this 'maverick' union by passing legislation in 1984–85 that allowed them to directly deregister a union whose activities were deemed 'contrary to the public interest'.

In 1988 a hostile alliance of governments, the ACTU and some of the most important left unions, including the BWIU and FEDFA, moved against the BLF. Over the course of the year the union was deregistered in Victoria, New South Wales and the ACT. This was not in itself the knock-out blow. The union had been deregistered before, as had the BWIU. Both had survived because other unions agreed not to poach their members. Now, however, the ACTU endorsed a campaign led by the BWIU to carve up the BLF membership. Union funds were seized and, with the blessing of the other building unions, the police carried out mass arrests of BLF members on construction sites. BWIU organisers summoned police to arrest BLF activists when they tried to get on to construction sites. However, loyal BLF members continued to battle away as a deregistered union without award coverage, with some success in Victoria. With the union's survival a real possibility, another round of repression followed. In 1987, the Cain Government in

Victoria despatched police to raid the BLF office in Melbourne in 1987 to sequester its resources. In the name of 'consensus politics', the BLF was crushed in the key eastern states.[36]

The left-wing unions were of rather more help to the Victorian nurses during their industrial campaign for higher pay in 1985–86. After striking for the first time in their history in late 1985, the nurses appeared to have won a victory. However, the ACTU then took over carriage of the dispute and submitted the nurses' claim to arbitration as an 'anomalies' case. The Commission handed down a derisory increase. Their failure to win a substantial rise fired up the nurses and in November 1986 they began what was to be a seven-week campaign, led by the recently elected Irene Bolger and her activist team. A mass meeting of 1000 nurses in Melbourne voted to strike for a pay rise and a cap on nurse–patient ratios.[37] For the first time in their history, nurses set up pickets outside hospitals.

The State Labor Government retaliated, threatening to deregister the union and charge nurses with manslaughter. There was enormous public sympathy for the nurses, but the ACTU and Trades Hall sought to patch up a backroom deal with the Government. In response, 1500 nurses marched on Trades Hall demanding that it stop its interference. If the nurses got little support from the peak councils, the left unions rallied in support of the nurses, with workers from many unions pledging action and financial support. Building and waterside workers levied themselves, held a one-day stoppage and marched through the city.

In December the nurses returned to work and their dispute was referred to the State Industrial Commission. Evidently impressed by their determined struggle, the Commission awarded the nurses a large pay rise and recommended increased staffing. The nurses' dispute was a big win for women workers, breaking through the stereotypes of a passive female workforce, and showing how determined strike action could win both solidarity and a decent wage increase.

The Accord's left-wing supporters argued that, even if it was not bringing about a planned economy, at least it was providing wage increases for all. However, even this argument became increasingly less credible. Following the continuation of Fraser's wage freeze until the first National Wage Case decision of September 1983, and the imposition of a 1 per cent Medicare tax levy, the wages share had fallen by nearly 5 percentage points in the 15 months to March 1984 (see Figure 2.1). Starting in September 1985, a fresh round of wage cuts took place. In the context of a sharp decline in the value of the dollar, which provided the Government with a pretext for cutting wages, the ACTU and Government renegotiated the Accord. The Government agreed to support full indexation for 1985 and the ACTU agreed to a 2 per cent wage discount at the following National Wage Case due in April 1986. This cut in real wages would be compensated by tax cuts in September 1986. The agreement to discount wages represented a substantial concession on the part of the unions. The national secretary of the Telecom workers' union, Bill Mansfield, had told members of his union in July 1984 that: 'If there is no full indexation, there is no Accord, it's as simple as that.'[38] Now indexation began to be discounted with the full support of the ACTU (see Table 5.1). By way of a sweetener, the Government agreed to support the ACTU's 3 per cent productivity-based pay claim, which would take the form of employer contributions to superannuation.

As the balance of payments and currency crises intensified in the first quarter of 1986, Treasurer Paul Keating made dire warnings that Australia was in danger of becoming a 'banana republic' in order to soften workers up for further cuts to their living standards. Not only would the next wage rise, already delayed by some months, be discounted by 2 per cent, but the following National Wage Case would also be delayed until early in 1987, at which time further discounting would be required. The promised tax cuts were delayed by three months and the Arbitration Commission ruled that employer contributions to superannuation would be phased in over two years and only following negotiations at an industry level. ACTU president Simon Crean lent his support to these cuts to real wages and refused to rule out further wage discounting. Award wages, which had fallen marginally by early 1985, now began to decline dramatically (Figure 5.1).

Left-wing defenders of the Accord were now left to grasp at straws. At the 1986 Broad Left Conference, featuring many left-wing figures from the unions, they were forced to acknowledge that the Accord was cutting real wages and that social security benefits were being squeezed. However, they pointed proudly to jobs growth, which would have accompanied a cyclical economic revival anyway, and warned darkly that, without Labor and the Accord by a big wages push, workers would face an incoming right-wing government led by Fraser's former Treasurer, John Howard. Destroying the Accord by a big wages push, they argued, would only pave the way for something much worse, just as the demise of the Social Contract between

Table 5.1 National Wage Case decisions under the Accord

Calendar year	CPI increase	National Wage Case increases	Operative date
1983	4.3%	4.3%	6 Oct 1983
	4.1%	4.1%	6 April 1984
1984	−0.2%	Deferred	
	2.7%	2.6%	6 April 1985
1985	3.8%	3.8%	4 Nov 1985
	4.3%	2.3% (2% discounted due to fall in $)	1 July 1986
1986	6.7%	$10 1st tier flat increase plus possible 4% (2nd tier)	10 March 1987
1987	9.3%	$6 flat increase	5 February 1988
1988	7.3%	3% plus $10 (award restructuring: SEP) after 6 months (approx. 5.2% in total)	Available from 1 September 1988 and 1 March 1989
1989	7.3%	$20–$30 in two instalments (approx. 6.0% in total) (SEP)	
1990	8.0%	2.5% (SEP)	
1991		Enterprise bargaining commences	
1993		Safety net adjustment of $8, with three further increases of $8 scheduled for 1994	

Source: Derived from M. Gardner & G. Palmer, *Employment Relations: Industrial Relations and Human Resource Management in Australia*, Macmillan, Melbourne, 1992, p. 336

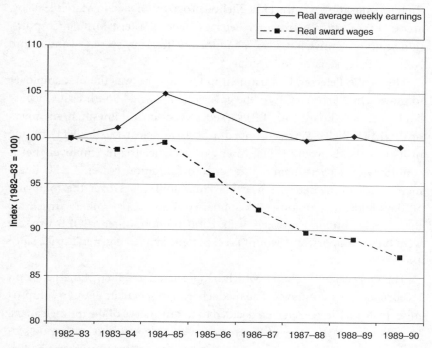

Figure 5.1 Wage levels 1982–83 to 1989–90
Source: ABS *Australian Economic Indicators,* Table 7.3, cat. no. 1350.0. Figure deflated by CPI to arrive at 'real earnings'

the British unions and the Callaghan Labour Government in 1978 had allowed Margaret Thatcher to sweep to power. This threat from the right was not imaginary; it did materialise in the mid 1980s. However, it emerged precisely because the Accord had paved the way for it, by demobilising the unions and legitimising right-wing economic policies.

The New Right challenge and the 'work practices' debate, 1985–86

While most large employers were content to reap the benefits of the Accord, a section of the capitalist class emerged in 1985 that favoured a direct attack on union rights. This 'New Right' comprised leading figures from the conservative parties, business-funded think tanks, right-wing law firms, employer organisations and a small number of business owners keen to challenge the award system and union work practices. In place of the traditional reliance on industrial tribunals, the New Right advocated using common law and executive power to break the unions. The most high-profile New

Right organisation was the H.R. Nicholls Society, formed in March 1986 by, among others, future Treasurer Peter Costello, Western Mining Corporation senior executive Ray Evans, and former Treasury secretary and future National Party senator, John Stone.

The Bjelke-Petersen Government in Queensland was the first employer to move. On 2 February 1985 the government-owned South East Queensland Electricity Board (SEQEB) sacked 1000 electrical linesmen, members of the ETU. Bjelke-Petersen hoped a decisive defeat for the ETU in one of its heartlands would signal to any other Queensland employer that it could rely on Government assistance to break union power.[39] ETU linesmen struck immediately. Power blackouts took place over the following 10 days and other unions took solidarity action. Coal miners struck for three weeks, building workers walked off the job, other SEQEB workers went out in support, and Mount Isa experienced its first general strike since 1965.[40]

The Queensland Cabinet, which had declared a State of Emergency on 7 February, began to waver. The media began to speculate about a compromise. Instead, Bjelke-Petersen decided to test the nerve of the union leaders. He followed up the State of Emergency with a slew of laws outlawing secondary action, closed shops and any strikes not endorsed by secret ballots overseen by the Industrial Commission. Police could arrest anyone deemed to be interfering with the power supply, thereby rendering illegal effective picketing of SEQEB facilities. The Government also threatened to invoke the federal secondary boycotts laws.

In this battle of wills the Trades and Labor Council (TLC) caved in and called off the solidarity strikes. The TLC, along with the ACTU, offered moral support and publicised the SEQEB workers' case, but refused to take resolute action. The ACTU called a 'blockade' of Queensland but this was largely a token gesture. The main strategy of the ACTU and TLC was to wind down the industrial campaign and to appeal to the Hawke Government to transfer the SEQEB linesmen to federal jurisdiction. Time was now on Bjelke-Petersen's side. After months of legal argument, the High Court ruled in favour of the Queensland Government, preventing federal intervention. The hopes of the SEQEB linesmen, by now entirely directed towards the legal process, were dashed.[41] Some were re-employed but most were scattered to the four winds.

Three months after the SEQEB sackings Jay Pendarvis, the owner of the Mudginberri Abattoir in Kakadu National Park in the Northern

Territory, announced plans to introduce contract labour in place of the union-negotiated tally system.[42] The contract labour system required meat-workers to kill more cattle for the same money. The 20-strong Mudginberri workforce, all members of the meat industry union (AMIEU), signed the contracts, claiming to be happy to work under the new arrangements. However, the AMIEU was concerned that the contracts undercut basic award entitlements such as minimum pay, sick pay, annual leave and workers' compensation. There was also no cap on working hours. The union decided to make a stand: if contract labour were introduced in one abattoir on these conditions, the entire tally system would come under threat. The union quickly established a picket line using members from the Katherine meat-works. The Mudginberri workforce refused to respect the picket but, when Commonwealth meat inspectors refused to cross, Pendarvis had to close his abattoir.

The right wing saw Mudginberri as a test case for its strategy of using the courts to break the unions. Pendarvis received extensive financial and legal support from the National Farmers' Federation (NFF) and the Northern Territory and Queensland governments. Peter Costello acted as barrister for Pendarvis, his fees paid by the NFF. Support for the AMIEU within the labour movement was less forthcoming. The ACTU Congress passed a resolution calling for support for the meatworkers and some unions made generous donations, but industrial support was lacking. Northern Territory waterfront and maritime unionists struck for 24 hours in solidarity in August, but otherwise the union was left to fight alone. It was not just the lack of concrete solidarity from other unions that was to blame. The AMIEU itself failed to pull out meatworkers from other sites to put pressure on the company's backers, the Territory Government and the NFF.

Through July and August 1985 the AMIEU was hit with successively larger fines as Pendarvis pursued his case through the courts. The union was ordered by the Arbitration Commission to call off the picket on the grounds that it constituted a 'secondary boycott', none of the picketers being Mudginberri workers. The AMIEU persisted with the picket and on 18 July it was fined a further $44 000 by the Federal Court, with $100 000 legal costs. The Court also authorised four accounting firms to enter the union's offices and seize its assets. In September, on the orders of the Arbitration Commission, the union eventually called off the picket. Pendarvis pursued the union through the Federal Court and in July 1986 was awarded nearly $1.5 million in damages, plus costs of around a million dollars. The power of the AMIEU in the Territory was severely weakened as other abattoirs followed Pendarvis' lead.

At the other end of the continent, another small employer with big business backers was in dispute with a union.[43] The Federated Confectioners' Association, a left bastion in Victoria that rejected the 'no extra claims' requirements of the Accord, was on strike for a 36-hour week at Dollar Sweets. In July 1985 the company sacked 15 of its 27-strong workforce for refusing to sign an agreement to work on the company's terms. The company quickly replaced the 15 strikers with scabs and maintained operations. The striking workers set up a picket for five months, demanding reinstatement as well as the 36-hour week. Transport and Telecom workers refused to cross the picket line, hampering the company's operations. Dollar Sweets became a right-wing *cause celebre*, with Peter Costello acting for the company. Dollar Sweets took the union to the Victorian Supreme Court alleging 'interference with contractual arrangements, intimidation, nuisance, and injury to the plaintiff'. The Court found in favour of the company, saying the picket was 'not a lawful form of picketing, but a . . . nuisance involving obstruction, harassment and besetting'. The Court issued an interlocutory injunction against the picket and ordered the union to pay costs. The union found no support from the ACTU, which condemned it on the grounds that its 36-hour claim was outside the Accord. Isolated and threatened with jail, union members lifted the picket on 12 December.

In each of these three cases, the employers were successful. Nonetheless, there was an overhead cost for business. If left to run unchecked, this aggressive strategy might jeopardise the national arrangements in place under the Accord. Big business did not, for the most part, relish the dismantling of the 'consensus' framework that had been established. Nor did the union leaders. They now began to consider how the New Right threat might best be defeated.

The New Right argument was that unions and the award system prevented flexible work practices. It was not just the New Right, however, who were active on this issue. The OECD's 1986 report *Labour Market Flexibility: Trends in Enterprises* recommended steps to increase the flexibility of labour markets, and 'labour flexibility' became the catchcry of governments and employers around the world. However, how was it to be best pursued? The New Right approach was to challenge arbitration and smash the unions. The majority in the employer camp, however, regarded this approach as high-risk – unions were still too powerful to be brushed aside.[44] Strong shopfloor organisation had faded in many workplaces, but at some larger worksites unions still had the capacity to prevent management from making unilateral changes to work practices. The ability of unions to resist a head-on attack was apparent from submissions to the Hancock Commission, which advised the Hawke Government *not* to reintroduce penal sanctions against strikes:

> It is clear from the submissions received and the discussions we had with many of those who presented views that there is an air of resignation abroad that the implementation of sanctions against unions is extremely difficult if not impossible.[45]

Mudginberri and Dollar Sweets had demonstrated that sanctions against unions were now *possible* if other unions did not rally to their cause. Whether they were *advisable*, however, especially if they were used at a major enterprise in a capital city, was another matter. It was not just that a frontal attack on unionism might be risky and counterproductive. It might also be unnecessary. After all, the ACTU had accepted wage discounting; might not other concessions be forthcoming?

On 3 September 1986, the Government convened a tripartite summit on work practices. The Prime Minister told the assembled union and business leaders:

> You can return to the processes of confrontation that haven't worked, or you can pursue the processes that we have brought into this country, of cooperative consultation. And good sense, rationality and proper perception of one's self-interest should leave no doubt, I suggest, as to what is the more appropriate course.[46]

Adventures by New Right employers were dangerous in this regard. Brian Powell, chief executive of the Australian Chamber of Manufacturers, described the 'extremists in the New Right' as 'fascists' who might wreck the 'new-found economic rationality among the union leadership which could be usefully employed to smooth the transition to a more productive labour market.'[47] The Confederation of Australian Industry agreed:

> . . . to indulge in escapist fantasies that all of these [industrial] problems could somehow be solved by getting rid of industrial tribunals and using the courts of law as the battlefield for industrial disputes takes the debate into a

dangerously irrelevant domain. If the only solution that such critics can come up with to resolve a dispute is to sue the union, then they have no solution at all.[48]

The BCA also supported the call for tripartite action to tackle restrictive work practices.[49] Even in Queensland the coal operators and cane-growers declined the State Government's offer of tough anti-strike legislation.[50]

The cost of pursuing the New Right strategy of confrontation was made clear at the Robe River iron ore mine in the Pilbara. In July 1986, Peko Wallsend, which had just taken ownership of the operation, notified mining unions of its intention to unilaterally change 200 work practices and slash jobs.[51] The unions took the company to the State Industrial Commission, which ordered a 30-day moratorium in order to allow negotiations to proceed. Peko ignored the Commission and went ahead and sacked 1300 mineworkers. After several weeks of a bitter dispute, during which the AWU held back the rest of the Peko workforce from striking, the case was referred back to the Commission, which ordered the company to reinstate the sacked workers. The company complied under protest but, as it did so, engineered widespread changes to work practices.

The dispute confirmed in the minds of many employers the risks of New Right tactics. The chief executive of the BHP Mount Newman mine in the Pilbara told *Business Review Weekly* under the headline 'Robe River: How Not to Tame a Union' that the dispute created 'misery, fear, intimidation, frustration . . . there must be a better way.' One of Peko's major corporate shareholders said that '[even if] the company has a big win, I don't see how they're going to maintain a satisfactory working relationship with their employees.'[52]

The mainstream employers and the Federal Government preferred to enlist union leaders in their pursuit of labour flexibility. They were pushing at an open door. The ACTU was concerned at the threat posed on its left by 'maverick' unions such as the BLF. It was also concerned by the threat from the New Right whose strategies, if widely adopted, could spell an end to the Accord. The union leaders therefore seized on labour flexibility as their own goal and sought to position themselves as responsible figures capable of bringing about the changes sought by business but without the risks of the New Right approach. The ACTU attack on the BLF, with the full support of the left unions, had shown the extent to which they were prepared to discipline the union movement. Business was reassured that the union leaders could be trusted to deliver.

The rise of productivity trade-offs, 1987–90

Over the course of 1987 and 1988 the Arbitration Commission, with ACTU support, rewrote the rules of wage fixing in Australia and set the course for two decades of industrial relations 'reform' legislation.[53] The centralised arbitration system that had been dominant for more than 80 years gave way to what was called 'managed decentralism'.[54] In the early 1990s this would lead to enterprise bargaining and, later still, to individual contracts and *WorkChoices*.

The two-tier decision, 1987

The first major step occurred in May 1987. It was a response not just to demands by employers, government and the ACTU for greater 'flexibility' in the wages system, but also to growing unrest among union members over falling wages (see Figure 5.1). Plumbers, metalworkers, transport workers, storemen and packers all expressed frustration at wage cuts in conditions of a booming jobs market and emerging skills shortages.[55] Workers knew their sacrifices were feeding rising profits.

In its May 1987 decision, the Arbitration Commission handed down two wage rises of $10 and $6.50 for all award employees, to be paid six months apart: the 'first tier'. This was to be supplemented by a 'second-tier' increase of up to 4 per cent, on an award-by-award basis, on condition that the relevant unions made trade-offs and gave a commitment to make no extra claims. These trade-offs involved changes to work practices, broad-banding and multiskilling. While all workers were to get the first-tier rises, the second tier, 'the restructuring and efficiency principle', was the key. The Commission emphasised that:

> . . . primary attention should be given to the principle dealing with restruc-
> turing and efficiency because of its potential to provide substantial benefits
> for employers, employees and the community as a whole.[56]

The ACTU was enthusiastic about the new productivity-based system, which it had helped design. It was at one with employers and the Federal Government on the economic tasks at hand, as the Commission noted:

> There were no essential differences between the parties . . . and [a]ll empha-
> sised the importance of maintaining international competitiveness, for con-
> tinued wage restraint, for a revival in private investment, for a restructure of
> the economy to promote manufacturing exports, and for increased efficiency
> and productivity.[57]

The notion of making pay rises conditional on trading away working practices was an innovation and reflected the exhaustion of wage discounting
from the Government's point of view. Wage restraint on its own was a fragile
means to lift the profit rate. By cheapening labour relative to capital, it only
discouraged companies from investing in new technology, and there were
clear signs of a slow-down of productivity in the 1980s. If productivity was
to rise, working arrangements had to change to enable more efficient use of
new equipment.

The emergence of award restructuring

Despite the initial commitment by all parties to the two-tier system, it
soon aroused significant opposition and survived for only 15 months. The
weak unions were confronted by employer foot-dragging and demands for
drastic cuts to working conditions. At the September 1987 ACTU Congress,
representatives of the retail and public sector unions complained about
their failure to win wage increases and employer pressure to surrender
long-standing conditions.[58] Six months after the introduction of the new
system, only 11 per cent of the workforce had won a second-tier increase.
By August 1988, the figure was still only 60 per cent.[59] The remaining 40 per
cent suffered a significant drop in real wages, as they had been granted only
two small pay rises (the first-tier increases of $10 and $6.50) since July 1986.
It was not just the weaker unions that suffered, however. AMWU research
officer Chris Lloyd recalls:

> We had a long two-year period, particularly after the second-tier, which the
> members did not like. It was, for them, a fundamental breach of what the
> Metal Workers had been about: never trade off your conditions with a boss.[60]

A pay rise to federal politicians of 12 per cent with no productivity strings attached only added fuel to the fire.

Working-class discontent with the two-tier wages system and the general environment of wage restraint in a period of strong jobs growth was most obvious in Victoria, where it took the form of street marches and strikes. In the first two weeks of June 1988, several mass meetings of shop stewards were held in Melbourne and a march of 1000 to the Arbitration Commission dis-rupted proceedings of the National Wage Case then in progress. The ACTU leadership received a roasting at these events and were loudly heckled.[61] The industrial offensive in Victoria climaxed with a 24-hour strike on 6 July, with half a million workers taking action. Melbourne's train and tram network was also brought to a standstill by eight days of industrial action by maintenance workers, and a national strike was only narrowly averted by the ACTU.[62] This brief lift in strike action was reflected in the election of John Halfpenny as secretary of Trades Hall and in gains by the left in the Victorian Public Service Association and the Victorian branches of the VBEF and FCU.[63]

As working-class frustration with the two-tier system was building, the Government and ACTU were considering how to take productivity bar-gaining to the next stage. In the middle of 1988 the Government published *Labour Market Reform: The Industrial Relations Agenda* in which Minister Ralph Willis argued that 'it is now time to take a quantum leap forward; to extend the process of reform and tackle more of the institutional barriers to labour market flexibility.'[64] This meant 'restructuring of awards to pro-vide the framework for incentives to skill formation, more flexible forms of work organisation, greater opportunities for career development and a better quality of work life.'[65]

The outcome of deliberations by the ACTU and Government was the Structural Efficiency Principle of the August 1988 National Wage Case deci-sion. Second-tier agreements had removed restrictive work practices in many industries. The Commission argued that award restructuring, involv-ing the complete rewriting of hundreds of existing awards, would allow an acceleration in the pace of change:

We consider it essential . . . that any new wage system introduced should build on the steps already taken to encourage greater productivity and efficiency. Attention must now be directed toward the more fundamental, institutionalised elements that operate to reduce the potential for increased productivity and efficiency.[66]

The National Wage Case allowed for a 3 per cent increase in wages from September 1988, with a further $10 six months after the first increase. It required only that unions commence negotiations over award restructuring. The August 1989 National Wage Case decision took the decision a step further. This provided for two pay increases of between $10 and $15, or 3 per cent – whichever was the greater – staggered at six-month intervals, to take effect only on the *ratification* of an award restructuring package by the Commission.

The unions and productivity bargaining

Union support for the two-tier system and award restructuring involved a significant shift on the part of the left-wing unions, who had traditionally been hostile to making wage increases dependent on improved productivity. In 1974 the AMWU's Jack Hutson decried the productivity agreements, which were making ground in the UK and had aroused the interest of Australian employers and the Whitlam Government.[67] In the UK, Hutson argued, productivity agreements had seen long-standing work practices torn up and shop steward organisation sidelined, with management taking 'sole control of the pace and character of production'. Rather than blindly following 'industry efficiency', he said; unionists should be asking: '. . . efficiency for whom? Their concern should not be the establishment of greater worker control by management but the imposing of workers control on management.'[68]

Thirteen years later the situation had changed, and 'industry efficiency' was now paramount in union thinking. The change in perspective was outlined in two important documents produced by the ACTU in 1987: *Future Strategies for the Trade Union Movement* and *Australia Reconstructed*. These spelled out the unions' willingness, under the rubric of 'strategic unionism', to embrace national competitiveness and productivity growth. *Future Strategies* explained the ACTU rationale:

> The economic circumstances have demanded that unions in pursuit of more jobs, greater job security and the capacity to increase living standards are more closely involved in the process of production and not simply in the

distribution of the receipts of production . . . unions must be interested and involved at company and industry level about training, investment, production methods, and industry policy.[69]

The ACTU argued that improved training programs, increased 'productivity consciousness' among union members, and greater union involvement in management were needed to lift productivity. 'Outdated' union structures based on traditional occupational demarcations were not to get in the way of changes to work practices. *Future Strategies* therefore set out an ambitious plan for union amalgamations along industry lines, with the aim of consolidating union membership in a dozen giant unions.

While *Future Strategies* focused on the internal operations of unions, *Australia Reconstructed* looked at steps to revitalise the economy. Jointly published with the Government's Trade Development Council, headed up by former AMWU research officer Ted Wilshire, *Australia Reconstructed* was the result of a study tour of Europe and North America by unions from both the left and the right, accompanied by officials from the Department of Industry. It recommended a National Development Fund to provide finance for business, with the money being drawn from industry superannuation funds, and a National Employment and Training Fund to boost skills in manufacturing industry. The significance of the document was indicated by Trade Minister John Dawkins, who wrote in the preface that:

> The contents of this report reveal the deep commitment by the senior union participants to maintaining international competitiveness, to reducing the balance of payment constraint and to enhancing productivity through changes in management and work practices.

Like the AMWU's earlier *Australia Uprooted* and *Australia Ripped Off*, *Australia Reconstructed* pointed to the baleful influence of financial speculation on the productive sectors of the economy. However, there was an important difference. Whereas these earlier documents were promoted as a left-wing intervention in debates within the union movement and, nominally at least, written from a socialist perspective, *Australia Reconstructed* was much more explicitly framed as an intervention in Government policy formation and was jointly endorsed by the left-wing and right-wing unions. The references to strikes and demonstrations that were scattered through the AMWU's earlier publications were nowhere to be found in *Australia Reconstructed*. Rachel Sharp commented:

> Any sign of moral outrage in the face of stark differences in the social condi-
> tions of the people is missing; the once muffled tones of the rhetoric of class
> struggle which marked the labour pronouncements of yesteryear are now
> entirely muted.[70]

Australia's senior union leaders now increasingly saw their role as de facto management consultants. In a letter to the *Sydney Morning Herald* in October 1988, the FEDFA branch secretary informed readers about a dispute at the NSW Electricity Commission (Elcom) over rostering:

> The FEDFA and other power industry unions are not interested in protecting
> inefficient practices and promoting overstaffing. We have been at the fore-
> front in identifying inefficient work and management practices and develop-
> ing proposals to restructure Elcom awards and workplaces – the underlying
> rationale being that greater efficiency and productivity will protect and
> enlarge employment.[71]

Nothing was to get in the way of the changes. Laurie Carmichael told the CPA journal *Australian Left Review*: 'We cannot concede to those who want to try and stop or delay it. Neither general historical or specific Australian circumstances will allow it.'[72] Asked whether he anticipated resistance to this message of union–management cooperation given his reputation as a former militant, Carmichael said: 'I would hope that there will be a change in their attitudes as there has been in mine.'[73] Those who did not support *Australia Reconstructed* received short shrift. At the 1987 ACTU Congress, in a rare display of dissent, NSW Public Service Association delegate Mary Kerr described *Australia Reconstructed* as a 'sinister document', only to have her congress ticket confiscated.[74]

To drive home the message of *Australia Reconstructed*, TUTA courses were devoted to instructing union officials and delegates in the benefits of 'strategic unionism'. Union officials and employers from the metal and vehicle industries undertook government-funded tours to Europe, the USA and Japan to learn more about 'international best practice' and to explore areas of mutual interest.

As the left union leaders became advocates of industry restructuring and business competitiveness, the historic divisions between left and right at ACTU congresses, already much attenuated by the mid 1980s, began to disappear. Bitter factional disputes no longer took place and leading positions were shared out without rancour. Right-aligned ACTU president Simon Crean, who won preselection to stand for Labor at the 1990 federal election, was replaced as president by the left's Martin Ferguson with no subsequent discernible shift in ACTU strategy or perspective.

Some outcomes of the productivity revolution

The union leaders' rationale for supporting increased labour flexibility and industry restructuring was that these would raise productivity, enhance business competitiveness, and thereby underpin secure employment and career advancement for well-trained workers. Union intervention in the process of industry restructuring would also embed trade unions at the centre of business decision-making. By taking the initiative, unions could offset the risk of New Right methods taking hold among Australian employers. Australian business certainly seized the opportunities presented by the new political environment. Between 1988 and 1990, employers at one-third of all workplaces with more than 20 staff undertook 'major restructuring of work practices'.[75] The same number introduced 'major new plant or technology'. In workplaces employing more than 500, the proportion rose to one-half.[76] What were some of the outcomes for workers?

A 1989 study by academics Malcolm Rimmer and Gianni Zappala reviewed 20 second-tier agreements. The common features were greater managerial discretion over the use of labour; the removal of some element of worker control over taking breaks; a reduction of penalty rates for unsocial hours; a rise in the proportion of casual and part-time staff; and the introduction of procedures that made it harder for unions to strike.

The metal industry second-tier agreement gave employers greater powers to hire on a part-time basis, to schedule rostered days off and to weaken job demarcation, traditionally one of the metal trades unions' most jealously guarded provisions. 'One in, all in' overtime guarantees were removed, giving managers the ability to select staff for overtime.

The agreement in the building and construction industry made provision for more flexible use of working hours, lifting restrictions on shiftwork. In the federal public service, unions agreed to tighter controls over absenteeism and the expansion of multiskilling. The Victorian retail industry introduced extended Saturday trading hours. Bank officers agreed to an increase in part-time staff, more managerial discretion over the timing of lunch breaks and rostered days off, an end to seniority-based promotion and the tying of salaries to managerial review.[77] At Ford, the VBEF agreed to changes to, or the abolition of, 104 different work practices. Rimmer and Zappala concluded that the changes to work practices conceded by unions as part of the second-tier agreements were 'impressive and valuable' for the employers.[78] All involved the trading away of hard-won conditions.

Union leaders were as keen as employers to use the second-tier to drive home significant changes to what BWIU national secretary Tom McDonald was later to call the 'many undesirable work practices that had developed during the earlier boom period'.[79] The *Financial Review* reported:

> In one instance recently, the central office of the AMWU sent back a deal to an AMWU steward because it involved a trade-off of wages in exchange for the lifting of industrial bans. In another, the union took an upfront role in suggesting to one company that the high rate of absenteeism needed to be addressed rather than the union simply offering to trade-off relatively trivial offsets like wash-up time or afternoon tea breaks.[80]

Employers therefore had grounds for thinking that significant changes to work practices were best engineered through negotiation with the unions, rather than New Right style confrontation. Rimmer and Zappala argued that:

> ... considerable gains in labour market flexibility can be won through existing Australian industrial relations institutions providing appropriate policies are adopted ... [This] lends support to those who emphasise gradual reform of labour market flexibility while accepting the existing authority of unions and industrial tribunals. The record of the second tier is that these parties have a good deal to contribute towards improving the labour market and that a joint or bargaining approach is practical and effective.[81]

What of award restructuring? In the vehicle industry membership, discontent with the trade-offs in the second-tier agreements of 1987 had been at least partly responsible for the defeat of moderate ALP-aligned leaders at the

Victorian and South Australian VBEF branch elections. Award restructuring was therefore implemented in late 1989 with an explicit commitment by the new left-wing leadership that it would avoid the trade-offs associated with the second-tier pay round and would lead instead to a genuine upgrading of workers' skills. In practice, award restructuring had little effect on workforce skills in the vehicle industry and may indeed have contributed to deskilling. Fifteen months after the restructured awards had been introduced, training opportunities in many car factories remained scarce, or even non-existent.[82] The VBEF concluded that:

> Whilst management evinced the view that award restructuring would over time deliver fewer, more highly trained workers in their enterprise, the evidence is that they have a current preoccupation weighted towards the shedding of labour and no proportionate increase in training.[83]

Delays in training led to increasing frustration among vehicle workers. The attitudinal changes so keenly sought by Laurie Carmichael were not much in evidence, according to a VBEF working party:

> The enthusiasm of management for award restructuring runs at a significantly higher level than that of the shop stewards and shopfloor employees, many of whom indicated that at the beginning of the exercise they had been imbued with optimism and hope. The initial perspective has gradually been replaced by cynicism . . . while changes had occurred to managerial style, and some traditional authoritarian methods had been dispensed with, there had been no genuine opening-up of the decision-making process, and workers' participation was only on terms decided unilaterally by management.[84]

Where employers faced strongly unionised workplaces, most notably in the public sector, they tended to negotiate changes to work practices.[85] Where the unions were weak, however, employers simply forced changes through. In 60 per cent of private sector unionised workplaces with more than 20 staff, union representatives were not even informed of significant workplace changes.[86]

If the second-tier agreements and award restructuring were delivering worse working conditions for many employees, the work of the Accord's much-vaunted tripartite industry councils was devoted to overseeing redundancies and closures. Under the Steel Industry Plan, BHP was awarded $360 million between 1983 and 1987 in industry assistance by the

Government as annual steel production rose from 175 tonnes per worker to 260 tonnes. Nonetheless, 21 000 workers lost their jobs.[87]

In 1988, the federal and New South Wales governments provided an aid package of several million dollars to the coal industry, which was suffering from an international downturn in prices and orders.[88] The employers took advantage of the situation to lay off hundreds of workers and push through the biggest downgrading of coal miners' conditions since 1949, including longer shifts, Saturday work and employer control over rostering.

Similar trends were under way on the waterfront under the auspices of the Waterfront Industry Reform Authority (WIRA). In June 1989, the Authority announced the loss of 1000 jobs and the removal of union control over the hiring and allocation of labour. With the shift to company-based employment, workers' jobs were tied to the fortunes of individual steve-dores, undercutting union solidarity and enhancing the ability of employers to hire and fire.

The position of trade unions by 1990

Although weakened by the Accord, trade unions did not disintegrate. Membership was stable between 1983 and 1990 (see Table 5.2) and in the latter year 80 per cent of all Australian workplaces with more than 20 staff had at least one union member. In the public sector, the figure was 100 per cent.[89] It was not just 'paper' membership either. Two-thirds of unionised workplaces had at least one union delegate on the premises[90] and there were in total approximately 50 000 union delegates nationally.[91] In one-quarter of unionised workplaces delegate committees existed, but in workplaces employing more than 500 the figure was as high as 63 per cent.[92] Even though unions had in many cases agreed to substantial changes to work practices, they still retained the ability to frustrate manage-ment when they chose. In 30 per cent of workplaces employing more than 200 staff and in which management sought significant 'efficiency changes', managers reported that trade unions were 'the major obstacle' that they confronted.[93]

Nonetheless, the overall trend during the 1980s was retreat, the start of the ebb tide. Union *coverage* slumped from 49 per cent in 1982 to 40.5 per cent in 1990 (see Table 5.2) as membership failed to keep pace with the

Table 5.2 Changes in union membership and coverage, Australia 1982–2007

Year	Membership (m)	Coverage (%)	Fall in coverage (percentage points)	*Annual* average fall in coverage (percentage points)
1982	2.57	49		
1986	2.59	46	3.0	0.75
1988	2.54	42	4.0	2.0
1990	2.62	40.5	1.5	0.75
1993	2.38	37.5	3.0	1.0
1996	2.23	31.3	6.2	2.1
1999	1.92	26.2	5.1	1.7
2002	1.86	23.4	2.8	0.9
2005	1.91	22.4	1,0	0.33
2006	1.79	20.3	2.1	2.1
2007	1.70	18.9	1.4	1.4

Source: ABS *Trade Union Members Australia,* cat. no. 6325.0; *Employee Earnings, Benefits and Trade Union Membership Australia,* cat. no. 6310.0
Note: This table presents union membership and coverage calculated by means of a household survey, as opposed to figures in Chapter 1, which present union membership and coverage sourced by means of a survey of trade unions themselves (ABS *Trade Union Statistics Australia*). The ABS discontinued the latter method in 1996.

expanding workforce. The strike rate, which had fallen dramatically with the deep recession and the introduction of indexation in 1982–83, fell further in the mid 1980s and never really recovered (see Figure 1.1). Union *activity* was substantially weakened where it mattered – among rank-and-file workers and union delegates.

The demobilisation of unions at the grassroots was not just a result of the weaknesses that existed at the time that the Hawke Government took power. As we have seen, it was also the result of ACTU policy. Ted Gnatenko explained:

> . . . the unions' method of dealing with the Hawke Government has resulted in alienating a large slice of the working population. For the past seven years, the workers have seen considerable erosion of their living standards without concerted action to defend them. It appears that we have almost forgotten how to struggle and how to campaign.[94]

Amnesia was not really the problem, however. The ACTU consciously *suppressed* struggle, and this fact was reinforced when the airline pilots joined the BLF as victims of ACTU 'discipline' at the end of the decade. On 26 July 1989, the Australian Federation of Airline Pilots (AFAP) lodged a 29 per cent pay claim on behalf of pilots at government-owned Australian Airlines (later absorbed into Qantas), whose wages had fallen significantly behind inflation and those of their peers at Ansett Airlines. The airline could afford to pay, but it was keen to weaken the union ahead of the proposed deregulation of the industry in 1990. Furthermore, the outcome of the dispute would have national significance. Had the company met the union's claim, or even half of it, it would have created a precedent for every other union to lodge similar catch-up claims. The ACTU and the Government decided that the pilots' union must not be allowed to succeed.

Representatives from Australian Airlines, the ACTU and the Government quickly conferred and decided to draw in Ansett Airlines, ensuring a united front by employers against the Pilots' Federation. The pilots' awards were cancelled and the union soon afterwards deregistered. In response, the Federation initiated a 'work to rule' and a ban on overtime, to which the companies immediately responded by threatening dismissal and standing down workers. In an attempt to manoeuvre around the law, 1647 domestic airline pilots resigned en masse. The company then served writs against both the individual pilots and the union, with the full public support of the Prime Minister.

The Government used RAAF planes and pilots to break the dispute, brought in overseas pilots as scab labour, and bailed out the airlines with tens of millions of dollars. It issued a farrago of lies about the pilots, suggesting that they were all millionaires and not worthy of support by the labour movement. The ACTU chimed in, with Bill Kelty telling the 1989 ACTU Congress that 'the pilots had declared war on ordinary Australian workers and the wage-fixing system.'[95]

In September, the airlines rejected an offer by the Pilots' Federation to return to work on pre-dispute conditions to allow negotiations to proceed. Instead, they offered re-employment only on individual contracts. In October, the Industrial Relations Commission (the renamed Arbitration Commission) certified new 'awards' for the industry based on individual contracts. The vast majority of pilots stood firm and remained loyal to the Federation. The union held regular meetings of members and staged noisy public rallies at the airports.

The pilots' determination was not enough to win the dispute, however. Backed by the bottomless pockets of the Federal Government, the airlines were willing to tough out the disruption. In November, the airlines sued the Federation and six of its leaders in the Victorian Supreme Court, claiming damages for various common law torts. The Federation was ordered to pay the airlines $6.3 million in common law damages and was effectively smashed. A small number of the pilots who had taken action were re-employed on individual contracts in subsequent months; the rest were forced to look for work elsewhere.

Trade unions had been broken in the past by attacks from employers, courts and governments. What the Accord added was the notion that unions could be smashed with the support of the ACTU. By attacking traditions of union struggle and solidarity, the ACTU undermined the fundamental principles on which trade unions could prosper and laid the basis for the membership crisis that was to follow in the 1990s and 2000s.

The 1990 federal election

At the March 1990 federal election, Labor was returned to office in an unprecedented fourth consecutive election victory. Nonetheless, this result was by no means a strong endorsement of the Government. Labor's primary vote fell to less than 40 per cent for only the third time since 1906 and it suffered a swing of more than 6 per cent, equivalent to that which swept Whitlam out of power in 1975. The fruits of the Accord must be regarded as a significant factor in Labor's declining popularity.

Seen from one perspective, the economic situation over the previous seven years had been relatively kind to workers. After the devastating recession and drought of 1982–83, the Australian economy benefited from the international economic upswing of the 1980s. Employment rose by 1.5 million. Many of these new jobs went to women workers: the female participation rate rose from 46.4 per cent in 1983 to 57.1 per cent in 1990, which meant that household incomes could rise even as real wages were declining.[96] Unemployment fell from 10 per cent to less than 6 per cent. Specific elements of the Accord benefited workers; most notable was Medicare which, while less generous than the original Medibank, was an improvement on the situation inherited from Fraser.

Nonetheless, the aggregate outcome of Labor's first seven years in power was a sharp redistribution of income and wealth from the working class to the capitalist class. Award wages fell dramatically between 1984–85 and 1989–90 (see Figure 5.1) and the wages share of national income fell to a 20-year low (see Figure 2.1). Such an outcome during a period of sustained economic growth was unprecedented. By contrast, the rate of profit recovered from its postwar nadir of 6 per cent in 1983 to reach 10 per cent by 1990 (see Figure 3.1) and the profit share of GDP lifted sharply (see Figure 3.2).

The redistribution of wealth from labour to capital was a conscious Government strategy: company taxes were cut from 46 per cent to 39 per cent, and the top marginal income tax rate was reduced from 60 per cent to 48 per cent. Meanwhile, social security became harder to access, and user-pays was introduced across a wide range of government services. Employment may have risen, but one-third of the increase was in part-time jobs. Furthermore, work was getting harder: full-time employees were working the equivalent of more than two weeks longer in 1990 when compared with 1983.[97]

The wealthy, by contrast, prospered in this period. Even after the 1987 crash, the stock market was still 150 per cent higher in 1990 than when Hawke took power, while the fortunes of the *Business Review Weekly* 'Top 200' rose from $7.3 billion in 1984 to $26.7 billion in 1990.[98] The Prime Minister was happy to be closely identified with Kerry Packer, Alan Bond and other high-profile businessmen.

The sharp swing against Labor at the 1990 federal election result can be seen as a reaction among Labor's working-class supporters to the fact that the benefits of the economic expansion of the 1980s went mostly to business and the wealthy, and that the ALP leadership so ostentatiously indulged and identified with the beneficiaries. After a minor leakage of votes at the 1984 and 1987 elections, Labor now began to experience serious political repercussions from its pursuit of an economically regressive agenda and work intensification.

Chapter Six

ENTERPRISE BARGAINING AND A REVIVED EMPLOYER OFFENSIVE, 1990–96

After several years of growth, the world economy slumped back into a deep recession late in 1990. The chief indicators of crisis were the same as those of earlier years – low profitability and excess capacity. Although the rate of profit in the United States (and Australia) had revived from its nadir in the early 1980s, it was still substantially below the level reached at the peak of the postwar boom in the 1960s.[1] This rendered the US economy, and with it the world economy, more susceptible to economic shocks and crises. The automotive industry, airlines and steel companies bled money. The consequences were mass retrenchment and plant closures. By 1992 there were 24 million unemployed in the OECD G7 economies.

In Australia, Treasurer Paul Keating lifted interest rates sharply in 1989–90, causing what he described as 'the recession that we had to have'. Manufacturing output fell by 8 per cent and profits by 40 per cent. Employers took to what was now euphemistically called 'downsizing' with a vengeance. Unemployment jumped from 6 per cent to 11 per cent, the worst performance in any Western economy (see Figure 4.2).

Committed to the Accord project, and with it the general health of Australian capitalism, union leaders sought to work with employers to find ways to restore business viability. As they saw it, costs of production had to be further reduced and the unions had to play their part. The agenda was spelled out in *Unions 2001*, a 1995 publication jointly authored by leading left officials and a New South Wales union think-tank:

With few exceptions, the imperative for Australian workers will be to achieve international competitiveness and best practice, and it will be within this disciplined environment that unions will have to operate. In many cases, unions will have to encourage workers and management to strive for best practice work and production techniques.[2]

John Dawkins, Treasurer from 1991 to 1993, explained the benefits of the union agenda to a business audience in 1994:

While the Business Council occasionally laments its lack of success and lack of influence, it and its predecessors have, by their proxies in the Government and the ACTU, achieved more than they could have expected from a Government of their friends.[3]

While business and government may have benefited from the union leaders' commitment to cost-cutting, in workers' eyes this commitment only succeeded in discrediting unions as organisations that would defend workers' rights. John Halfpenny summed the situation up succinctly in 1994: 'At a time when we are more popular than ever in the boardrooms and cabinet rooms, we are less popular in the workplace.'[4] Union membership and union coverage, already in decline, plunged further. By the time of Labor's defeat in March 1996, Australian unionism could count on 400 000 fewer members than in 1990 and the lowest rate of union coverage since 1914. With unions in serious decline, the union-busting tactics of the New Right, spurned by mainstream employers in 1986, were now taken up more widely, helped along by supportive government legislation.

A new phase in the productivity revolution

The introduction of enterprise bargaining

Enterprise bargaining had first been flagged by the 1985 Hancock Commission review of arbitration, which recommended that employers should be able to 'opt out' of arbitration and negotiate separate stand-alone agreements with unions, certified by the Arbitration Commission. To this end the Hawke Government made provision in its *Industrial Relations Act 1988* for enterprise ('certified') agreements, known as s.115 agreements after the relevant clause in the Act. Similar moves were under way in the New South Wales State industrial jurisdiction following a review of the State system of tribunals by Professor John Niland, a noted supporter of collective bargaining. Nonetheless, the new provisions in the federal and New South Wales jurisdictions had little attraction for employers and for the most part they simply gathered dust.[5]

The main drive for enterprise bargaining, however, came not from government or employers but from the ACTU.[6] By the middle of 1989 the ACTU was under fire from union leaders, who were reporting angry and frustrated members demanding the opportunity to strike for higher wages. In February 1990, the ACTU and Government negotiated Accord Mk VI, under which the two parties agreed to promote enterprise bargaining following the conclusion of award restructuring. According to Chris Briggs, 'enterprise bargaining under the Accord Mk VI was to be a safety valve for defusing pressure in labour market hotspots.'[7] But the wage rises that resulted came at a heavy cost.

During National Wage Case hearings in early 1991 the ACTU and Government urged the Industrial Relations Commission to grasp the nettle of enterprise bargaining and hand down new wage-fixing principles. They were supported by most employer associations except the MTIA, which feared the consequences of decentralised bargaining freed from the disciplinary effects of arbitration. In the early 1970s, and again ten years later, members of the MTIA had experienced at first hand the capacity of stronger unions to extract substantial wage increases by striking. The Full Bench of the Commission shared the MTIA's concerns, and in its April 1991 determination rejected the ACTU–Government joint submission, declaring that employers and unions were insufficiently 'mature'. Instead, the Full Bench urged unions and employers to persevere with award restructuring. Chris Briggs records that the decision 'sent the ACTU leadership into a blind fury', with Kelty telling the press that 'It is a sickening decision but there is no reason for the trade union movement to eat the vomit.'[8] For the first time in years the ACTU endorsed a wages push to put pressure on the Commission and the strike rate jumped.

At the subsequent National Wage Case in October 1991, a chastened Full Bench obliged the Government and the ACTU and handed down new principles to govern enterprise bargaining. These principles followed the broad lines advocated by the Accord partners. The Commission would certify enterprise agreements negotiated directly between employers and trade unions, with the proviso that any wage increases be based on 'the actual implementation of efficiency measures designed to effect real gains in productivity'. Such efficiency measures must involve consideration of a 'broad agenda' of items, subject to the condition that agreements did not involve 'a reduction in ordinary time earnings or departures from Commission standards of hours of work, annual leave with pay, or long service leave with pay' (the so-called 'no disadvantage test'). Unions could not 'double-dip' by claiming wage rises from National Wage Cases in addition to increases from enterprise bargaining. In effect, the 'absorption' of arbitrated wage increases that had been defeated in 1968 had now reappeared in a different guise.

Given that many of the 'efficiency measures' mandated by the Commission were likely to involve further trading away of workers' conditions, the ACTU and Government had to provide some incentive for workers and unions to enter into enterprise agreements. The leaders of the stronger unions felt confident that they could derive wage rises within an industry framework without sacrificing much. However, many unions lacked the capacity to negotiate wage increases at the level of individual enterprises, or could make gains only at the cost of substantial trade-offs. With unemployment at 11 per cent, enterprise bargaining was likely to be self-defeating for such unions. Furthermore, many employers, as opposed to employer associations, were initially sceptical about enterprise bargaining – they were wary of a system that might open the door in the strongly organised sectors to a new explosion of 'over-award' payments. Nearly two years after the new enterprise bargaining principles were handed down, fewer than one in eight workers were covered by registered agreements.[9] Steps had to be taken by the Government to force the pace. This was made easier by a shift to the right, which was taking place elsewhere in the political establishment.

The Labor Government's shift away from its traditional support for the award system was occurring in tandem with a further move to the right in the Liberal and National Parties. The Queensland Nationals had been at the forefront when the Bjelke-Petersen Government passed legislation in 1987 allowing for 'voluntary employment agreements' – essentially, non-union site agreements. In 1991 the Greiner Government in New South Wales had banned union closed shops, opened up scope for non-union enterprise deals and removed the public interest test for enterprise agreements, thereby lowering the floor of conditions.[10] Similar legislation was also put in place by newly elected Liberal governments in Tasmania in 1992 and in South Australia in 1994. It was in Victoria and Western Australia, however, that the conservative parties went furthest. Within a month of taking office in October 1992, the new Kennett Government in Victoria proposed to scrap the system of State tribunals and replace them with a regime of individual and collective contracts underpinned by a threadbare safety net. In Western Australia the Court Government passed two waves of anti-union industrial relations legislation in 1993 and 1995. Wherever the conservative parties took government, departmental heads in the public services were given instructions to squeeze out the unions. Payroll deduction of union dues was cancelled in many states and the consultative committees established by Labor state governments in the 1980s were shut down. Membership of public sector unions declined severely in state jurisdictions in Victoria and WA.

The election of John Hewson as Liberal leader in 1991 marked a shift to the right among the conservatives' federal leadership as well. In November 1991 Hewson unveiled harsh economic and industrial relations policy proposals, known as *Fightback!*[11] These were modelled on the neoliberal policy revolution then unfolding in New Zealand and involved aggressive union-busting, the introduction of a goods and services tax, extensive privatisation, reduced youth wages, drastic cuts to unemployment benefits and the gutting of the public health system.[12] Business groups rallied behind the Coalition in the run-up to the March 1993 election. John Ralph, the chief executive of mining giant CRA, and McDonald's boss Peter Ritchie helped to draft the Opposition's industrial relations policy and joined Hewson's 'kitchen cabinet'.

This was the context in which the federal Labor Government sought to aggressively push the pace of enterprise bargaining in the federal jurisdiction. In mid 1992 the Federal Government matched the New South Wales Government and removed the public interest test for enterprise agreements. Nine months later, having seen off the Liberal challenge in the Government's surprise re-election in March 1993 (more on this below), Keating immediately announced his intention to give enterprise bargaining a boost. He told the Institute of Company Directors in April that he intended to pass legislation that would make enterprise agreements 'full substitutes' for awards, with awards and arbitrated wage increases operating only as a safety net.

The ACTU leadership was taken aback. It favoured a gradual shift to enterprise bargaining but wanted to see the award system maintained. Keating, however, was now proposing to adopt the thrust of the Liberals' industrial relations platform. Relations between the two Accord partners chilled and Industrial Relations Minister Laurie Brereton was heckled when he addressed the 1993 ACTU Congress to promote the Government's forthcoming Industrial Relations Reform Act. Nonetheless, Keating and Brereton understood that the ACTU would not mount a serious challenge to the Government. Despite claiming to have 'drawn a line on non-union enterprise bargains',[13] the ACTU did nothing to hinder passage of the Reform Act in October 1993. Wilfully ignoring the fact that the Labor Government was now making provision for non-union enterprise agreements, ACTU president Martin Ferguson told a meeting of employers that such agreements were an imported aberration quite contrary to the traditions of the 'fair go' upheld by all decent Australian employers, the Labor Government and unions alike.[14]

Labor's 1993 Reform Act represented a significant attack on the award system and elevated enterprise bargaining to the primary mechanism of wage determination. As well as allowing for non-union agreements and the transformation of awards to mere 'safety nets', National Wage Cases were to be replaced by 'safety net adjustments', set sufficiently low to ensure that workers could not rely on them to improve real wages. In the first safety net adjustment late in 1993, the Commission handed down an increase of eight dollars, with a further three increases of this size to follow in 1994. Even these proposed meagre increases proved too much, and the third increase was deferred until September 1995. It became clear that workers could no longer rely on arbitration to secure decent wage rises and would be pitched, willy-nilly, into enterprise bargaining. The take-up rate of enterprise bargaining began to accelerate and by 1995, 2000 agreements had been certified by the Commission, with unions in manufacturing, construction, transport and storage, public administration and defence at the forefront.

The Reform Act introduced a 'right to strike', but this right was encumbered by so many qualifications that workers' ability to strike was actually reduced. In particular, 'protected' strikes could only take place at the expiry of an enterprise agreement during a Commission-sanctioned 'bargaining

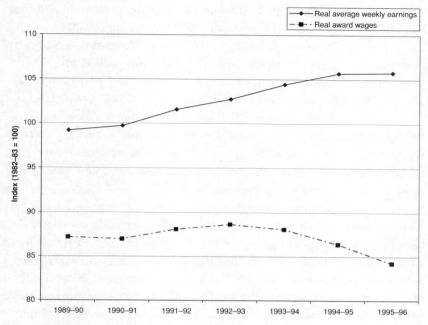

Figure 6.1 Wage levels 1989–90 to 1995–96
Source: ABS *Australian Economic Indicators,* Table 7.3, cat. no. 1350.0. Figure deflated by CPI to arrive at 'real earnings'

period'. Unless they happened to coincide with the bargaining period, strikes to protect union delegates; to respond to redundancies or major changes to work practices; or to prevent work in unsafe conditions were now legally 'unprotected' and could open up unions to heavy fines.

The content of enterprise agreements

The ACTU had enthusiastically promoted enterprise bargaining in the early 1990s. Workers now had to face the consequences. Two Government publications in 1993 and 1995, reviewing the results of a survey of 11 000 workers and the first 1000 certified agreements, provide insights into the effects of enterprise bargaining.[15] As opposed to the meagre safety net adjustments to awards, enterprise bargaining lifted real wages (Figure 6.1). After years of cuts to wages, workers welcomed the increases. Forty-five per cent of workers reported in 1994 that they were 'better off' as a result of enterprise bargaining.[16] Only one-sixth reported that they were 'worse off'.

However, wage rises could only be bought at the expense of working conditions or by conceding managers more power to deploy workers without constraint. Tom McDonald, leader of the newly formed Construction, Forestry, Mining and Energy Union (CFMEU), complained in 1995: 'At times the public perception seems to be that workplace bargaining is all about trading away hard-won award conditions.'[17] This was quite false, he averred, as 'The long-term aim of workplace bargaining is to develop a new workplace culture based on flexibility, cooperation and democracy and the win/win principle of mutual benefits.'[18] The actual experience of enterprise bargaining, however, demonstrated that the public perception was rather more in tune with the reality than was McDonald.

The most significant change resulting from enterprise bargaining involved ceding power to employers to determine working hours and the allocation of labour.[19] Eighty per cent of companies reported that they had changed hours of work. This involved extending daily 'ordinary hours' within which no penalty rates applied, the introduction of 24-hour operations, and a lengthening of the working day. At Alcoa, continuous shift work was introduced and the working week extended from 38 to 42 hours. At Richmond Council in Melbourne, the working day was extended from 7.2 hours to 7.7 hours in exchange for a one-off lump sum payment. In many enterprises, employers were now able to bank rostered days off, allowing workers to take them only in quieter times of operation rather than on a scheduled basis. At Australia Post, the 1994 agreement offered shift workers the 'right' to sell back their extra one-week leave entitlement, thereby diluting award provisions for annual leave.

In order to make extended working hours and weekend work financially viable, employers used enterprise bargaining to cut penalty rates and shift loadings. At the Commonwealth Bank and the Advance Bank, weekend and evening work at ordinary rates was introduced. At Email Appliance plants, ordinary hours were extended to between 6 a.m. and 6 p.m. At a Thiess Linfox joint venture the shift penalty was cut from 50 per cent to 15 per cent.

Such concessions demonstrated the weakness of the 'no disadvantage' test. Furthermore, the 'no disadvantage' test could itself be waived under 'exceptional' conditions. Citing 'economic circumstances', Bonds extended ordinary working hours to 7.00 a.m. to 10.30 p.m. at its clothing factory in northern New South Wales. The Bonds agreement contained no guarantee of minimum weekly hours and allowed a working week of up to 48 hours.

Notwithstanding the 'no disadvantage' test, the agreement was duly certified by the Commission.

Changing working hours was not just a matter of getting the existing workforce to work more 'flexibly'. It also involved increasing the proportion of the workforce employed on precarious conditions. Forty per cent of agreements registered in the private sector in 1994 provided for increased use of part-time, contract or casual labour.

The second set of changes resulting from enterprise bargaining involved the breaking up of common conditions. Agreements in the liquor trades, for example, created a two-tier workforce with overtime payments eliminated for new employees and existing casuals, but maintained for existing full-time workers. The evident intention was to eliminate overtime pay altogether in the long term, but in the short term the effect was to divide the workforce. In the oil industry, the traditional pattern of company-wide bargaining was replaced by bargaining section by section. The consequences of this became clear in August 1995, when offshore workers on strike were left to take action without support from their onshore workmates. Attempts to divide and rule were also evident at Telecom, where management split the organisation into 22 'business units', each with its own employment conditions.

Enterprise bargaining, in combination with the disputes over amalgamations, led to increasing divisions between unions. The AWU had long promoted itself to employers as a 'moderate' union willing to negotiate concessions on working conditions in exchange for sole coverage. It now used enterprise bargaining to force out other unions at Mount Isa Mines and in the Queensland tourist industry. At the Coca-Cola bottling plant in Sydney, management struck a single-union deal with the ETU and cut out the previously dominant Miscellaneous Workers' Union because the Electricians agreed to changes to conditions that had been blocked by the 'Missos'.

Enterprise bargaining invariably introduced new classification structures, a redefinition of jobs, multiskilling and reorganisation of work involving a 'broadening of responsibilities' and the 'removal of restrictive work practices and demarcation barriers'. These were often promoted as job-enriching and opening up career paths for unskilled workers. However, the consequences were more commonly work intensification and loss of jobs. While one-third of workers covered by enterprise agreements in 1994 reported that their ability to use their skills had increased, and two-thirds said that the range of tasks performed had risen over the preceding

12 months, more than half reported increased effort and stress. More than three times as many workers reported reduced job security, less opportunity for promotion and less career development as compared to increases in these conditions.[20]

One aim of enterprise agreements was to bring about what managers called 'continuous improvement' of work practices using 'benchmarking' and 'best practice'. At Melbourne City Council and the Australian Tax Office workers had to 'benchmark' their work against the costs of providing the same service in the private sector. Seven hundred workers at the Federal Government Patents Office won a pay rise of 2 per cent, but only on condition that they helped cut costs by $1 million.

Far from providing 'a framework of employee protection', as the Keating Government suggested, most enterprise agreements allowed business to cut jobs unhindered. In return for a pay rise of 6 per cent spread over two years, Qantas was given the unions' imprimatur to cut staff from 21 200 to 18 000. In public sector health and education, wage increases through enterprise agreements were dependent almost entirely on productivity increases achieved through reducing staffing levels. The result was increased class sizes, fewer nurses on each hospital ward, the closure of wards and reduced patient service.

The involvement of unions in promoting the trade-offs had serious implications that extended beyond the union leaders to shopfloor organisation. An organiser for the AMWU explained:

> When the union and management come along and say 'let's change things', there can be strong resistance, especially in hard, dirty work environments where the culture can be pretty tough. When the shop steward, who is their mate and their own representative, is saying the same thing about the need for change, things can get pretty ugly for the people involved.

At the ANI Bradken foundry in Brisbane such tensions led to a fist-fight between the union delegate and another worker in 1993, both of whom were summarily dismissed.

The return of the New Right

With no sign of a wages breakout following the introduction of enterprise bargaining and with the new system's evident success in breaking down working conditions, employers increasingly warmed to the advantages that might accrue from further decentralisation of the wages system. The MTIA broke from its support for arbitration and embraced the new agenda. With the steady erosion of union power in the workplace and supportive legislation in place at federal and state levels, a number of employers now saw an opportunity to resume the New Right offensive that had been put to one side in 1987.

CRA was at the forefront of the employer offensive and used individual contracts as a weapon to eliminate trade unions. Individual contracts were first used in the company on a mass scale in 1991 at the company's Tiwai Point aluminium smelter in New Zealand to break a 1200-strong union base. The company then turned to Australia and went through its sites one by one. In 1992 CRA sacked 130 workers at its Weipa (Queensland) bauxite mine and imposed individual contracts. In 1993, the company overcame union opposition to contracts at its Hamersley Iron site operations in the Pilbara and its new gold mine at Cobar (New South Wales). In the following year it shifted award workers onto contracts at its Bell Bay smelter in Tasmania and got employee support for a non-union contract at the Boyne Island smelter in Gladstone.

The main lure used by CRA to encourage individual contracts was a significant increase in wages and related conditions, along with a refusal to negotiate an enterprise agreement. The result was a marked difference in wages between workers on contract and those who remained on the award. For example, workers on contract at the Weipa bauxite mine enjoyed a salary advantage of about $15 000, better superannuation and medical benefits, and a week's extra leave. The financial costs of paying these benefits could easily be borne because labour costs were a relatively small factor in CRA's cost structure. By breaking the unions, the company gained complete flexibility in how its capital equipment was used. Workers on contracts had no say about where they worked or about their shifts or roster arrangements and were subject to management's 'right' to hire and fire at will. They could be required to work on any job at any pace for almost unlimited hours.

CRA's success encouraged other employers. In March 1992, APPM went on the attack at its pulp and paper mill at Burnie in Tasmania, seeking to abolish a wide range of over-award conditions and to exclude the Printing and Kindred Industries Union (PKIU) from negotiations.[21] When management instructed boiler operators to train non-union white-collar staff so they could operate the plant in the event of a strike, the dispute escalated and sackings followed. The union struck and set up a picket line that shut down the plant.[22] The picket line became a focal point for the town, with up to a thousand APPM workers and their supporters at the mill gates at any one time.[23] At this point the ACTU intervened; it was not opposed to the change in work practices that the management sought, so much as the company's attempt to lock out the union. If successful, the process of de-unionisation would have accelerated. ACTU president Martin Ferguson negotiated a face-saving agreement with the company that maintained union involvement but conceded many of the company's demands for changes to work practices. In many respects this was a precursor to the more famous waterfront dispute that was to follow six years later.

The more aggressive employer stance became clear even in companies traditionally regarded as 'union-friendly', such as Qantas and the Common-wealth Bank, where management threatened to stop collecting union dues during disputes in 1993. The union-busters were assisted by decisions in the tribunals and the courts. In 1993 the Industrial Relations Commission ruled against applications by the PKIU to incorporate into a union agreement a company that had negotiated a non-union agreement with its staff. The Commission found that the non-union agreement had been freely entered into by workers and that the union had no business intervening.[24] In 1994 the Industrial Relations Court rubber-stamped CRA's strategy of paying workers on award rates less than those on contract at the company's Bell Bay site in Tasmania. In 1995, the Court also ruled that unions had no right to be involved in negotiations at the non-union Asahi metals company.

The Federal Government also came to the assistance of employers seeking to bar unions from their premises. Optus was praised by Laurie Brereton in 1994 when it offered its workforce a non-union agreement that contained no provision for any guaranteed pay rise. The Minister's office offered financial support to any company interested in following Optus' lead,[25] and in 1995 Brereton also intervened to support Asahi's successful bid in the Industrial Court to keep unions out of negotiation over new working arrangements.

Working-class resistance

Despite the employers' offensive, workers still retained a capacity to resist collectively and in some important episodes were able to score victories of their own. Fuelling the resistance was the fact that the arguments for sacrifice, so successful in winning workers to the Accord and wage restraint through the 1980s, had worn very thin after a decade of wage cuts, rising profits and, in the early 1990s, a deep recession. The National Australia Bank, which cut thousands of jobs during and after the recession, reported profits of $2 billion in 1994–95. Coles Myer cut employment by 31 000 between 1989 and 1993 and in the latter year reported profits of $400 million. The All Ordinaries stock market index surged from 1270 in December 1990 to 2100 by October 1993. Workers understood that they were the victims of a process of restructuring that appeared to be rewarding only business investors.

There were two fronts for workers' resistance: conservative state governments and condition-cutting enterprise agreements. With regard to the first, state labor councils mounted defensive action against attacks by conservative governments on several occasions in the 1990s. In 1991 the NSW Labor Council organised a one-day State stoppage in protest at the Greiner Government's Industrial Relations Bill. In the following year it was the Victorian Trades Hall's turn to bring workers into the streets. The recession had been deepest in Victoria and there was already enormous bitterness in working-class communities. The Kennett Government's harsh anti-union legislation, together with an announcement of large-scale school and hospital closures, sparked a major backlash. On 10 November, 800 000 Victorian workers struck and an enormous crowd of 150 000 marched in Melbourne against the Government's plans. Public meetings, stop-work meetings and smaller strikes were held in every corner of the State. Kennett was rattled.

At this very moment, when Trades Hall had built significant momentum behind its campaign, secretary John Halfpenny offered the Government a 'Christmas truce'. Trades Hall aimed to use the strikes and demonstrations as leverage to start negotiations with the Government over its plans, rather than to use the collective power of the unions to frustrate them. With workers back at work and off the streets, Kennett now had some breathing space and the campaign began to lose momentum. Continuing working-class hostility to Kennett was revealed in two further street marches of 80 000 in March 1993 and 50 000 in May, but at this point Trades Hall called off the campaign. The industrial legislation and the cuts went ahead and Kennett won re-election in 1995. Nonetheless, the mass mobilisation had achieved two important gains: it frightened many employers from using the anti-union laws to their full potential and it laid the basis for some further bitter fights against the Kennett Government in the next six years.

The Western Australian Trades and Labor Council (TLC) also organised large demonstrations in 1993 against the newly elected Court Government's 'first wave' industrial relations reforms. The unions failed to stop the legislation, but two years later workers in Western Australia were out on the streets again against the Government's 'second wave'. The TLC organised widespread industrial action, civil disobedience and street protests to force the Government to remove the most draconian aspects of the laws in the State's upper house.[26] In South Australia, the United Trades and Labor Council organised mass demonstrations and State-wide one-day strikes in 1995 in protest at the conservative Brown Government's plans to shackle unions and impose swingeing public-sector cuts.

These examples demonstrate the willingness of the state labor councils to fight attacks by conservative governments. The labor councils also mobilised opposition to the Coalition's 'Fightback' election campaign over the summer of 1993. Against all odds, Labor returned to power at the March 1993 Federal election with an increased majority and a swing of 5.5 per cent. Working-class electorates in Sydney and Melbourne recorded swings of 10–15 per cent, testimony to workers' continuing desire to resist the neoliberal onslaught represented by the Liberals.

Despite the mass involvement in anti-government protests and strikes, resistance to the emerging neoliberal agenda was limited in two ways. First, street marches and strikes were used mostly as token protests rather than as the start of a program of sustained industrial action to prevent the implementation of the legislation, as was clear from the Victorian experience. Second, the unions mounted no such protests when similar attacks were mounted by Labor governments. Union leaders may have heckled Brereton at the 1993 ACTU Congress, but they did not organise any street marches or mass protests against the Reform Act, which contained many of the same provisions as the Greiner Government's legislation of two years earlier.

The second front on which workers fought in this period involved unsatisfactory enterprise agreements. One of the earliest cases was a campaign by postal workers to reject a proposed enterprise agreement in New South Wales in 1991. In the following year, Toyota's Port Melbourne plant rejected a proposed enterprise agreement four times. At Franklins warehouses in

Sydney, workers took a stand in April 1994 against 'engineered work standards', or speed-ups, and an increase in the number of casual staff. Members of the National Union of Workers (NUW, formerly the Storemen and Packers) struck for a week during negotiations, forcing the company to retreat on speed-up and concede an immediate pay rise of $25, with another $10 to follow. One of the most outstanding campaigns against a poor enterprise deal involved New South Wales firefighters in 1994. The firefighters rejected their proposed agreement several times. Mass meetings, work bans and a publicity campaign to reject trade-offs enabled the union to win a much-improved agreement. In August 1995, National Rail Corporation employees rejected a draft enterprise agreement and undertook a one-day strike against the introduction of driver-only operations and longer shifts.

Workers rejected poor enterprise agreements even in areas of traditionally weak union organisation. Employees overwhelmingly threw out a proposed agreement at the Sheraton Wentworth Hotel in Sydney in 1994, even after the same deal at the company's hotel in Melbourne had been promoted by the ACTU and Government as a model agreement. Clerks at the Colonial Mutual bank rejected an enterprise deal offering 4 per cent when they heard that their general manager was paid a salary package of $600 000. In the clothing industry, where employment and union membership had fallen dramatically over the previous two decades, workers at Yakka's four factories in Victoria struck in August 1995 and won a 9 per cent pay rise while defeating plans to scrap tea breaks. Staff at the Bank of Melbourne and the Bendigo Bank, both predominantly non-union companies, prevented their employers from pushing through non-union enterprise agreements.

Where workers accepted first-round enterprise agreements, they were less easily convinced in the following round. Ford workers in Melbourne accepted one of the earliest agreements in 1991, which gave them a 5 per cent pay rise at the expense of meal allowances and dirt money. In 1993 they were ready to fight when management asked for reductions in sick leave for long-serving staff. Led by junior stewards and other shopfloor activists they struck for four hours and subsequently engaged in minor sabotage of plant and equipment. Although the VBEF later secured acceptance of the agreement, 600 workers still voted against the deal.

It was by these sorts of actions that workers were able to frustrate management's ability to carry through a wholesale rolling back of working conditions. Senior managers reported to University of New South Wales researchers in 1993 that the biggest obstacle to implementing change was 'employee resistance'.[27] They complained about 'employee caution and hesitation around change', 'staff scepticism and apathy to change' and 'commitment problems'. Managers reported that 'the front-line distrust the motives of top management and fear for their job security', and also named 'communication failures' along with 'industrial relations issues'. Management 'had difficulty getting the message through' owing to 'union inflexibility', 'entrenched industrial relations attitudes' and 'the strength of the union'. These reports reveal that unions were still hanging on, but resistance was not enough to halt union decline.

The two faces of unionism

The most obvious factor that emerges from an overview of trade unions in the early to mid 1990s is the stark contrast between the relatively comfortable position of those in leadership positions when compared to the collapse of membership at the base.

As a result of the wave of mergers and amalgamations that had started in 1988, the number of federally registered unions fell from 143 to 72 between 1989 and 1993. Those union leaders left standing had become heads of large organisations with political clout to match. In 1993 the 11 largest unions, accounting for two-thirds of total union membership, had on average 150 000 members, an annual income of $25 million in membership dues and 289 staff.[28] Every large union had property holdings and investment portfolios. Union leaders also sat on the boards of industry superannuation funds. They were therefore significant figures on the political, industrial and commercial scene. This was particularly evident at the most senior echelons of the union movement. ACTU secretary Bill Kelty was often seen in the company of trucking magnate Lindsay Fox and in 1995 weighed into a boardroom dispute at Coles Myer on behalf of Fox and his ally, executive chairman Solomon Lew.[29] Kelty was also an ex officio appointment to the Board of the Reserve Bank.

On retiring, senior union leaders had several attractive career options. One was Parliament. ACTU president Simon Crean was elected to Parliament at the 1990 federal election and immediately joined the Hawke Cabinet. He was followed onto Labor's front bench by his successor as

ACTU president, Martin Ferguson, at the 1996 election. Another possible destination was the arbitration tribunals. Such was the ACTU's enthusiasm for the new system of enterprise bargaining that the Government appointed ACTU assistant secretary Iain Ross to head up the new Enterprise Bargaining Division of the Industrial Relations Commission, where he served the workers' cause on a salary five times average weekly earnings.

The private sector also held its attractions. Union leaders regarded by employers as 'a safe pair of hands' had always enjoyed the option of switching sides to serve business, albeit with some censure from their former comrades. In the 1990s, however, business men and women were upheld as 'great mates' in the ACTU's new glossy magazine *Workplace*, which featured breathless interviews with mining and pastoral boss Janet Holmes à Court, the CEO of BTR/Nylex, and senior managers from Lend Lease. In this political environment, behaviour that might have once been frowned upon in a union leader, such as quitting the movement to work in private business, now became more common. Qantas provides one study of such a phenomenon at work. As of mid 1994, Qantas senior management featured three former union leaders: group general manager for industrial relations Peter Marsh (formerly secretary of the Victorian Trades Hall), group general manager Barry Robinson (also formerly a senior unionist), and executive general manager Ian Oldmeadow (formerly senior ACTU industrial officer responsible for the aviation industry).[30]

For others, board positions beckoned. On his resignation as NSW Labor Council secretary in 1994, Michael Easson embarked on a new career as a business director with several major companies. Anna Booth, secretary of the Textile, Clothing and Footwear Workers Union until 1990, was appointed to various board positions with the Commonwealth Bank, the Shopping Centre Council of Australia, the Sydney Harbour Casino and Westpac Bank. Union leaders had well and truly come in from the cold as far as business was concerned.

If the senior leaders of the union movement were prospering during the Accord, the union *base* was in free fall. Between 1990 and 1993, during the worst period of redundancies, union coverage fell by 3 percentage points. In the following three years, as enterprise bargaining took hold and as the job market began to slowly pick up, coverage fell at twice this rate (Table 5.2). The proportion of workplaces with an active union presence fell from 24 per cent in 1990 to 18 per cent in 1995.[31]

Other than creating bureaucratic empires, the wave of union mergers in the first half of the 1990s had done nothing to rebuild union membership.[32] In some significant cases (for example FIA/AWU and AMWU/VBEF), mergers were followed by years of fratricidal disputes and court cases that absorbed union finances and further diverted attention from recruitment. Certainly there is no evidence that the mergers contributed to enhanced democratic accountability or membership empowerment. In 1995, three-quarters of delegates belonging to merged unions reported that the amalgamation had not improved their say in the union, nor their contact with full-time officials, their ability to recruit new members, or their capacity to deal with issues in the workplace.[33]

While enjoying their relatively privileged position during the latter Accord years, union leaders were also aware that this was built on sand. The continuing decline in union coverage undermined their position in the long run, as it was encouraging businesses such as CRA to push unions aside. Union leaders could see the threat posed by non-union enterprise agreements. They also understood that, with a change of government in Canberra, their privileged access to government ministers would end. They therefore had an incentive to address falling union membership, but sought to do so without challenging the agenda of workplace reform to which they remained committed.

In March 1993 the ACTU published *Future Directions*, a paper offering steps to revive union membership that was endorsed at the 1993 Congress. In *Future Directions*, the ACTU argued that unions needed to address union decline head on. It proposed a series of measures: a wider variety of services to members, including a union Visa card and discount shopper scheme, the continuation of union amalgamations, the building of democratic structures in the union movement, and a revival of recruitment campaigns. In pursuit of new members, the ACTU introduced in 1994 its Organising Works program, involving the recruitment and training of what Martin Ferguson described as 'flying squads of highly motivated young recruiters who will go out and sell our message to key groups of young workers'.[34] The ACTU also invested millions of dollars in union publicity campaigns and in union call centres, in an attempt to draw in more members.[35]

These initiatives did little to halt the decline in membership. They failed to address the obvious factor – that the Accord, with its decline in real wages in the 1980s, followed by the trading away of working conditions, had made trade unionism less attractive for workers seeking to defend their conditions of employment. Ferguson promised a more 'active', 'democratic', 'responsive and flexible' union movement, but not one that would *fight* or seek to reverse the damage. On several occasions, the ACTU choked off the opportunity for a serious defence of workers' interests. While union leaders grumbled about Keating's Reform Act, Kelty prevented their complaints from developing into a rupture with the Government. In 1994, as unemployment began to fall and pressure built for a wages push, Kelty warned unions not to engage in 'leapfrogging' (that is, rival unions making successive claims to maintain pay relativities), or industry-wide demands (so-called 'pattern bargaining'). The strike rate fell to a postwar low (see Figure 1.1), and the ebb tide continued to flow against the unions.

In 1995 the ACTU had the opportunity to push back CRA at the company's bauxite mine at Weipa in far north Queensland. Most of the company's workers, facing high prices and attracted to the town by the prospect of making good money fast, had signed individual contracts. Seventy CRA workers, however, stood firm and insisted on union representation. The company tried to wear them down, delaying collective negotiations over improved conditions for more than two years. In frustration the workers struck in October 1995. Several weeks of high drama followed, with wharfies and coal miners striking in Queensland and New South Wales, and dockyard workers walking off the job in Sydney. A wide range of unions in the power, shipping, oil, rail, road, airline, chemicals and manufacturing industries also offered to take action.

At the 1995 ACTU Congress, Kelty promised to draw 'a line in the sand' over Weipa. However, the ACTU leadership had no intention of escalating the dispute into a national stoppage that would seriously hurt the company. Instead Kelty called on the wharfies to return to work after four days on strike and pulled Bob Hawke out of retirement to present the union case to the Industrial Relations Commission. The Commission ultimately ruled in February 1996 that the 70 workers had the right to union representation, but had no right to the same pay and conditions as the contract workers *unless* they were willing to work under the same terms, including 12-hour shifts. The Commission thereby confirmed the validity of CRA's basic strategy. By refusing to leverage the industrial power of the unions in a sustained way, the ACTU lost an opportunity to halt union-busting in the mining industry.

At the 1995 ACTU Congress, president Martin Ferguson boasted of the unions' continued 'discipline and restraint in the face of deliberate, politically motivated provocation' and their 'persistence in playing a powerful role in reshaping the Australian community as a major force driving microeconomic reform'.[36] This 'discipline and restraint' was evident in June 1995 when the ACTU signed Accord Mk VIII with the Government. This, the final version of the Accord, offered low-paid workers paltry safety net adjustments of between $9 and $14.

At a time when the profit share of GDP was at record levels, the ACTU leadership was simply unwilling to mount a serious fight to improve real wages and defend workers' conditions. It thereby contributed to, rather than slowed, the steady decline of union membership. The senior leaders of Australia's unions faced no organised opposition. The networks of union militants once held together by the various left-wing organisations, and which could have led such an opposition, had vanished by the 1990s. For the most part, the union leaders were secure in their posts, more concerned by membership-raiding by rivals than by a revolt by their members. True, grassroots resistance did on occasion lead to the dumping of union leaders. In the Queensland branch of the State Public Services' Federation two leading officials were forced to resign in 1994 after Queensland public servants rejected an enterprise agreement. In the same year the federal secretary of the Finance Sector Union, an enthusiastic supporter of 'workplace reform', was forced to quit after ANZ Bank workers voted 7000 to 5000 to reject a 1.5 per cent pay rise in exchange for a substantial lengthening of ordinary time working hours, weekend work and further staff cuts. Unfortunately, however, such cases were the exception rather than the rule.

The 1996 election and the end of the Accord

Following his Government's re-election in 1993, Keating promised to 'bring home the bacon' for workers who had suffered during the recession. Nonetheless, privatisation and labour market 'reform' were pushed further, and other natural Labor constituencies, including university students, were hit harder with increased charges. Award wages continued to decline in value – by 5 per cent between 1993 and 1996, and by a full 16 per cent when compared to their value in 1983. The increase in average weekly earnings

Table 6.1 Distribution of household incomes (after taxation and government benefits are included) 1994–2004

Income quintile	Share of total household disposable income (%)		Average real household disposable incomes (1993–94 prices) ($)		Change in real household disposable incomes (%)
	1984	**1994**	**1984**	**1994**	**1984–94**
Lowest	6.3	5.8	192.13	174.82	−9.0
Second	12.1	11.4	365.67	340.07	−7.0
Third	17.9	17.4	543.27	517.77	−4.7
Fourth	24.8	25.0	751.37	745.77	−0.7
Highest	38.8	40.4	1176.68	1205.46	+2.5
TOTAL	**100.0**	**100.0**	**605.54**	**596.84**	−1.4

Source: ABS *Australian Social Trends 1997*, cat. no. 4102.0, pp. 117 and 118

arising from enterprise bargaining in the early 1990s began to flatten out once again by 1996 (Figure 6.1). Much was made by the Government of its 'social wage' program, whereby wage restraint was offset by improvements to social welfare and a progressive tax system. Nonetheless, even when these factors are taken into account, only the top 20 per cent of households saw any overall lift in their incomes over the decade to 1994 (Table 6.1) and income inequality registered a sharp increase during the tenure of the Hawke and Keating governments.[37]

There was a substantial increase in employment of more than 650 000 between 1993 and 1996, but more than one-third of these jobs were part-time.[38] For those with full-time jobs, work was just getting harder with longer hours. By 1996, workers were working the equivalent of four more weeks over the course of the year when compared to 1983.[39]

Business, by contrast, did well from the Keating Government. Productivity, which had been stagnant in the first five years of the Accord, began to lift quite sharply in the 1990s.[40] Company tax, which had fallen from 46 per cent to 39 per cent in the 1980s, was cut again to 33 per cent in 1993. By 1996, the profit share of GDP was 5 percentage points higher than in 1983, equivalent to more than $20 billion, and the rate of profit rose to its highest level since 1974 (Figure 3.1).

The ongoing failure of Labor to deliver for the working class generated resentment among its supporters. It had only narrowly held on to power at the 1990 election, but revived its fortunes at the 1993 poll in the face of widespread fear among the working class about the threat posed by the Coalition's anti-working-class manifesto *Fightback*. In 1996 workers' patience with Labor was exhausted and the Government was not going to get another chance. Opposition leader John Howard, having learned from the Coalition's 1993 debacle, pitched the conservatives as a force that could deliver a 'relaxed and comfortable' Australia. Queensland Labor Premier Wayne Goss's comment that voters were 'waiting with baseball bats on their verandahs' to turf out the Keating Government captured the mood.

On 2 March 1996, the Keating Government was finally confronted with the reality of its unpopularity. Labor was voted out with a swing of more than 6 per cent and polled its lowest percentage primary vote since 1906. One-third of union members voted for the Coalition parties. After years of declining membership, the atrophying of grassroots activism and a lack of willingness by the union leaders to fight for workers' rights, the unions were now vulnerable to a full-blown attack by the incoming Howard Government.

Chapter Seven

UNIONISM IN A COLD CLIMATE, 1996–2004

Workers and their unions in 1996

Three elements defined the union movement during the first three terms of the Howard Government (1996–2004). One was an ongoing employer and government offensive against the working class. The economy grew throughout this period. The rate of profit continued its recovery. Nonetheless, international competition continued to bear down on Australian business, and this compelled employers to cut costs wherever possible. The Federal Government for its part encouraged employers to confront the trade unions, which still retained significant power to frustrate managers in their core areas of strength. It passed a series of laws that made it increasingly difficult for unions to operate and used a combination of sticks and carrots to cajole and entice employers into using these laws.

The second feature of trade unionism in these years was a working class that was battered and bruised and had lost the networks of militants that could have organised a fight-back, but which was at the same time increasingly bitter towards government and employer attacks and the sacrifices that it was expected to make in the name of international competitiveness. Steady economic growth created jobs, unemployment fell, and real wages rose for most workers, but at the cost of work intensification and longer working hours. Job insecurity and household debt were persistent concerns.[1] Housing was becoming increasingly unaffordable, at least partly because of a strong demand for rental stock by wealthy investors provided tax breaks by the government. Many workers were experiencing a 'joyless recovery' in the 1990s and understood the effects of the ongoing employer and government offensive. This class antagonism meant that, when a call to fight was given by their leaders, workers responded enthusiastically.

The problem was that such leads were rarely given. The third characteristic of the union movement in these years was a reluctance on the part of union officials to fight the Government and employers. The union leaders understood that the government and employers were seeking to squeeze them out; late in 1995 Kelty had promised the Coalition that, if the solidarity strike in support of the workers at CRA's Weipa site had been 'a sonata', the Coalition would be treated to 'the full symphony, with all the pieces, all the clashes and all the music' if it enacted anti-union legislation on winning office. In practice, however, the union leaders constrained the struggle to those channels that were likely to lead to defeat or a poor compromise at best. At times they simply capitulated without a fight.

In other words, the stance that the union leaders had adopted during the Accord years was maintained in its essentials, even in the very different political environment of the Coalition Government. In place of fighting, the union leaders thrashed around for other strategies that could halt the decline of unionism and mitigate the full effects of the employer and government offensive. In most cases these did little to rebuild unionism. Where unions were able to recruit in large numbers, this was invariably the result of strikes.

The broad strategic orientation of the union leaders during the Howard Government was apparent in their post mortems of the Accord. Not surprisingly, the ACTU, which had invested so much in the Accord and had enjoyed unprecedented authority during its lifetime, was least willing to entertain any criticisms. In August 1996, new ACTU president Jennie George confessed that the ACTU 'didn't appreciate enough how much people were actually hurting in that process of change and how much anxiety there was and the loss of job security that was affecting our traditional constituency',[2] but was essentially unapologetic. The economic and industrial changes introduced by Labor had been necessary. The problem was 'reform fatigue' within Labor's working-class constituency. In March 1997 George argued that 'Keating's "big picture", now as fashionably disparaged by some as it was once applauded, did provide a coherent and inspiring portrayal of social democracy in the 1990s' and two years later the ACTU argued that the Accord 'delivered significant social and industrial improvements' to the union movement.[3]

The ACTU officers were not alone in their positive assessment of the Accord. George Campbell, national secretary of the AMWU, wrote at the end of 1996 that the Accord had been 'more beneficial for workers and the Australian economy than would otherwise have been achieved in its absence, since it achieved significant structural change to the Australian economy with limited social dislocation and cost.'[4] Campbell then listed these 'benefits' as the facilitation of microeconomic reform, a cut in real wages of 14 per cent between 1987 and 1991, a rise in the share of profits, and substantial gains for employers – thus providing an illustration of the ACTU 'disconnect' that George had alluded to three months earlier. 'History,' he concluded, 'will judge the Accord quite favourably.' In September 1997 Campbell was appointed to a Senate seat by the Carr Labor Government in New South Wales.

Other union leaders were rather more critical, either explicitly or implicitly. The CFMEU national executive condemned the Accord for cutting real wages, reducing union membership and undermining 'the consciousness and fighting capacity of trade unionists'.[5] Without directly criticising the Accord, Doug Cameron, Campbell's successor as AMWU national secretary, reviewed the experience of the AMWU during the 1990s as follows:

> We have sought real partnerships [with employers] and been betrayed; we have promoted co-operation, not capitulation; we have benchmarked; we have introduced teams; we have talked endlessly about training and competency with almost no results for the bulk of our members; we have innovated; we have been flexible; we have restructured the Award; we have simplified the Award; we have strived for best practice in manufacturing workplaces; we have bargained and bargained and bargained.
>
> None of this has been enough for government or employers . . . the workers have been abandoned to market forces and the latest fads, such as downsizing, contracting out and re-engineering.[6]

Important though these criticisms were, they suffered from a series of problems. The CFMEU may have condemned the Accord in May 1996, but the BWIU (which subsequently became part of the CFMEU) had endorsed all eight versions of the Accord while Labor was still in power, a fact Jennie

George pointed to when confronted by the CFMEU's resolution. Further-more, the left officials were simply not serious. No attempt was made by the left leaders to force out of office those in the ACTU who had enthusiastically prosecuted the Accord for 13 years. Kelty was re-elected as secretary with-out opposition at the 1997 ACTU Congress and continued to be revered by his successors. The most serious limitation of the retrospective criticisms, however, was that they had little practical effect. The political climate may have become more harsh under Howard, but the union leaders, both left and right, continued to preach industrial peace and collaboration with the employers. Their greatest hope was simply a return to the Accord environ-ment of tripartite industry committees, where they could once again find a seat at the table. They criticised the decline in wages that had occurred under Labor but they had no intention of rebuilding a union movement that would fight. Importantly, none criticised the systematic squashing of strikes or the crushing of the BLF and Airline Pilots.

These three elements – employer and government aggression, a willing-ness by workers to respond when given a lead, and the essential reluctance of the union leaders to vigorously fight for workers' rights – were demonstrated in full in two major episodes in the first three years of the Howard Gov-ernment: the struggle over the Workplace Relations Act and the waterfront dispute.

Two early clashes

The *Workplace Relations Act 1996*

After promising a 'relaxed and comfortable' Australia during the 1996 elec-tion campaign, the Howard Government quickly revealed its real agenda when it tabled the Workplace Relations Bill in Parliament. The Bill was designed to accelerate the processes under way in the later years of the Keating Government – a declining role for arbitration and the award system – but accompanied by a much more trenchant attack on trade unions. Individual contracts, known as Australian Workplace Agreements (AWAs), were to receive pride of place in the array of industrial instru-ments. An Employment Advocate was given the job of promoting AWAs and policing union activity. Awards were to be stripped back to 20 'allowable matters', removing among other things all caps on the use of part-time and casual employment. Unfair dismissal legislation was to be weakened.

Secondary boycotts provisions, prohibiting solidarity industrial action, were to be reintroduced into the Trades Practices Act, giving them extra legal bite. The Bill prohibited all forms of compulsory unionism and preference arrangements. The payment of wages by employers to workers on strike was banned and the Industrial Relations Commission was given greater power to prevent industrial action. The Bill also marked the abolition of the Trade Union Training Authority.

When the details of the Bill became public in April, the ACTU leadership described it as 'the most malicious and vindictive piece of legislation that the country has ever seen'. Nonetheless, it accepted that the legislation would go through in some form. It therefore adopted a short-term and a long-term strategy.[7] The former involved attempts to draw the teeth of the Bill by lobbying senators. The ACTU held negotiations with the Democrats and Independent senator Brian Harradine, at which it argued that the Coalition had no mandate for its extreme measures and that the Bill flouted Howard's pre-election 'rock solid guarantee that no worker would be worse off'. The ACTU also lobbied individual Coalition Government MPs, with Jennie George writing to female Coalition members asking them to 'raise their voices' against attacks on women's rights. The ACTU also launched a case in the High Court on the grounds that the legislation was not within the competence of the Commonwealth. These were the immediate moves. The long-term strategy was to campaign for the defeat of the Coalition Government at the next federal election: this would involve a sustained program of raising 'community awareness'.

An important element of the parliamentary and public awareness campaigns was a series of union rallies to protest against both the Bill and the August 1996 Budget, which was predicted to include hundreds of millions of dollars in spending cuts and the privatisation of the Commonwealth Employment Service The ACTU hoped that the rallies would sway the Democrats, convince workers of the need to take a stand against the Coalition Government's attacks, and highlight Labor's opposition. The ACTU planned to bring the campaign of rallies against the Bill and the Budget to a climax with a National Day of Action (NDA) on 19 August, the day before the Budget was handed down. The NDA was to involve a series of mass rallies in the capital cities and a Cavalcade to Canberra, drawing thousands of workers from Sydney and Melbourne to protest outside Parliament House.

Workers took every opportunity to protest. Thousands flocked to union rallies over the three months leading up to the NDA. On 17 May, 2000 members of the CFMEU and MUA, which had launched a mutual defence pact, marched in Sydney in protest at threats by the Government to crush the MUA. The National Tertiary Education Union (NTEU) held two national strikes on 30 May and 7 August to protest against higher education funding cuts, with nearly 30 000 taking part in demonstrations. Also on 30 May, 150 000 construction workers struck against proposed cuts to travel allowances. On 11 July the construction unions were out again, with 5000 marching in Melbourne. A march in Canberra convened by the CPSU on 6 June to protest against staffing cuts drew 4000 onto the streets. In the last week of July, 11 000 Telstra workers rallied at mass meetings in protest against plans to privatise the company, and tens of thousands of public servants marched in Melbourne against staffing and service cuts. The strike rate, which had been in steady decline for years, lifted sharply. Thousands of students and Aboriginal people also protested during these three months against cuts to higher education and attacks on Indigenous rights.

The NDA on 19 August therefore looked set to be a success. The ACTU plan was to get a large crowd of unionists to attend a set-piece demonstration on the lawns some distance from Parliament House itself. It would last approximately 90 minutes and would be addressed by Labor leader Kim Beazley and other VIPs. The demonstrators would then return home, leaving the ACTU leaders to meet the Prime Minister and to lobby the Democrats. The first part of the agenda went according to plan. Several left unions pulled out all stops to get members to the capital; the New South Wales branch of the AMWU alone organised 47 buses, and the CFMEU also brought large contingents of members. Aboriginal groups and student unions also brought out significant numbers. By 12 noon some 20 000 protestors had assembled.

In the following two hours, however, the plan fell apart. Contingents of CFMEU members, students and Aboriginal people bypassed the official route and approached the forecourt of Parliament House. Other union contingents, seeing the growing crowd at the forecourt, assumed that this was the official rally and joined in, as did several thousand other protestors who had been at the official demonstration but were curious to see what was going on. Two thousand or more then marched up to the doors of the building, where they laid siege to it. *Canberra Times* journalist Ian Warden captured the carnival atmosphere as the demonstrators sought to assert their claim to the 'people's house':

> And all of this, this milling, burning and shouting in a tidy, clean, ceremonial place the planners and managers have always sought to keep unsoiled by anything as spontaneous as free people flexing their democratic pecs and abs. Impertinent but agile protestors climbed up and across the holy marble parapet of the Great Verandah in front of the building and hung their banners there. Eureka and Aboriginal flags even hung across the holy marble parapet of the nation's sacred stainless steel coat of arms. Nothing was sacred, and the hitherto aloof, superior and polished parliament, however inexcusable the damage done to it yesterday, seemed for a few exciting hours to be a popular amenity.[8]

Cheered on by the crowd, between 500 and 1000 of the protestors then pushed open the first set of doors to Parliament House, forcing the police to retreat inside. Unable to get any further, some of the demonstrators then sought a different route via the gift shop where they pushed out a window. After police reinforcements rushed to the scene the protestors were driven back and 49 arrested.

While those on the official platform had no idea of the dramatic events occurring a few hundred metres away, other union leaders very quickly became aware of the situation. The secretary of the ACT Community and Public Sector Union (CPSU) tried in vain to keep people from walking across to the forecourt. The CFMEU leaders were more successful. On realising that many CFMEU members, including some organisers, were leading the charge on the doors of Parliament House, the national officers of the CFMEU hurried over to drag them away. The CFMEU component of the breakaway demonstration dispersed, but a significant number of unionists remained for the duration.

The breakaway demonstration unleashed a media firestorm, with vivid accounts of a 'riot' at the seat of government. The Government whipped up an atmosphere of panic, demanding that the Labor Party condemn what it called an assault on democracy. The ALP leaders did not need much persuasion. Opposition leader Kim Beazley referred to the protestors as 'louts' and 'lunatics' while his deputy, Senator Gareth Evans, described them as 'crazy, self-indulgent bastards' whose actions were 'ugly, un-Australian, stupid and indefensible'.[9] The problem for the ALP leadership, however, was that, by cooperating with the Government's attempts to construct the event as simply an issue of 'law and order', they allowed the Government to set the terrain for debate about the entire incident and lost the opportunity to make any headway criticising the harsh budget.

The ACTU also recoiled in horror. After some initial confusion on the day, Jennie George and Bill Kelty joined the media attack. George condemned the 'wanton violence and wanton destruction' by those whose 'action and behaviour had nothing to do with the mainstream of the union movement' and who did 'serious damage' to it. The ACTU would disown anyone charged for taking part in the protest and 'would not walk away from responsibility' for disciplining union officials who were involved. The right-wing union leaders were even more aggressive. Senior right-wing officials wrote to the Australian Federal Police Association apologising for the violence of the protestors, and criticised the ACTU leadership for its 'unsatisfactory organisation' of the rally. Coverage of the Cavalcade in the journals of right-wing unions condemned the 'storming' of Parliament House and carried photographs and names of CFMEU organisers allegedly involved in the breakaway demonstration. The left-wing unions attacked the hypocrisy of the right-wing leaders who had gone along with the media condemnations while doing nothing themselves to defend workers' rights. Nonetheless, they too disowned the protest and Doug Cameron from the AMWU and Stan Sharkey from the CFMEU announced that any of their union officials found to have been involved would be sacked. In the wash-up at the next ACTU Council meeting held on 3 September, Council declared that 'These acts of violence and destruction of property are totally abhorrent to the union movement and any person found to be involved should receive no support or comfort from our movement.'[10]

Just as Hawke had urged delegates to 'cool it' during the Kerr Coup, the ACTU now sought to lower the temperature of working-class anger against the anti-union laws. The ACTU resolved not to call any more public rallies. Henceforth the focus would be on raising 'community awareness' (the electoral strategy), delegates' meetings to advise union members of progress with the campaign, and the despatch of more delegations to lobby the Democrats and right-wing senator Harradine. The campaign against public sector cutbacks was likewise confined to a marginal seats campaign to prepare for the next election, a public awareness campaign, and the formation of a 'network of respected persons'.

The ACTU capitulated all the way along the line. Fearing that the Government would call a double dissolution election if the Democrats blocked the Workplace Relations Bill or insisted on unacceptable amendments, the ACTU worked with the minor party to develop amendments that would be acceptable to both the Democrats and the Government. When these were subsequently incorporated into the Bill and passed in the Senate, the ACTU refrained from publicly criticising the Democrats for allowing the Bill to proceed.

The Waterfront dispute

Having secured its anti-union legislation, the Government sought to press ahead. However, it faced a problem in doing so. Business lobby groups stood four-square behind the Government's efforts to marginalise unions, but the same was not true of individual employers, many of whom were not prepared to risk a major confrontation with unions. Collectively, employers understood the benefits that would ensue from a decisive shift of power from unions to business; but it was in each employer's *individual* best interests to avoid the necessary confrontation. Consequently, it was up to the state to push employers into carrying out attacks on unions using a combination of sticks and carrots.

The Howard Government was certainly not the first to deal with employer hesitancy in this way. The Hawke Government's Accord, with its no extra claims clause, was aimed not just at unions but at employers too. The Government wanted to prevent employers from caving in to any 'maverick' unions determined to break indexation. Likewise, it took action by the federal and state Labor governments to break the power of the BLF in 1986, whereas individual construction companies had been prepared to buy industrial peace by making concessions to the union. In 1989 it was the Federal Government's use of the RAAF that had allowed the domestic airline carriers to beat the airline pilots. John Howard and Workplace Relations Minister Peter Reith now wielded the machinery of the Australian state to launch further attacks on unions and to prod employers into action.

In the name of 'workplace reform', government inspectors and the Employment Advocate were unleashed to root out activism in core areas of union organisation. Early targets included the construction industry, the waterfront, coal mining and the meat industry.[11] In relation to construction, it was not enough that the Labor Government had destroyed the BLF in New South Wales and Victoria. Now all union activism had to be purged from building sites. The Government published a National Code of Industry Practice in May 1997, which required all employers seeking Government tenders for major infrastructure projects to attack the CFMEU.[12]

The waterfront was a particular focus of Government animus. The Maritime Union of Australia (MUA) and its predecessors, the WWF and SUA, had been thorns in the side of conservative governments for decades, and Howard now resolved to break waterfront unions once and for all. A conspiracy against the MUA began to take shape in the first half of 1997.[13] Meetings involved Workplace Relations Minister Peter Reith, Transport Minister John Sharp, Patrick Stevedores' CEO Chris Corrigan, Don McGauchie and Wendy Craik from the National Farmers' Federation (NFF), and a number of senior industrial lawyers and departmental advisers. A strategy document endorsed by the Howard Cabinet in July called for a full-scale attack on the MUA.

The conspiracy advanced on a number of fronts. In September 1997, International Purveyors, owned by US mining giant Freport McMoran, attempted to bring in non-union labour to operate facilities in Cairns. Threats by the International Transport Workers Federation to black-ban Freport's port operations brought this to an abrupt end. In the same month Corrigan re-engineered his corporate structure to create a series of labour-hire shelf companies, thereby removing Patrick from any direct responsibility for the employment of wharfies. Meanwhile Patrick, with Government support, sent 30 former and serving military personnel to train in Dubai in readiness to work as scab supervisors and managers in Australia. The secret plan was exposed in the media and the subsequent threat by the International Transport Workers Federation to ban shipping saw the Dubai government quickly withdraw the scabs' work permits.

Undeterred, Patrick locked out its workforce at Webb Dock in Melbourne in January 1998, sub-leasing the site to a non-union front company established by the NFF, which then proceeded to train a fresh non-union workforce. The Government readied the Australian Competition and Consumer Commission to take retaliatory action should a strike eventuate. Stories were planted with current affairs programs to create public resentment against 'lazy and overpaid' wharfies. Stan Wallis, head of the BCA, declared that big business was 'prepared to wear any amount of costs' in a campaign to destroy the MUA, and business made pledges of close to $100 million to the NFF over the course of the dispute.

The ACTU leadership was now confronted by a frontal assault on one of Australia's landmark unions. Unlike the smashing of mining unionism in the remote reaches of Western Australia, the elimination of the MUA would be in full view of the media and would occur with the explicit backing of the Government. To abandon the MUA would have left the field clear for the virtual eradication of unionism and, with it, much of the political power and influence of the ACTU leadership itself. And so, at the 1997 ACTU Congress, Kelty promised that the union movement's resources would be thrown into defending the MUA, on the proviso that the union accept further rounds of waterfront 'reform'.

The attempt to break the MUA climaxed on the night of 7–8 April with the sacking of 1400 Patrick wharfies and their replacement by an army of scabs. Union leaders swung into action to rally their members to support the MUA. The MUA and its supporters organised what they called 'community assemblies' at all the major ports to protest at the sackings and to put pressure on the Government. The original intention of the MUA was that these were to operate within the law. Picketers could approach drivers and ask them to respect the picket lines, but if drivers chose to drive through, picketers would not seek to block their way. This was the way it remained in Brisbane. Indeed, a delegation from the Queensland TLC was sent to the Police Commissioner to seek assurances that adequate numbers of police were dispatched to ensure order was maintained.[14] Nonetheless, in Fremantle and Melbourne and to a lesser extent in Sydney, the community assemblies developed very quickly into blockades that prevented the movement of containers out of the ports whether by truck or train. Patrick could unload ships and put cargo on trucks and trains, but these were prevented from leaving the ports, paralysing the company. In Sydney and Melbourne alone, approximately $500 million worth of cargo was stranded on the dockside.

Thousands of unionists rushed to back the wharfies. If the MUA was beaten, no union was safe. Workers had already indicated their willingness to strike in support of the wharfies. On 20 March, 12 000 construction workers in Melbourne had stopped work for a day to demonstrate their support for the union, and on 2 April AWU members in the oil industry promised to strike the moment that Patrick's workers were sacked. But not only unionism was at stake. The dispute had the potential not only to save jobs on the wharf but also to inflict a major blow on the credibility of the Howard Government.

Over the course of April a wide array of workers took direct action in support of the wharfies. Warehouse employees from the big supermarket chains, building and construction workers, truck drivers, metalworkers, vehicle workers and coal miners all stopped work and turned up in large contingents to lend support to the wharfies' cause. When it was reported on 20 April that WA Premier Richard Court's brother was set to break the picket line in Fremantle with a convoy of farmers' trucks, workers at P&O, the other waterfront operator, struck in protest. At a delegates' meeting in Brisbane on 16 April, Queensland TLC secretary John Thompson told the mass meeting of 1500 that his office had been swamped by faxes from unionists demanding State-wide industrial action and that his main job had been 'putting out fires' around the State. A mass meeting of 3000 delegates convened by the Victorian Trades Hall voted to hold a rally in support of the wharfies on 6 May.[15]

The community assembly marshalled at East Swanson Dock in Melbourne was the most impressive feature of the entire campaign. The Melbourne picketers were determined that no trucks would pass. They laid railway tracks across the road and welded them together as a 'community arts project'; they arranged concrete blocks across the entrance road to East Swanson; and they overturned a trailer to block traffic. TWU members planned to block Footscray Road with their trucks if any non-union driver tried to force entry.

Union officials put into place a system at East Swanson to coordinate the work of thousands of MUA supporters. Each union was rostered to provide picketers for particular time-slots. A telephone tree of thousands alerted supporters when the police made hostile moves. At any one time several hundred workers and supporters would be at the Melbourne picket line, bringing food, drink, ideas, laughter, song and skills. The festive atmosphere, the solidarity and the sense of purpose affected all.

The most dramatic mass action at East Swanson Dock occurred on the night of 17–18 April. Following a tip-off that 1000 police would be arriving to break up the picket line and cart people off to detention centres, thousands of workers, students and pensioners flocked to the dock to meet an imminent police attack. With arms linked, packed in tightly behind barricades of concrete blocks, cars and railway tracks, 4000 picketers stood their ground. At 8 a.m. they were joined by 2000 construction workers, thereby encircling the police and forcing them to retreat. At another entrance to Swanson Dock, after a police push had cleared out the picketers, the dock was re-taken by a detachment of 1000 MUA supporters. No cargo moved into or out of the entire Port of Melbourne. This was the biggest victory won by the trade union movement for many years, a fact clearly recognised by business: the shares of Patrick's owners, Lang Corp, promptly fell by 13 per cent.

Sydney and Fremantle also put on an impressive display of solidarity. In Sydney hundreds showed up to protest outside Patrick's operations at Darling Harbour and Port Botany in Sydney. Once picketers were seized by the police and taken off the road, many went straight back to join the picket. New South Wales trucking companies met and decided to refuse to send their drivers through the picket lines. In Fremantle there were similar scenes, with up to 2000 wharfies and their supporters making the movement of trucks difficult if not impossible.

Despite the injunction against the Melbourne picket by the Victorian Supreme Court on 20 April, and despite increasingly desperate calls from politicians and farmers for the police to break up the pickets, the sheer size of the union mobilisation in Melbourne made the police unwilling to act. In Sydney, the police were completely outnumbered: when they were ordered in to break up the lines, more than 160 took sick leave. In Fremantle, in protest at a raid by riot police on the Patrick picket line at 2 a.m., a crowd of more than 2000 determined picketers quickly gathered, demonstrating that the police were in for a fight.

The campaign by the wharfies and their supporters tapped international solidarity, in particular from the International Transport Workers Federation. Japanese and Filipino workers demonstrated in support. In India, Indonesia, Holland, PNG and South Africa, waterfront workers took solidarity action to support Australian wharfies. In California, wharfies defied their own repressive industrial laws and refused to handle ships that had been loaded by scab labour in Australia.

Working-class support for the MUA was also evident in the more than $1 million raised by unions. Thousands personally contributed money, many taking out payroll deductions. P&O wharfies, instructed by the union leadership to take on work redirected from Patrick's operations, donated between $50 and half of their pay each shift to help out those who had been sacked.

Very quickly the Government was pushed onto the defensive by the actions of the mass pickets. Far from there being mass resentment at the 'lazy and overpaid wharfie', public sympathy was much more evident for the watersiders who, after all, had been sacked and driven off the waterfront by security guards with ferocious dogs. Business was increasingly alarmed. Reg Clairs, Woolworths' chief executive, expressed the fears of business leaders, saying that if the unions mounted widespread strikes in support of the wharfies the consequences for profits would be enormous. The Government was under increasing pressure the longer the dispute dragged on. What had begun as an attempt to break the MUA quickly developed into a situation where the MUA and its supporters could have broken the Government, or at the very least inflicted serious damage on it and its industrial laws.

The community assemblies were one crucial element of the campaign and, indeed, developed into a far larger component of it than originally anticipated. Not even the most optimistic MUA supporter had expected the pickets to attract hundreds of unionists and supporters around the clock, peaking at several thousands during emergencies. Nonetheless, if it was the mass pickets that were crippling Patrick's operations, the focus of the MUA and ACTU was on the legal case to have the wharfies reinstated. The MUA applied to the Federal Court for reinstatement of the wharfies on the grounds that they had been dismissed by the company because they were union members, thereby violating the Government's own 'freedom of assembly' provisions of the Workplace Relations Act. The legal focus meant that strikes in support of the wharfies were regarded as marginal if not counterproductive. The MUA and ACTU regularly denounced calls for a national campaign of strikes to support the wharfies as a 'gift to the Coalition', as it would render the unions liable to incur millions of dollars in fines under secondary boycotts legislation. Further, it might 'inconvenience the public' and undermine the public relations campaign.

The legal focus of the campaign seriously weakened the ability of unions to draw on traditional sources of solidarity. Breaking decades of tradition, the MUA leaders instructed members to crew ships that had been loaded or unloaded by scabs, much to the disgust of seafarers who would gladly have black-banned the ships. Likewise, MUA members at P&O were kept at work, although chief executive Richard Hein made it clear that his company would pursue any cost-cutting measures extracted by Patrick.

Some left-wing union leaders and organisers were less reluctant to break the law. The CFMEU regularly organised large contingents of workers to stop work on building sites to march to the pickets, and sometimes they were joined by the TWU and AMWU. On other occasions, union officials simply turned a blind eye to workers acting site by site. It was in Melbourne, where the officials of the Trades Hall and individual unions were under most pressure from militants, that the union leaders were prepared to go furthest.[16] In the days immediately after the sackings on 7 April, containers were still getting out of East Swanson Dock by rail. The union officials were nervous about preventing the passage of trains for fear of incurring heavy fines. On 10 April, a group of socialists and other militants argued successfully against the officials to picket the railway tracks, with the result that no containers moved out by train. Patrick responded by taking out an injunction against the picket. The picket was maintained, but union officials were clearly fearful about the legal consequences of defying the court. At the Trades Hall delegates' meeting on 16 April, secretary Leigh Hubbard hedged around the question of whether to endorse the defiant action. Jerome Small describes what happened next when a socialist shop steward from the Postal Workers' Union got up to speak:

> Winning the dispute depended on having an effective picket; having a picket meant breaking the law; who was prepared to break the law to defend the wharfies? Thousands raised their hands.
>
> At the next delegates meeting, it was the Trades Hall Secretary himself, running to catch up with the mood of the membership, who asked every delegate to raise their hands if we were prepared to break the law.[17]

The mass pickets, the effective shut-down of Patrick operations, and the preparedness of workers to turn out in force to prevent scabbing, created an unfortunate situation for the courts. One option canvassed by the Federal and High Courts during their deliberations over the course of April and early May was simply to award the MUA members damages for their lost jobs and to allow Patrick to continue its shelf company operations with scab labour. Nonetheless, the learned judges were sufficiently acquainted with the facts on the ground to understand that such a decision would have only fuelled an escalation of the situation. Probably they remembered the O'Shea strikes and the impossibility of simply imposing legal decisions entirely at variance with industrial reality. And so on 23 April the Federal Court ordered the reinstatement of the wharfies. An outraged Corrigan appealed on the basis that he should not be required to re-employ staff when the company was at risk of liquidation (through its own financial engineering). He received short shrift and the High Court upheld the Federal Court decision on 4 May, albeit with the significant rider that administrators of the shelf companies set up by Patrick would have the power to liquidate them at any time. On 7 May, bowing to the inevitable, Patrick relented and the wharfies marched back through the gates.

The result was a great defeat for the Howard Government's attempt to destroy the MUA, an outcome celebrated at the largest turn-ups at May Day demonstrations for many years in Brisbane and Sydney on 3–4 May and by a massive march of 80 000 in Melbourne on 6 May. In each of its major aims – to break the MUA and to use this as the first step for a broader offensive, to introduce scab labour onto the wharves, and to give itself an electoral boost – the Howard Government had failed outright. What the Prime Minister had described in parliament on the morning after the sackings as a 'defining moment in Australian industrial history' and a 'fight back by the people of Australia' against union power turned out to be a significant embarrassment for the Government. Far from being a vote-winner, the mobilisation in defence of the MUA and the reinstatement of MUA members hurt the Coalition Government. Peter Reith had become 'damaged goods' for the Government and did not attempt another direct confrontation of this kind.

But the wharfies paid a heavy price in the deal negotiated with Corrigan in the months following their reinstatement. In the face of significant opposition among wharfies, particularly at the Sydney Port Botany operations, MUA secretary John Coombs and ACTU assistant secretary Greg Combet negotiated a package with Patrick that delivered over 600 redundancies out of the 1400-strong workforce, mass casualisation, the contracting out of many key functions, and the loss of penalty rates. The union also sacrificed control over the allocation of workers to jobs (the 'order of the pick') and agreed to a performance-based bonus system, allowing Patrick much greater freedom to allocate and discipline staff. As it had threatened, P&O then followed suit, sacking 450 of its 1300 workers and introducing dramatic changes to work practices with union endorsement.

The MUA dispute demonstrated the two logics of union action. One was the logic of mass mobilisation that was the instinctive response of union activists and, indeed, many union organisers, and on which they acted, in many cases defying the law. The other was going through the 'proper channels'. This took the form of the legal challenge. Unfortunately, the focus on the legal challenge, and the subordination of the campaign to this tactic, meant that the ACTU and MUA sacrificed the best opportunity in many years to turn the tide against the government and employer offensive. Furthermore, their commitment to workplace reform and collaboration with employers meant that the taste of victory was soured by large-scale concessions. Once the MUA leaders were recognised as legitimate bargaining parties by Patrick, following the reinstatement of the wharfies, they were prepared to accept any sacrifices on the part of the workforce.

The union campaigns against the Workplace Relations Bill and against Patrick Stevedores convey a good sense of the main features of Australian unionism in the late 1990s. The common experience of work intensification, cut-backs to the social wage, and attacks on their rights at work meant that many workers were open to demonstrating their opposition to these attacks. The ACTU's public awareness campaigns found a ready audience among workers who did not need to read the fine details of the Workplace Relations Bill to understand that it was another attack on their rights at work. They were not disoriented by the government and media campaign to portray wharfies as 'overpaid bludgers' because they had a keen understanding of the many ways in which the media and conservatives had denigrated workers over the years. When their union leaders provided an opportunity to resist, many workers seized it with both hands. In doing so, they also nudged their union leaders to the left.

The problem was that the ACTU was not prepared to give a bold lead to workers to defy the law, seeking only to use demonstrations and pickets to give it extra leverage in court and in lobbying politicians. Furthermore, in neither case did the leaders provide any mechanism for union delegates to play any role in determining the course of the campaign. During the waterfront dispute there were no elected MUA dispute committees and no means for MUA members to vote on campaign strategy or tactics. Where significant opposition to the final settlement appeared in Sydney, the national office simply squashed it. Workers could fight back, therefore, and do their best to resist the ongoing Government offensive, but significant changes in the operation of the unions were needed if these fight-backs were to play a role in rebuilding trade unions from the bottom up.

The anti-union offensive continues

Following its defeat on the waterfront, the Howard Government suffered a significant swing against it at the October 1998 election. Its two-party vote actually fell below Labor's and it lost 14 seats in the lower house. Undeterred, the Government introduced its More Jobs, Better Pay Bill in early 1999. Popularly known as the 'second wave' of industrial reforms, key features of the Bill included measures to increase the take-up of the unpopular AWAs, a further reduction in the allowable content of awards, the exemption of small business from unfair dismissal laws, and more restrictions on unions and their ability to organise and strike. The ACTU resumed its Senate lobbying campaign, but the left-wing state labor councils and some individual unions, fresh from their mobilisations in support of the MUA, preferred a more defiant response. On 11 August 1999, the South Australian United Trades and Labor Council organised a demonstration of 10 000 in Adelaide.[18] On the following day 100 000 unionists and supporters marched in Melbourne, with building workers striking for 24 hours. Having faced flak on their left after allowing the passage of the Workplace Relations Act in 1996, and under pressure to make a stand against the Coalition following the MUA victory and a decline in their Senate vote at the 1998 election, the Democrats blocked the Bill, which did not make its way through to a final reading.

Nonetheless, the union victory over the 'second wave' legislation was not typical of the Howard years. Retreat and defeat were more common. Outright union-busting was still gaining ground in the mining industry. In the Western Australian iron ore industry, BHP, which had traditionally distinguished its policies from the anti-unionism of Rio Tinto (re-badged CRA), decided to follow suit in the late 1990s, and by 2003 one-half of its Pilbara workforce was on individual contracts.[19] The CFMEU faced a rash of union-busting attempts in the Queensland coal industry. In August 1997, mining company ARCO sacked its entire unionised workforce of 312 production and engineering workers at its Gordonstone mine in central Queensland. The CFMEU members were offered their jobs back on individual contracts. At the subsequent tribunal hearing, the Commission ruled that the workers had been unfairly dismissed but did not order reinstatement. ARCO paid off the workforce and sold the operations to Rio Tinto, which reopened the mine with non-union contractors.[20]

The ARCO case was an indication that lockouts were becoming an increasingly common feature of Australian industrial relations after having virtually disappeared in the decades following the Great Depression.[21] One such case involved Kerry Packer's Consolidated Meat Group, which early in 2002 locked out its 1200-strong workforce at its Rockhampton abattoir in Queensland. Management offered to reopen the plant only on condition that the workers agree to revert to the minimum award conditions. Facing permanent closure, the workforce eventually agreed to the company's terms.

Even short of lockouts, however, employers continued to use a variety of means to undercut established conditions and attack unions. In 2000 the Commonwealth Bank began to shift large numbers of non-managerial staff on to AWAs.[22] In the federal public service, conditions of employment and managerial practices that had once been used as a means to attract staff – secure employment, regular hours, superior leave entitlements, training and career progression and consultation with staff and staff unions – were now held up as evidence of extravagance and waste. 'Market testing' was now used to strengthen managerial prerogatives and reduce conditions of employment to those prevailing in the private sector. Departmental heads were selected and assessed on their willingness to push trade unions aside.

Enterprise bargaining was used to make obsolete any notion of a standard five-day, 37-hour week. Penalty rates were cashed out to allow much greater shift work and weekend work, clauses limiting the use of part-time and casual work were abolished, and 152-hour 'months' were introduced allowing employers to vary the working week almost at will. Work classifications were collapsed, and 'agency agreements' in the public service undermined the ability of unions to mobilise 'all-in' campaigns.

Unions in the airline industry were hit by a series of blows. For a number of years, efforts had been made to establish a third airline in Australia to break open the duopoly of Qantas/Australian and Ansett on domestic routes. Backed by the deep pockets of Richard Branson, Virgin Blue was eventually successful in building a sustainable operation based on employment conditions significantly lower than the industry standard. Virgin's start-up was followed in September 2001 by the closure of Ansett with the loss of thousands of jobs. Qantas used the downturn in traffic following the 9/11 terrorist attacks to axe thousands of jobs and slash employment conditions. The company met the Virgin challenge by setting up Jetstar with staff employed on lower pay, lower staffing ratios and worse conditions than those enjoyed at Qantas. Qantas then used the inroads established at Jetstar to attack conditions for Qantas staff. In 2004 the airline commenced a major program of outsourcing and casualisation and threatened to relocate maintenance work to overseas and regional operators.

The Federal Government kept up the pressure on the construction unions. Between 1997 and 1999 the Employment Advocate had devoted extensive resources to identifying and trying to break closed shops in the construction industry. Nonetheless, at the turn of the century, the CFMEU was still very much a live presence at the big CBD construction projects. The major contractors in many cases turned a blind eye to the union's activities, fearing disruption of work and the imposition of penalties for late completion of projects. Peter Reith's successor as Minister for Workplace Relations, Tony Abbott, was determined to bring the employers and unions to heel. In 2000 the Employment Advocate produced a ten-page report alleging intimidation, 'rorts' and violence in the industry, which effectively constituted a frame-up of the CFMEU. The Government then used this report as the basis to establish a Royal Commission in July 2001, headed by Justice Terence Cole, to review the industry's allegedly low productivity, inadequate training and skills base, rampant industrial action, and poor standards of occupational health and safety.[23] The real agenda of the Commission was clear in the allocation of its time, 90 per cent of which was spent in investigating allegations adverse to the union and just 3 per cent on those adverse to the employers.[24] The CFMEU organised protests of hundreds of building workers outside Commission hearings. Cole's first report in August 2002 led to the formation of the Interim Building Industry Taskforce. The Taskforce, headed up by former National Crime Authority police investigator Nigel Hadgkiss, had extensive powers to search premises, interview 'persons of interest' and conduct phone intercepts.

Justice Cole handed his final report to the Government in March 2003.[25] Cole's report recommended stringent action to weaken the grip of the building unions, including the establishment of a new watchdog, the Australian Building and Construction Commission, which is discussed further in the next chapter. The CFMEU did its best to maintain operations in the new environment. Despite its sweeping powers, the Taskforce was not able to mount a single successful prosecution of CFMEU officials or members in its first 18 months. When John Setka, a Victorian branch organiser, was summoned in October 2003 to appear before the Melbourne Magistrates Court on charges laid by the Taskforce, 10 000 building workers rallied outside the Court in his defence.[26]

In the university sector, years of funding cuts had taken their toll on staff conditions in the form of larger class sizes, lay-offs, and rapid casualisation of staff. The NTEU leadership failed to offer any kind of serious resistance. Nonetheless, the NTEU held at bay some of the Government's more ambitious goals and the union was therefore in the Government's sights.[27] In September 2003, the Government intervened during a round of enterprise bargaining in the universities to demand that management offer AWAs and take action to reduce the role of unions on their campuses.[28] Managements that refused to do so would not have access to an additional $400 million in university funding. The vice-chancellors opposed the tying of university funding to industrial relations demands, but nonetheless agreed to the new conditions. Their protests were mollified by the Government sweetener that they be allowed to raise HECS charges for students by 25 per cent.

University staff were in no hurry to sign AWAs. To 'rectify' this situation, Minister Brendan Nelson unveiled the Higher Education Workplace Relations Requirements (HEWRRs) in 2004.[29] All universities were now required to promote AWAs, eliminate unions from university committees, remove any limits on the employment of casual and part-time employees, lift restrictions on management's rights to fire staff, and curtail the NTEU's freedom to organise.[30] University managements that fulfilled the HEWRRs were given a 5 per cent increase in funding which still, however, left them substantially short of the funding per student that they had enjoyed when the Government first took office in 1996.

Union efforts to reverse decline

Unions faced a hostile operating environment. The arbitration system no longer provided benchmark pay rises for all workers, awards were becoming increasingly irrelevant in determining conditions of employment for millions of workers, and the Government appeared hell-bent on making life difficult for unions to organise. Union membership continued to slide – from 2.2 million in 1996 to 1.9 million three years later (see Figure 7.1). The cancellation of dues check-off and closed shop arrangements

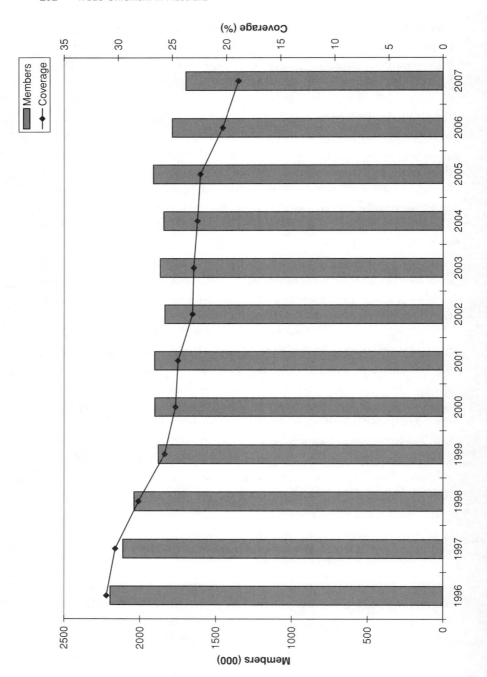

spelled financial crisis for many unions, which were forced to slash staffing and administration costs. [31]

None of the strategies arising from the ACTU publications *Australia Reconstructed* and *Future Strategies* had had any success in halting the decline of union membership. Union amalgamations, a centrepiece of *Future Strategies*, had succeeded in rationalising union structures but had done nothing to lift recruitment. The unions had signally failed to meet the two-year target of 200 000 new members set by Bill Kelty at the 1995 ACTU Congress. Instead, membership fell by nearly 90 000.

Concern among union leaders about declining membership resulted in the adoption in 1999 of *unions@work* [*sic*], a document drawn up by the ACTU following a tour of Europe and North America by leading officials from both left and right factions. *Unions@work* incorporated strategies developed by US trade unions in response to their steady loss of membership over several decades.[32] *Unions@work* was followed in 2003 by *Australian Unions: Strategies for Growth*. These documents emphasised the need to build strength in workplaces with an established union presence, to recruit in new areas, to use information technology to improve delivery of union services, and to promote a 'strong union voice in wider society'. The emphasis on strength in the workplace was implicit recognition of the impact that suppression of workplace activism during the Accord years had had on the engine room of Australian unionism. Stronger workplace activism was essential to rebuff employer efforts to exclude unions and was the only guarantee of union growth.

Union leaders took heart from surveys by the NSW Labor Council which demonstrated that, although only one-quarter of the workforce were members of trade unions, a further one-quarter were sympathetic. They tried a variety of methods to recruit from this pool of sympathetic non-members.[33]

←——————————————————————————————————————

Figure 7.1 Union membership and coverage 1996–2007
Source: Australian Bureau of Statistics *Trade Union Members Australia*, cat. no. 6325.0; *Employee Earnings, Benefits and Trade Union Membership Australia*, cat. no. 6310.0
Note: This figure presents union membership and coverage calculated by means of a household survey, as opposed to figures in Chapter 1, which present union membership and coverage sourced by means of a survey of trade unions themselves (ABS *Trade Union Statistics Australia*). The ABS discontinued the latter method in 1996

Specialist organising teams were established in a number of unions, in some cases pooling resources among several erstwhile competitors. This was particularly evident in the burgeoning call centre, hotel and gambling industries.[34] In the Pilbara mining region, four unions shared resources to establish the Pilbara Mineworkers' Union.[35] Using house calls, one-to-one meetings with workers, organising committees and contact with family members, the new organisation was able to recruit quickly.[36]

The Liquor, Hospitality and Miscellaneous Union (LHMU) campaigned to boost membership for two years at the Sydney Star City Casino. The campaign involved a range of activities by on-site members, organisers and supporters from outside the industry and resulted in significant recruitment and a revitalisation of union activity during enterprise bargaining negotiations. The climax of the campaign was a 24-hour strike.[37]

Unions sought to develop closer relations with a variety of community campaign groups. The most significant was the struggle to win compensation for James Hardie Industries workers who had contracted asbestosis. A union ban on the use of James Hardie products on construction sites and demonstrations of 5000–10 000 in Sydney and Melbourne in 2003–4 gave real muscle to the retired workers' demands for compensation and ultimately led to satisfaction of the victims' claims in 2005.

The decline in union coverage and membership began to slow at the turn of the decade and by 2002 the process had virtually stopped (see Figure 7.1). Although no reliable account has been kept, it is likely that the greater emphasis on a 'recruitment and organising culture' among union organisers may have contributed to this welcome development. However, other factors are likely to have been more important. The banning of closed shops in state and federal jurisdictions during the 1990s was responsible for a significant decline in membership.[38] However, once the initial exodus of 'conscript' members had left, this factor lost its urgency.[39] Another factor was changes to the structure of the workforce. In the 1990s union coverage was adversely affected by rapid growth in casual employment, traditionally non-union. It was also hit hard by large-scale cuts in public service employment, where union coverage is traditionally relatively high. In the 2000s the casual share of the workforce stabilised, with most growth coming from full-time jobs. In addition, employment in the state and federal public services began to recover. Both of these developments contributed to the levelling-out of union coverage rates. Finally, strong employment growth in the economy more generally may have helped offset the fear of dismissal among workers who were considering joining unions.

Some combination of these factors contributed to halting decline, but they did not help to rebuild unionism as an *active* force. This required a preparedness on the part of unions to fight for workers' rights, including using tactics such as strikes and bans. It is here that the efforts of the ACTU to revive the union movement faltered. Despite the contribution that strikes could play in boosting recruitment and breathing life into unions, the ACTU saw no role for them. *Unions@work* referred to membership 'activism', but this in practice tended to involve anything but strikes, preferring city rallies, petitions, election campaigning in marginal seats, and liaison with community organisations. The strike rate continued to fall to successive record lows, despite strong growth in employment (see Figure 1.1).

Union leaders justified their reluctance to strike on the grounds that restrictive industrial relations legislation had made most strikes, in particular solidarity actions, legally hazardous. Unions therefore had to pursue other avenues, in particular the use of the courts and public relations campaigns. However, the reluctance to strike or use militant tactics was not, at its heart, an issue of legal constraint. The Victorian rebel unions had demonstrated in 1969 that determined action could break even the most restrictive laws. The fundamental problem was that the union leaders did not actually *want* to fight, preferring 'partnership' with business. These were not just the right-wing union leaders, for whom partnership was always their preferred mode. This inclination was also evident among the left-wing leaders. In 1999 the new left-wing 'Workers First' leadership of the Victorian branch of the AMWU referred approvingly to Accord-style consultative committees: 'The national industry plans of the 1980s provided examples of limited but significant success in policy innovation . . . the challenge now is to build on this approach.'[40] The Victorian leadership advocated the establishment of a Victorian Manufacturing Council, comprising representatives from business, government and unions, with an agenda of 'workplace change and innovation'. In earlier years, Sweden, with its high union membership and extensive welfare state, had been the preferred model for advocates of union–business partnership. Now, however, the AMWU held up Singapore and Ireland, characterised by strongly anti-union governments and/or threadbare welfare states, as 'successful regional economies' that Australia might emulate.[41]

The pursuit of partnership with business meant that union leaders consistently frustrated relations with other forces that could have proven to be genuine allies of the labour movement and chose instead to work with those who were the workers' adversaries. In the late 1990s left-wing environmental activists in Melbourne launched Earthworker, to build bridges between environmentalists and the mining and forestry unions and to prevent the mining and forestry companies from playing them off against each other. The Victorian Trades Hall provided resources for Earthworker and initially encouraged it. Very quickly, however, the project came under intense pressure from the forestry division of the CFMEU, which preferred cosy relations with the timber companies and state governments in Victoria and Tasmania, in the belief that workers could trust them to secure jobs for their members. Relations between the forestry division and the environmental campaigners quickly became heated, with the result that Earthworker was shut down in 2001.

As elsewhere, partnership with business did nothing to protect workers' jobs and conditions. While employers were grateful to the forestry division leaders for lobbying state Labor governments for wider access to old-growth forests in Victoria and Tasmania, their gratitude did not extend to guaranteeing forestry workers their jobs. They continued to use mechanisation and technological upgrading to slash forestry employment. And, in an echo of the warm support extended by the VBEF to Malcolm Fraser in Geelong in 1975, the leaders of the forestry division welcomed John Howard to the stage at a mass meeting in Tasmania during the 2004 election campaign as a defender of forestry workers' jobs.

Most union leaders condemned the forestry union leaders for extending a welcome to the conservative leader in 2004, but the forestry leaders' strategy of pursuing partnership with business, and ignoring or downplaying relations with the union movement's natural allies, was not unusual. Union leaders had been making modest efforts for some years to recruit young workers and students. Labor councils in Sydney and Melbourne experimented with Young Unionist Networks and took the union message to festivals, campuses and high schools. And yet, when a massive opportunity to relate to young workers and students came along during the anti-war mobilisations of late 2002 and early 2003, the unions were missing in action.

A clear majority of Australians opposed the looming US attack on Iraq, and on the weekend of 15–16 February 2003 the largest demonstrations in

Australian history took place. Across Australia, 800 000 protestors marched against the impending war. Had the unions put themselves at the centre of this movement, they would not only have provided it with much needed political leverage and organisational capacity; they would also have enjoyed a great opportunity to relate to thousands of anti-Government protestors. However, the union leaders did virtually nothing to mobilise members to join the rallies and union involvement was a pale shadow of what it had been during the Vietnam Moratoriums. Unlike the 1970 Moratorium, which was called under the slogan 'Stop Work to Stop the War', the left-wing union leaders called no strikes or walk-outs to participate in the rallies. Indeed, their efforts were shown up by the churches, which did more work to build the demonstrations than did the unions.

Rather than seeking partnership with employers, a more aggressive strategy to fight for workers' rights would have been more beneficial in rebuilding union power. Every episode where unions actually fought in this period resulted in strong membership growth. The one-day strike at the Sydney Star City Casino in 2000 resulted in 630 new members for the LHMU. Strikes for higher wages by the National Tertiary Education Union in October 2003 and by the Victorian branch of the Australian Education Union in February 2004 netted these unions more than 1000 new members in each instance,[42] while 600 workers joined the Association of Professional Engineers, Scientists and Managers, Australia (APESMA) at the non-union IT company EDS when it launched a fight for higher wages in 2004.

Instead of building unions by organising strikes, union leaders all too often sought to make gains by body-snatching from other unions. The most egregious example occurred at Rio Tinto in the Pilbara in 2003.[43] After three years of successful collaboration, mining unions won a major victory in 2002 when Rio Tinto workers rejected a non-union enterprise agreement. The workers demanded that the company negotiate a union enterprise agreement, using the relatively favourable Western Australian jurisdiction. Unbeknown to the local AWU representative, however, the national leadership of the AWU had negotiated a 'sweetheart' arrangement with Rio Tinto under the federal jurisdiction, freezing out the other three unions and imposing inferior terms and conditions on the workforce.[44] Collaboration between the unions in the Pilbara collapsed in the ensuing acrimony.

Unprepared to mount the kind of activity that would rebuild union power, union leaders placed their hopes in the ALP. At successive federal elections in 1998, 2001 and 2004, unions spent millions of dollars in advertising and marginal seat campaigns. The latter involved allocating union staff, officials and delegates to particular constituencies deemed vulnerable for the Coalition, in the hope that union resources could tip the balance to Labor. In some instances union campaigning contributed to the defeat of Coalition candidates, but unions received little in the way of thanks from the ALP. The situation can be contrasted with the late 1960s and early 1970s, when the preparedness of unions to strike gave union leaders the power to influence ALP policy, and Labor's parliamentary leaders regularly spoke out in support of trade unionism. Now, with unions in a weak state, it was the Labor parliamentary caucus that called the shots. Successive Labor leaders distanced themselves from the unions in the name of party 'modernisation'. A review of the party's operations under the short-lived Crean leadership led to a reduction in union representation at state conferences from 60 per cent to 50 per cent in 2002. Crean's successor, Mark Latham, used his time as Labor leader to mount a series of gratuitous attacks on trade unions. Then, with the election of Kevin Rudd as Labor leader in December 2006, union leaders were pushed to the back of the queue in the quest for Labor's support, as we shall see in the next chapter.

To summarise, thirteen years of close collaboration with the Hawke–Keating Labor Government had weakened the Australian union movement and placed it in a precarious position when the Coalition Government took power in 1996. The Coalition proceeded to kick away many of the remaining institutional props that had supported trade unionism. The decisions of the Government were reinforced by judgments from courts and by an increasing preparedness by employers to 'take on' trade unions where they had previously cooperated.

It was not a rout. The campaign for the MUA in 1998 demonstrated the willingness of many thousands of workers to take militant action in defence of trade unionism. The problem was that, for the most part, their leaders refused to lead, seeking means other than strikes and defiance to turn back the attacks. They were, however, conscious that declining membership was significantly weakening their position in relation to government and employers. They therefore embarked on a series of internal measures aimed at boosting membership. However, recruitment was not the same as rebuilding *activism*, the only guarantee of sustained union recovery or, indeed, survival. The union leaders were uninterested in reviving unions on the basis of *struggle*, as this ran counter to their desire for partnership with business and to their general timidity. With the re-election of the Howard Government at the October 2004 election, the leaders' innate industrial conservatism prevented the unions from taking full advantage of the massive backlash provoked by the re-elected Government's WorkChoices legislation.

Chapter Eight

WORKCHOICES AND THE DEFEAT OF THE HOWARD GOVERNMENT

WorkChoices

The context for WorkChoices

Although the *Workplace Relations Act 1996* represented the most drastic anti-union legislation for several decades, the Federal Government was constrained for its first nine years in office because it lacked a majority in the Senate. With the achievement of a majority in both houses following the 2004 federal election, Howard proposed a total overhaul of the federal arbitration system, which took shape in the *Workplace Relations Amendment (WorkChoices) Act 2005*.

One interpretation of WorkChoices, initially promoted strongly by the ACTU and ALP, was that it resulted from a single-minded right-wing 'ideological' obsession on the part of John Howard, supported by conservative lawyers and business lobby groups. In a speech to the National Press Club in June 2005, ACTU secretary Greg Combet explained:

> . . . John Howard is offering the realisation of a long-held IR prejudice. His is a backward-looking agenda to cut labour costs, to find our economic way in the world by preying on the weak and vulnerable, by attacking fairness and democratic principles.[1]

Combet argued that WorkChoices was a 'radical', 'reckless', 'irresponsible' and 'biased' plan.[2] 'Irresponsible' because it was not in the interests of business to pursue a strategy based on cutting wages. Such a strategy would not address 'the real economic priorities facing Australia'.[3] Australian business would benefit far more by fixing problems in infrastructure investment, skills, and research and development, which were resulting in 'slow growth in high-value exports, under-performance in the generation of highly skilled jobs, and sluggish productivity in the tradeable goods sector'. The ACTU put itself forward as a partner for business in a productivity revolution that could fix these problems.

ALP leader Kim Beazley likewise suggested that the Prime Minister did not understand the modern economy and operated with 'a mindset that still lives with a picture of the world that in the mid-1970s may have had some truth to it but now has no truth at all.'[4] The Howard Government had benefited from the productivity gains ensuing from Labor's reforms of the 1980s and 1990s, Labor argued, but was now jeopardising the benefits by ignoring infrastructure development. The result was that 'the productivity surge has faltered.'[5] Labor promised business that it could revive the surge by:

> investing in the skills and education of our workforce, investing in research and development, investing in better use, more efficient use of infrastructure, investing in better information technology infrastructure, reducing the complexity of regulations, so that we're more productive.[6]

Beazley slammed the Liberals on the floor of Parliament for their efforts to cut workers' wages:

> We in the Labor Party will never fight a class war like that, because we do not believe in it. We do not believe in class war; they do. We believe in cooperative flexible labour relations . . . You introduce into Australia an element of latent class war that we do not want, that is against the Australian spirit of the fair go and against the Australian spirit of equality.[7]

The notion that WorkChoices was simply the result of an 'ideological obsession' of an old man increasingly out of touch with the 'modern economy' missed the point. WorkChoices possessed a logical coherence and addressed real problems in Australian capitalism and, from a capitalist point of view, was an equally valid response to problems confronting it. Despite a long period of economic growth starting in 1992, and a steady revival in the rate of profit and the profit share under way since 1983, Australian capitalism in 2004 faced some serious problems: substantial trade deficits, susceptibility to world financial markets that were increasingly reliant on speculation, and a profit rate that was still lagging behind the figure experienced during the postwar boom years.[8]

The Australian capitalist class was enjoying a record profit *share*, but what mattered to it most was that the *rate* of profit, the return on its investment, needed to be boosted. This explains why, even in the context of the economic growth of the 1990s and 2000s, major companies reporting substantial profits engaged in continuous attacks on their workforces in the form of redundancies, contracting-out, longer hours of work and reduced conditions of employment. They had no choice from the perspective of capitalists who wanted to prosper in an increasingly globalised economy – not to do so would have meant falling behind their rivals. The BCA and the Australian Chamber of Commerce and Industry (ACCI) urged the Government to engage in another round of labour market 'reform', not because their leaders were zealots who did not understand the needs of modern business, but because they understood that the Government had a 'once in a lifetime opportunity' of a Senate majority to allow employers to cut wages for the less skilled, change work practices almost at will, remove any constraints on employers' ability to hire and fire, and push aside trade unions. With the economy growing quickly and unemployment low, the Government did not necessarily expect that large wage cuts were on the *immediate* agenda for many businesses but, by establishing the necessary legal framework now, it was preparing the scene for a future recession when such measures might be needed. The International Monetary Fund and the World Bank urged the Government on.[9]

The use of WorkChoices to weaken trade unions had a further benefit for the Government. Even though union power was much weaker than in the 1970s, Australian unions still retained an ability to resist the Government's ambitions to foster a society run entirely in the interests of the capitalist class through cuts to the welfare system, implementation of user pays throughout the public sector and so forth. Unions therefore had to be marginalised and weakened wherever possible. It was no coincidence that the Government also used its Senate majority in 2005 to pass legislation designed to cripple student unionism, another potential source of opposition to the Government's mission.

Still, the idea that WorkChoices represented an 'ideological obsession' by the Howard Government did rest on some undoubted facts. Howard and other senior Cabinet ministers including Peter Costello and Tony Abbott *did* have a long-term objective of crippling Australian trade unionism that was ideological in its consistency and passion. But this was not irrational from the perspective of Australian capitalism. The Howard Government's enactment of WorkChoices was not the product of its attachment to an obsolete ideology but, rather, reflected a long-term characteristic of the Australian state – its preparedness to intervene to discipline not just unions but also individual capitalists who might not follow through on measures that benefited the capitalist class as a whole. WorkChoices was not the only strategy possible that would serve this end – we will see later that Australian business was prepared to live with an amended version of WorkChoices under the Rudd Labor Government – but it certainly did not run counter to the interests of Australian capitalism.

Features and effects of WorkChoices

What were some of the specific features and effects of WorkChoices? First, it promoted a much expanded role for AWAs. It further weakened the ability of unions to negotiate collective agreements, abolished the no disadvantage test, and undercut the base conditions provided by the award system. WorkChoices proposed to drive conditions down with the introduction of its Fair Pay and Conditions Standard, which was now the baseline for all contracts and agreements. This comprised a Federal Minimum Wage (initially set at $12.75 per hour), four weeks' annual leave (up to two weeks of which could be traded off for cash), 10 days' personal or carer's leave, 52 weeks' unpaid parental leave, and a standard working week of no more than 38 hours (but which could be packaged into monthly or half-yearly formats). The Minimum Wage would be set by a new Australian Fair Pay Commission. AWAs could now be 'negotiated' with five-year terms, rather than three years. Consistent with the Workplace Relations Act, AWAs could be offered on a 'take it or leave it' basis to new staff and would override any relevant award or enterprise agreement for the individual concerned.

Every study done on the impact of AWAs indicates a deterioration in conditions of employment for the majority of workers covered by such agreements.[10] This much was clear even before WorkChoices.[11] With the removal of the no disadvantage test, most protections simply disappeared and business took advantage of the new environment. More than 300 000 new AWAs were registered in the first 12 months of WorkChoices. In a sample of 998 AWAs lodged between May and October 2006, the Government's own Workplace Authority (the re-badged Office of the Employment Advocate) found that the majority lacked penalty rates for work in unsocial hours, shift loadings, overtime loadings, public holiday payment, and annual leave loadings.[12] Thirty per cent made no reference to rest breaks, one-quarter did not include declared public holidays, and one-third made no provision for wage increases during the life of the agreement. One in six removed all award conditions, replacing them with only the Government's five minimum items. Rates of pay were systematically lower for most workers on AWAs as compared to those on enterprise agreements.[13] In one-half of cases, workers on AWAs reported that they had had no opportunity to negotiate their content.

Behind the statistics lay the stories of the 29 Cowra abattoir workers who were sacked and then invited to reapply for only 20 positions on much inferior conditions, a practice upheld by the Workplace Ombudsman (the former Inspectorate) following an investigation. Three hundred fellow meatworkers at the Lobethal Australia abattoir in the Adelaide Hills were forced onto five-year AWAs, which cut pay by between $200 and $300 a week.[14] Young workers at Bakers Delight in regional Victoria were confronted with management demands to give up paid sick leave and annual leave entitlements in return for a pay increase of 75 cents an hour, while casual workers at Darrell Lea in Victoria were pressured into signing AWAs that slashed penalty rates for weekends and public holidays.[15] It was not just workers in the most precarious positions who were badly treated. Two dozen maintenance workers at Boeing operations in Williamtown, New South Wales, struck for nine months in 2005–06 in protest at being forced onto AWAs, which paid $15 000 less than the industry going rate.

The impact of AWAs was particularly harsh for women in low-paid jobs, for whom one national study found 'significant negative outcomes in relation to employment security, the level and predictability of pay and hours, overall earnings and employee voice and say'.[16] These included women like Annette Harris, the Spotlight worker from Coffs Harbour, New South Wales who was asked to trade in all her penalty rates for a two cents per hour pay increase. Then there was 20-year-old trainee diving instructor Brooke O'Mara, who was paid $30 a day for 10-hour shifts over three months in the summer of 2007, with no entitlement to annual leave or sick leave. The Ombudsman ruled that she was not entitled to the award rate because she was under 21.[17] The removal of unfair dismissal rights from more than one-third of the workforce further exacerbated the impact of WorkChoices on female workers in precarious jobs.[18] WorkChoices unleashed a spate of sackings of pregnant women, staff on sickness leave or those off work recovering from injuries sustained in the workplace. In the first year of WorkChoices, the Human Rights and Equal Opportunity Commission received a 60 per cent increase in workplace-related complaints.[19] Even though the economy was growing and unemployment was low, average weekly earnings adjusted for inflation fell by half a per cent for full-time adult workers in WorkChoices' first year of operation, but for women working in the private sector, by a full 2 per cent.[20]

WorkChoices intensified the trend under way since the late 1980s of employers seizing greater control over the number and scheduling of hours worked by employees.[21] One-third of all workers surveyed in a major study of WorkChoices agreements experienced a reduction in their real pay at the same time as their hours remained the same or increased.[22] There was a ripple effect throughout working-class communities. More than 40 per cent of New South Wales workers reported in 2007 that they had a friend or family member negatively affected by the new regime.[23]

Facing sustained public hostility to WorkChoices after one year of operation and fearing the electoral consequences, the Government reintroduced a weak version of the no disadvantage test – the Fairness Test – in July 2007. The Fairness Test required employers to demonstrate that they had provided some financial or other compensation for the cancellation of core award conditions. However, this was so widely flouted by employers that by September 2007 the Workplace Authority had been forced to reject one-half of the 54 000 AWAs that had been submitted to it, on the grounds that they failed to meet the standards of even this weak safeguard.[24]

WorkChoices targeted trade unions and encouraged employers to exclude them from work premises. Both the Workplace Authority and the Minister for Workplace Relations were empowered to strike out clauses in employment agreements that enabled unions to operate effectively – those that prohibited AWAs, banned independent contractors or labour hire, allowed industrial action during the term of an agreement, provided for trade union training leave or pay for attendance at union meetings, mandated union involvement in dispute procedures, or provided for redress for unfair dismissal. Anyone seeking the inclusion of such 'prohibited content' was liable to fines of $6600 (individuals) or $33 000 (unions or employers).

Under WorkChoices, employers were under no obligation to bargain in good faith with a trade union, even if the entire workforce nominated the union as their preferred bargaining agent. WorkChoices also further restricted the right of union organisers to enter workplaces to sign up new members, attend to grievances, or confirm that employers were abiding by the relevant award or legal codes. Union officials could now only enter workplaces and hold discussions with members where the union was party to an industrial agreement or award, and could only hold such meetings during meal or other breaks, and at a place nominated by the employer.

Union membership was hard hit. Between August 2004 and August 2005, union membership rose by 70 000. Over the following two years, as WorkChoices took effect, it fell by 216 000, or more than 11 per cent (see Figure 7.1). Union coverage fell by 3.5 percentage points, the steepest drop in coverage since the mid 1990s.

WorkChoices also sought to make strikes virtually impossible. Under the Workplace Relations Act, strikes had only been considered 'protected', and therefore immune from tort action, during a 'bargaining period', which occurred at the expiry of an enterprise agreement. Any strike outside this bargaining period was unprotected and the IRC had the power to stop it. WorkChoices drew the noose even tighter. All unprotected industrial action became automatically unlawful, and the IRC was now *required* to order its cessation. Tougher penalties were introduced for unlawful strikes, including new essential services legislation. Compulsory secret ballots were required before any strike. A strike could not be 'protected' if a non-unionist was involved, and the IRC could order a 'cooling off' period where the action was harmful to a 'third person', such as another business or individual. The IRC could suspend or terminate protected action that it believed to be part of 'pattern bargaining', a form of industry-wide bargaining.

The strike rate, already at record lows in 2005, plummeted further under WorkChoices. Comparing the three quarters leading up to March 2006, the date when WorkChoices took effect, with the six quarters that followed, the average number of new disputes each quarter fell from 109 to 34.[25] This compares with a quarterly average of 447 at the start of the Accord in 1983 and more than 600 during the 1970s.

WorkChoices created a climate of intimidation and fear. Two hundred workers on AWAs at BHP Billiton's Mount Newman iron ore mine in Western Australia signed a petition in May 2007 complaining about 'an atmosphere of intimidation and victimisation' of workers at the worksite.[26] They complained to the ABC's *7.30 Report* on 11 June that management was forcing them to work in unsafe conditions and that they were afraid to hold up production to rectify the problems.[27] With no union protection, no protection against unfair dismissal and no effective right to strike, the workers felt powerless to act.

The pressure on workers and unionists was particularly intense in the construction industry, where the *Building and Construction Industry Improvement Act 2005* and the *Independent Contractors Act 2006* were used together with WorkChoices to establish an extraordinarily repressive regulatory regime. The former was passed following the recommendations of the Cole Royal Commission (see Chapter 7) and cemented in place the Building Industry Taskforce, now renamed the Australian Building and Construction Commission (ABCC). The Commission's main aim was to make it impossible for the building industry unions to organise effectively.[28] Strike action was practically banned and the ABCC had a particular brief to eliminate 'no-ticket, no-start' arrangements on building sites where they still existed. The Commission was aimed squarely at the CFMEU; rather than repeat the kind of high-risk operation seen on the waterfront, the Government sought to cripple the CFMEU with repeated fines, including up to $22 000 for individuals and $110 000 for organisations. Assets could be sequestered and compensation awarded to parties affected by industrial action was uncapped. The ABCC had extraordinary powers of surveillance over individuals and organisations. It was allowed to question workers who had no right to remain silent, and to prohibit them or their lawyers from speaking to anyone else about their cases. Jail terms of up to six months were prescribed for those refusing to attend or answer questions put by the ABCC.[29]

The Independent Contractors Act complemented the Building and Construction Industry Improvement Act. Traditionally the building unions had been able to regulate the conditions of work of vulnerable subcontractors on construction sites by incorporating them under the terms of the enterprise agreement negotiated with the head contractor. They were treated as de facto employees and thereby received the relevant industrial protections afforded employees. The new Act made such arrangements illegal; henceforth subcontractors with grievances had access only to the much more expensive and time-consuming avenue of redress through commercial law.

The extraordinary powers of the ABCC were soon put into use. Within two years of its establishment, the Commission had mounted 64 prosecutions, mostly against unions and union officials.[30] In the first action of its kind, the ABCC sued 107 individual unionists working on the Leighton Kumagai Perth to Mandurah rail line who had struck in February 2006 in protest at the sacking of their union delegate. CFMEU members demonstrated around the country in their thousands in support of their victimised comrades, but in November 2007 the Federal Court fined 91 of the 107 workers amounts of up to $10 000.[31] The activities of the ABCC and the new legislative regime allowed formerly 'union-friendly' employers, such as Leighton subsidiary John Holland, to adopt a much more aggressive strategy. Using an 'employer greenfield agreement', a bizarre WorkChoices legal instrument whereby the company 'negotiated' an agreement with itself and used this 'agreement' to set the terms under which it employed staff for the first 12 months, John Holland built a new wharf in Port Hedland without any union involvement.

In order to promote this draconian new legal framework, the Government spent $121 million on advertising WorkChoices in electronic and print media.[32] In addition, large numbers of staff and resources from the Department of Workplace Relations were devoted to promoting the new system. The director of the Workplace Authority, Barbara Bennett, a public servant and nominally independent of the Government, was used in a saturation TV and newspaper advertising campaign in the months leading up to the 2007 election in an attempt to win public support.

The 'Your Rights at Work' campaign

Facing the harshest attack on trade unionism in recent history, the ACTU launched a campaign to defeat the Howard Government. Focus groups conducted by a public relations company on behalf of the ACTU in early 2005 revealed that workers were concerned about the Government's industrial relations plans even before WorkChoices was tabled in parliament. Chief concerns were the proposed removal of unfair dismissal protection, the greater scope for employers to use individual contracts to break established award conditions, and the potential for a race to the bottom in low-skilled occupations. Basing its campaign on findings from this research, the ACTU focused on the rights of *working families*, rather than *union* rights, and adopted the slogan 'Your Rights at Work: Worth Fighting For' (henceforth YRW).[33]

After the 2004 election the ACTU initially appeared to have no intention of calling demonstrations or any form of collective action, saying it had no plans to cause 'industrial trouble'. Instead, the ACTU spoke of a long and 'disciplined' campaign aimed at defeating the Government which, in the aftermath of the 2004 election, was not thought to be a realistic prospect until 2010. The ACTU also encouraged unions to try to 'firewall' their conditions by bringing forward their enterprise bargaining negotiations to ensure that agreements were certified before WorkChoices became law.[34] Some of Australia's strongest unions, including the CFMEU, AMWU and ETU, pursued this strategy and negotiated hundreds of enterprise agreements early in this way, with employers agreeing to do so in return for a discounted wage increase.

If collective action was not part of the ACTU's initial thinking, by late summer 2005 the leaders of the left unions in Victoria had begun to reconsider this stance when the severity of the Government's proposed legislation became apparent. They organised a series of well-attended delegates' meetings in February and March leading to a Trades Hall meeting of 1800 delegates that voted for a national day of action (NDA) on 30 June. The call for national action was initially rejected by the leaders of the other labour councils, citing the risk of fines, and the ACTU executive voted against the proposal. At this late stage, ACTU secretary Greg Combet was still reluctant to mount any kind of resistance, preferring to engage in private lobbying of the Prime Minister to dilute the legislation and avert any confrontation with the Government.[35] Nonetheless, despite the ACTU's weak response, momentum began to build in April and May and other labour councils started to move, beginning with Western Australia and Queensland followed by New South Wales, which called its own day of action for 1 July.

The first NDAs (30 June–1 July) were an enormous success. More than a quarter of a million unionists and supporters marched across the country, from the 120 000 in Melbourne to the smallest events of a couple of hundred

Table 8.1 Attendance at Your Rights at Work demonstrations 2005–07

Date	Location	Attendance	Sponsor
1 May 2005	Brisbane*	15 000	Qld Council of Unions (QCU)
30 June 2005 (& 1 July: NSW)	National	270 000	Individual labour councils
15 Nov 2005	National	550 000	ACTU
1 May 2006	Brisbane*	25 000	QCU
28 June 2006	National	250 000	ACTU
30 Nov 2006	National	250 000	ACTU
22 April 2007	Sydney	40 000	Unions NSW
7 May 2007	Brisbane*	25 000	QCU
26 Sept 2007	Melbourne	35 000	Vic left unions

* *Note:* These were the Queensland Council of Unions' annual Labour Day rallies and were not called specifically 'Your Rights at Work' events. Nonetheless, YRW was the central theme of these rallies.

in regional and country towns. It was the largest union-led mobilisation in Australian history and, outside the February 2003 demonstrations against the Iraq war, the largest ever protest on a national scale.

The success emboldened the union leaders and encouraged the ACTU to enter the field. There followed three ACTU NDAs in November 2005, June 2006 and November 2006. The largest attendance at a single rally was 250 000 in Melbourne on 15 November 2005, with a further 300 000 protesting elsewhere around the country on that day (Table 8.1).

The mass rallies were preceded and supplemented by an extensive campaign of television, newspaper and radio advertising that reinforced union warnings about the threat posed by WorkChoices to working families. In addition, the unions commissioned call centres to cold-call workers at home to advise them of the dangers presented by WorkChoices and to urge them to join unions. The ACTU website received a major overhaul providing advice on every aspect of WorkChoices and the YRW campaign. The ACTU also established a recruitment hotline that allowed workers to sign up to a union by telephone.

YRW campaign stalls were set up at shopping centres, rock concerts, festivals and sports contests. Union barbecues and touch football matches were organised in parks and public spaces. Banners were hung off union buildings in areas of high public exposure, and dozens of media events were staged. To pay for the massive costs involved, the ACTU established a fighting fund, levied unions and sought individual donations, raising millions of dollars. ACTU approaches to leaders of major community, social welfare and religious organisations, many of whom declared their opposition to the legislation, also helped get the message across.

The union campaign of public relations and mass rallies had a significant effect in coalescing and sustaining mass opposition to WorkChoices. Indeed, the Government's reform package had never enjoyed public support. It had not been flagged by the Government in its 2004 election campaign and from early 2005, when its plans became public, WorkChoices became a significant electoral millstone around the Government's neck. Coalition support fell from 48 per cent in February 2005 to 37 per cent in October at which point it partially recovered, only to fall back again to 34 per cent by March 2007 (Figure 8.1). ACTU research in March 2007 suggested that 11 per cent of voters had already switched their vote away from the Coalition because of *WorkChoices*, and a further 14 per cent were considering doing so.[36]

These results showed that union-bashing no longer worked in the way that it had for Malcolm Fraser three decades earlier: far from pulling people towards it, the Howard Government only chased away support by positioning itself as a hard right-wing party on industrial relations. WorkChoices ran contrary to the general sympathy that existed in the community towards trade unions. A NSW Labor Council survey in summer 2005 revealed that 90 per cent of workers earning less than $60 000 disagreed with the statement that 'Australia would be better off without trade unions.' The proportion of the workforce dissatisfied with the performance of trade unions fell to 25 per cent, down from 43 per cent nine years earlier. The proportion of Australians believing that 'unions have too much power' fell to 37 per cent, the lowest figure ever recorded.[37] Labor's repeated promise to 'rip up' WorkChoices and its support for the YRW rallies significantly helped its position – support for the ALP rose in opinion polls following each of the four NDAs (Table 8.2).

No amount of Government advertising could turn this around. By July 2005, 60 per cent of Australians were hostile to WorkChoices. This figure remained solid throughout the following two years in successive national surveys despite the Government's advertising blitz.[38] The Government's

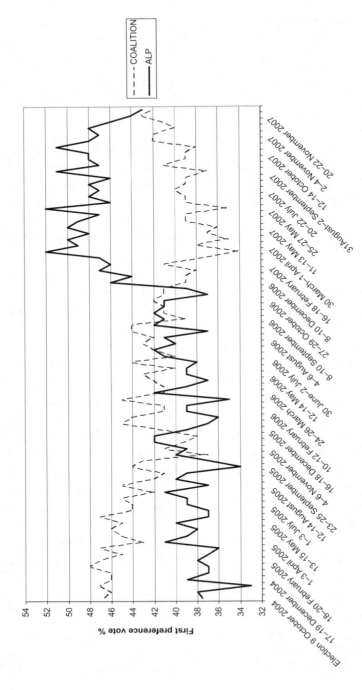

Figure 8.1 Voting intentions 2004–07 (federal elections, first preference)
Source: Newspoll

Table 8.2 Your Rights at Work NDAs and ALP first preference support

NDA	ALP 1st preference support immediately prior to the NDA	ALP 1st preference support immediately following the NDA	ALP YRW 'bounce'
30 June–1 July 2005	37%	39%	+2%
15 November 2005	39%	42%	+3%
28 June 2006	38%	41%	+3%
30 November 2006	39%*	46%	+7%*

*An important additional factor accounting for the sharp lift in Labor support at this time was the election of Kevin Rudd as Labor leader on 4 December 2006.

Source: Newspoll (www.newspoll.com.au, accessed 1 March 2008)

polling may have partially recovered from its low of 34 per cent in April 2007, but WorkChoices remained as unpopular as ever. The reasons were plain. Within 12 months of its taking effect, 21 per cent of Australians felt that they were personally worse off as a result of WorkChoices and only 5 per cent felt better off, despite falling unemployment and robust economic growth.[39] A confidential Government briefing paper in April 2007 concluded that the millions of dollars spent by the Government on advertising had been a complete waste of money:

> The two images that have formed in the community's minds . . . are, firstly, that of a pendulum that has swung too far in favour of employers (especially big business), and secondly, that of the little guy pitted alone and unprotected against the might of the big corporations and their lawyers (and the Government).[40]

The briefing paper reported that 'key emotions' aroused by WorkChoices were 'fear, panic, insecurity, cynicism, distrust and disempowerment'.[41] In a selection of 133 messages posted to the ACTU YRW website in May 2006, WorkChoices was described by respondents as 'Dickensian', 'turning

Australia into a two-tier American-style society', 'destructive and damaging' and 'frightening'.[42]

Such was the hostility to WorkChoices that state Labor governments were able to use the issue as a vote winner to buttress their own fortunes. This was the case in Victoria, where the Bracks Labor Government coasted home in the November 2006 state elections by campaigning hard against Work-Choices. It was also true in New South Wales, where the unpopular Labor Government led by Morris Iemma was able to win re-election in March 2007 despite widespread dissatisfaction with his Government's performance in health, education and transport.

The advertising campaign and the street marches were very success-ful components of the YRW campaign. They can be contrasted to other elements that were either unsuccessful or even undermined the drive to ultimately 'rip up' WorkChoices. One failure was the intensive ACTU lob-bying effort aimed at persuading two senators to block the legislation in the Senate: Family First's Steve Fielding and National Party maverick Barn-aby Joyce. Petitions were collected in their thousands and lodged with these politicians. However, Joyce supported the legislation after minor amendments. The second was a High Court challenge mounted by the state Labor governments, supported by several unions, which argued that the Federal Government's use of its Corporations Power to take over the state industrial relations systems was unconstitutional. This also failed, as the High Court ruled in favour of the Federal Government, something that was widely predicted beforehand given the conservative composi-tion of the High Court after a decade of appointments by the Howard Government.

The major limitation with the YRW campaign, however, was that its focus on getting Labor elected tended to dictate the content and scheduling of the entire campaign. The long-term strategy, geared towards an election two-and-a-half years after the campaign launch, meant that the YRW days of action were scheduled with such time lags between each one that no momentum could be sustained. After the first two, attendance dropped off, and local organising to get workplaces to stop work to attend the rallies became increasingly lackadaisical. Once it became clear in the latter half of 2006 that Labor was in with a fighting chance to win the 2007 election, the ACTU called no more NDAs but threw all of its energy into marginal seats campaigning.

The ACTU and the right-wing unions and labour councils had not been enthusiastic supporters of the NDAs at the beginning and at the MCG rally in Melbourne in November 2006 the ACTU revealed its new slogan – 'Worth Fighting For' was replaced by 'Worth *Voting* For'. The Queensland Council of Unions issued a press release on 14 November 2006 following the High Court decision, which summed up the approach of these union leaders: 'Ballot box now the only choice for workers.' In the 12 months leading to the November 2007 election the energies of the ACTU and most of its affiliates were devoted almost entirely to electoral work.[43] Hundreds of thousands of dollars were spent by the ACTU in setting up and staffing YRW 'community groups' in 25 Liberal-held marginal seats, each with a full-time paid convenor, to direct the work of hundreds of volunteers to get the Labor vote out on election day.[44]

While the decision to call no more NDAs might have been expected of the ACTU and the right-wing unions, more surprising was the decision by the Victorian Trades Hall to abandon mass action after November 2006. It was left to the building unions and the ETU in Victoria to call one final rally in Melbourne, two months before the federal election.

The focus on election campaigning was rooted in the union leaders' preference for a resolution of the issue by conventional constitutional means. The electoral orientation gave the union leaders their rationale not to call strikes: the one weapon that, if used intelligently, could have destroyed the ability of the employers to actually use the legislation. The O'Shea campaign had demonstrated that strikes in the maritime, transport, energy and construction industries could have broken WorkChoices. The ACTU, however, had had no intention of challenging the penal powers in 1969 by mass strikes and, nearly 40 years later, it had no plans to strike out WorkChoices either. Union leaders labelled mass strikes against WorkChoices 'a gift to the Coalition'. Their solution was the ballot box, with Sharan Burrow, president of the ACTU, telling a public meeting in Brisbane in August 2007: 'I tell workers who are anxious about WorkChoices. You don't need to strike. You don't need to organise a picket line. You just have to vote.'

Again, it was not just the ACTU but the left unions as well that sought to avoid an industrial confrontation with the Government over WorkChoices. Right from the outset, Leigh Hubbard, Victorian Trades Hall secretary, argued that defiance was not an option, telling the ABC's *7.30 Report* that 'We will have to work within the system . . . They are the cards that are dealt.' The left-wing unions, which were by and large the stronger ones better able to strike with effect, used the 'firewalling' strategy to duck a fight over WorkChoices in 2005. Not only did 'firewalling' force these unions to concede ground in wage negotiations, in order to persuade employers to bring negotiations forward, but it also isolated the weaker unions, who were not in a position to push employers to do this. In the meantime, until such time as Labor was elected, workers had to wear WorkChoices, allowing employers to force hundreds of thousands of workers onto AWAs and inferior conditions.

While the initial ACTU slogan was 'Your Rights at Work, Worth Fighting For', fighting was mostly absent from the campaign itself, which focused not on workers' capacity to stop WorkChoices by strikes but on their status as *victims*. Thus the media advertising, as well as the speakers and videos presented at the NDAs, focused mostly on cases where individuals or groups of workers had been abused under the new laws not, with the occasional exception, where they had stood together and defeated an employer attack.

The refusal of the union leaders to call strikes to break WorkChoices reflected their general stance during the whole campaign, which was to defuse hostility to business, to focus public anger only on the Howard Government, and to position themselves as the force that could offer business what it wanted – higher profits – but through collaboration with the unions rather than by a frontal attack. The ACTU leadership used the experience of the Accord as evidence that it could deliver. Burrow explained:

> . . . We were the architects – with the employers I might say – in a more concil-
> iatory and consensual environment led by a Labor government, of the skilling
> environment, the multi-skilling environment, that actually drove productiv-
> ity . . . We're actually absolutely committed to growing the economy and
> growing productivity, but let's do it on the basis of skill, of economic growth
> through increased industry investment, through infrastructure development,
> through new industries.[45]

Union action to resist WorkChoices was only aimed at the 'maverick' bosses. 'Mainstream' employers, by contrast, were potential allies. After the first NDA in June 2005, Burrow apologised to business for any inconvenience caused by workers walking off the job. Two years later, reflecting on the fact that in the first half of 2007 the Workplace Authority had rejected

25 000 AWAs from 4000 employers, Burrow blamed the situation on the 'complexities' of the legislation, not on the general impulse by employers to cut costs by attacking workers' rights. Burrow bridled at Liberal Party advertisements that attacked unions as 'anti-business', declaring them 'an insult to working families':

> The job of all unions is to protect secure, well paid employment for Australian working families. To achieve this we need profitable businesses that value their workers. The idea that unions would somehow want to undermine business is, frankly, absurd. Under a Labor Government we would want to work with employers to grow the economy and increase the opportunities for Australian workers.[46]

This desire to forge common ground with business meant that the union leaders consistently hosed down calls by militant unionists for a more resolute campaign of strikes and work bans. In contrast to 1969, when networks of militants and left-wing union leaders pressed ahead with strikes in the face of opposition from the ACTU and Victorian Trades Hall, these networks had vanished by 2005. The leaders of the ACTU and its affiliates were under no threat from their left and remained in control of the campaign throughout.

As YRW became increasingly geared towards the electoral contest, so it became hostage to the Labor Party. With Labor increasingly looking a racing certainty to win the 2007 election following the election of Kevin Rudd as Labor leader in December 2006, the ACTU allowed Rudd and his deputy Julia Gillard to push Labor's industrial relations policies steadily to the right, offering the unions less and less in return for their unstinting support.

Labor's industrial relations platform, entitled *Forward with Fairness*, was released in two stages over the course of 2007. The first draft, released in time for the Labor conference in April, maintained Labor's promise to scrap AWAs. It flagged the introduction of a 'safety net' of 10 legislated national employment standards, to form the benchmark for a revised no disadvantage test. It included a requirement that employers bargain in good faith if workers opted for union representation, and it partially restored unfair dismissal rights to workers in small businesses. Labor also promised to abolish the Workplace Authority and the Fair Pay Commission and to create a new institution, Fair Work Australia, to absorb the legal and judicial functions of the industrial tribunals and the courts.

Other elements of *Forward with Fairness* were copied directly from Work-Choices – the requirement that unions undertake mandatory postal ballots before striking, the prohibition of pattern bargaining, and the restrictions on the right of union officials to enter workplaces. Political strikes were banned, as were any closed shop or union preference arrangements. Where strikes threatened to 'cause significant harm to the wider economy or to the safety or welfare of the community', Fair Work Australia could 'end the industrial action and determine a settlement between the parties'. Strike pay by employers was prohibited. Labor promised to 'abolish' the ABCC, but only in order to roll it into a specialist division of Fair Work Australia.

Unions would certainly not be receiving any special favours from Labor under Rudd or his deputy. Gillard warned building unions that there would always be 'a tough cop on the beat' under a Labor Government and, in a National Press Club speech in May 2007, she reassured business:

> I am from the political party that deregistered the BLF. That happened in Victoria under the Cain Labor government. Any suggestion that Labor's track history isn't one of insisting on tough compliance is a suggestion that simply doesn't pass the test of analysis.[47]

Although awards were to be a feature of Labor's new system, they could be drastically 'simplified' under *Forward with Fairness*. Award conditions removed by the 1996 Workplace Relations Act were not to be reintroduced. Unfair dismissal rights were to be restored, but were heavily circumscribed by the discriminatory requirement that workers in small organisations employing fewer than 15 staff had a probationary period of one year; workers in larger organisations had six months.

As for the Independent Contractors Act, Julia Gillard wrote to the Independent Contractors Association, a right-wing lobby group:

> Labor's policy is that independent contractors are small businesses which should be regulated by commercial law and not industrial law . . . Labor believes unions should not be permitted to interfere in commercial arrangements involving contracts, and the key tenets of freedom of association should be respected at all times.[48]

Despite quickly attracting the description 'WorkChoices Lite', *Forward with Fairness* received unanimous support from delegates at the ALP conference in April 2007. Although 15 union officials had circulated a document before the conference condemning the restrictions on the right to strike, none of them voted against the policy. And despite the fact that it failed to meet virtually every plank of the policy adopted by an October 2006 ACTU special conference, the ACTU issued a press release praising *Forward with Fairness* as 'giving great hope to working families because it means that under a Labor government basic rights at work will be protected.'[49] *Forward with Fairness* would give 'working families a very clear choice at the Federal election'.[50]

If the union leaders played up the differences between the two parties' policies, so too did business, which reacted to *Forward with Fairness* with manufactured horror and a sustained lobbying and advertising campaign aimed at persuading Labor to retreat further. Business had realised that the ALP was likely to win the election. Rather than try to hold back the tide, business representatives sought to ensure that Labor's industrial relations policy retained as much of WorkChoices as possible. They were successful. This became clear on 28 August when Kevin Rudd and Julia Gillard released Labor's Implementation Plan for *Forward with Fairness*.

The central element of the Implementation Plan was a delay in 'ripping up' WorkChoices. Labor's planned legislation was not to take effect until January 2010, to allow 'extensive consultation' with unions and business in the name of 'maximising certainty'. AWAs would continue until expiry, potentially as late as December 2012. Employers using AWAs expiring before January 2010 could roll these into 'individual transitional employment agreements'. In addition, the new policy allowed employers a number of options to retain 'flexible' individual arrangements. All awards and enterprise agreements were to contain a 'model flexibility clause' to 'allow' staff to negotiate individual arrangements with their boss, so long as these were not inferior to the relevant award or agreement. AWAs would no longer be allowable, but common law contracts could override the relevant award. Unfair dismissal rights would be partially restored but there was to be no access to protection for staff laid off because of 'genuine redundancy' or technological change. Fair Work Australia was to have no power to order the reinstatement of staff in companies employing fewer than 15 staff if reinstatement were 'not in the interests of the employer's business'.

Labor policy was particularly strict on strikes and union rights. Any industrial action taking place outside the bargaining period, or without a secret ballot, or on political grounds, would be met 'with the full force of the law', with Fair Work Australia empowered to take immediate action to order a return to work. This would apply, as Gillard admitted, to workers attending any future YRW rallies under a Labor government. Construction workers found no relief. Labor had promised in 2006 to abolish the ABCC, from which most unionists in the construction industry had drawn the conclusion that the institution and its coercive powers would simply disappear. Labor's policy in April had already shattered that belief by providing that the ABCC's powers would be rolled into a specialist division of Fair Work Australia. Now Labor said the ABCC would itself be maintained in its current form and with its current powers, budget and staff until 2010.

Business crowed. BHP welcomed the 'considerable policy progress' by Labor, while Rio Tinto found 'some positive elements'.[51] *The Australian* thought 'Rudd had done well in preserving business safeguards and individual contracts for the high paid' while the *Financial Review* noted that 'Labor has now adopted many of the *WorkChoices* initiatives it previously opposed.'[52]

Forward with Fairness was a sharp rebuff to the ACTU. After all, Labor was now prepared to retain many of the policies that the party had voted against when they were first tabled by the Government in its first three terms in office. In some important respects *Forward with Fairness* was harsher than the Workplace Relations Act of 1996, which the ACTU had described at the time as 'the most malicious and vindictive piece of legislation that the country has ever seen'. Nonetheless, having committed to an electoral strategy, the ACTU leaders had no alternative but to smile, albeit through gritted teeth. They criticised the lengthy transition period and the restrictions on unions' rights to organise but described the policy as 'an important step towards restoring rights for working families' and, again, as 'ensuring that workers have a real choice at the next Federal Election.'[53]

Some union leaders were less supportive. John Robertson from Unions NSW (the renamed NSW Labor Council) described the revised policies as 'a sop to big business': by retaining many elements of WorkChoices,

Labor had only 'created confusion in the minds of working people' about the actual differences between the policies of Labor and the Coalition.[54] Similar criticisms were made by left-wing officials. Michele O'Neil, national secretary of the Textile, Clothing and Footwear Union, urged the ALP to reconsider its policy,[55] while CFMEU national secretary John Sutton said that:

> It was disappointing Labor allowed itself to be bullied by big-business inter-
> ests . . . There was no reason for it. The Government's industrial relations
> policy is poison with the public, and it's not like there was any pressure from
> the electorate for Rudd to buckle.[56]

Such criticisms, however, won no support from the ACTU and did not prevent the unions from devoting a further one million dollars to electoral campaign expenses in October.[57]

Rudd brushed aside union criticism of *Forward with Fairness*:

> Obviously a number of the unions may be disappointed with elements of
> what we put forward. I understand that. Our job, however, is to govern in the
> national interest – it's not to govern in the interest of big business and it's not
> to govern in the interest of any individual trade union.[58]

In reality, Rudd's 'national interest' resolved itself into precisely the interest of big business.

The situation in the lead-up to the 2007 election was very different from that on the two previous occasions when Labor had taken government, in 1972 and 1983. In 1972, working-class militants were on the offensive and the political and business establishment was in retreat, giving the union leaders considerable bargaining power in shaping Labor policy and forcing it to the left. In 1983, the militants were industrially and politically disoriented but still capable of mounting strikes on their own initiative, and business was looking for an alternative to Fraser. The union leaders could therefore appeal to business and the ALP as a force capable of disciplining workers in the name of consensus. By 2007, however, union activists had been in retreat for 25 years, strike levels and union coverage were at historic lows, and business was confident and eager to further unwind the industrial gains that workers had won during the postwar boom. The union leaders were therefore in a weak position to make demands on Labor.

The ALP leadership understood this balance of forces only too well: union support for Labor at the election was certainly appreciated, but it would be on Rudd's terms. Many union leaders, by contrast, were of the opinion that if Labor lost the election, unionism would be dead in Australia. They approached Labor as supplicants, allowing the parliamentary leadership to dictate the terms of the relationship. In a painful snub on election eve, Rudd declared that trade unions would not enjoy any special relationship with a Labor Government, that rebuilding union membership would never become his Government's responsibility, and that if pursuing 'the national interest . . . means having a fight with any trade union in the future about any matter, I am more than prepared to do so.'[59]

Rudd declared open season on any union leader who appeared to disrupt Labor's message of controls on unions and wage restraint. In April 2007 he greeted a timid criticism of *Forward with Fairness* by AMWU national secretary Doug Cameron with an invitation to 'get used to the 21st century.'[60] In May he personally instructed the party national secretary to request the resignation from the ALP of ETU Victorian Secretary Dean Mighell after the ABCC leaked video footage of Mighell boasting about tricking employers into paying higher wages. In November, Western Australian CFMEU state secretary Joe McDonald was also expelled from the party in the context of a series of charges of 'trespass', none sustained.

None of this, however, meant a severance of relations between the parliamentary and industrial wings of the ALP. The Shadow Cabinet included many former union officials, most notably former ACTU presidents Simon Crean and Martin Ferguson, but also including Nicola Roxon, Stephen Ludwig and Lindsay Tanner. Furthermore, many union officials had been preselected for parliamentary seats. Greg Combet was parachuted into the safe seat of Charlton, New South Wales with the assistance of the national office, while Doug Cameron and Bill Shorten were able to use the enormous factional power of the AMWU and AWU to win preselection for the Senate and lower house respectively. They were joined at the hustings by ACTU assistant secretary Richard Marles and, from South Australia, LHMU secretary Mark Butler and SDA secretary Don Farrell.

The 2007 federal election

With the poll called for 24 November, the YRW electoral campaign shifted into a higher gear. The ACTU allocated each of the 25 marginal seats campaign groups an extra $50 000, ran intensive television advertising, and galvanised union members living in marginal seats. Six thousand unionists were involved in some form of electioneering. More than two million leaflets were distributed, 40 000 people were canvassed through a door-knocking campaign and 5000 volunteers handed out how-to-vote cards at 835 polling booths on election day. The efforts of the ACTU and its affiliates were certainly noticed: Coalition candidates complained that they faced opposition on two fronts, one headed up by Labor and the other by the ACTU. Crucial to the ACTU's calculations was the Senate. It was clear that Labor could not achieve a majority in both houses, that the Democrats were going to be eliminated, and that passage of Labor's industrial relations legislation would therefore depend on support from the Greens and Family First in the Senate. YRW how-to-vote cards therefore advised voters to support Labor in the lower house and told them: 'Do not vote for the Liberal or National Party in the Senate.'

On all the traditional criteria used by political pundits to predict election results, the Howard Government should have been a clear winner. The economy had grown throughout its 11 years in office. Unemployment had fallen to 4.2 per cent, the lowest since 1974, and economic forecasters were predicting a sunny 2008. The Coalition led the ALP by a wide margin, 56 per cent to 20 per cent, on the key question as to which party was the better economic manager. And yet despite these favourable economic circumstances, the Coalition was swept out of office with a swing of nearly 6 per cent, with the Prime Minister losing his seat – only the second time that this had occurred in Australian history. Labor's primary vote, at 43 per cent, was its highest since 1993 and, when taken together with the Greens vote, also up, the parties of the left polled more than 50 per cent of the primary vote.

The election result could be understood primarily as a referendum on WorkChoices and the Government's wider economic agenda. The more that Government advertising reminded workers of WorkChoices, the more solid was their opposition and the more that they looked to Labor to save them.[61]

Further, the aggregate figures for economic growth and unemployment only tell a very partial story about the fortunes of the Australian working class during the years of the Howard Government. Clearly there had been economic growth, and skilled workers had enjoyed increased real wages, even if wages for less skilled workers had fallen under WorkChoices. Low unemployment had made it easier for workers to get jobs. Enhanced family benefits had lifted household incomes for those with children. These phenomena help explain why the Coalition enjoyed a 36-point margin as the better economic manager. However, when the survey question was altered to 'which party is better at handling the economy *in a way that helps ordinary working people*', the Coalition's 36-point lead was transformed into an 11-point deficit, or 36 per cent to 47 per cent.[62] In John Howard's 'aspirational society', class turned out to matter after all.

The benefits of the economic boom during the 1990s and 2000s were unevenly distributed. By 2005, the income share of the richest 10 per cent of the population was higher than at any time since 1949.[63] The wages share of GDP reached a 37-year low (see Figure 2.1) and the profit share a record high (see Figure 3.2). The disparity between workers and the super rich became more and more extreme. In 1992, the remuneration of the typical executive in one of Australia's top 50 companies was 27 times the wage of the average worker. Ten years later the multiple had risen to 98.[64] *WorkChoices* widened the gap still further. While average weekly earnings rose by only 3 per cent (in nominal terms) in the first year of WorkChoices, total annual compensation for chief executives rose by 30 per cent.[65] Allan Moss, chief executive of Macquarie Bank, topped the list in 2006 with a package of $33 million, equivalent to 747 times average weekly earnings.[66]

It was not just wages and bonuses, but the tax system too that had been skewed in favour of the well-off in the Howard years. Income tax was made more regressive and those with substantial superannuation were rewarded with sizeable tax breaks. Families with private health insurance or who sent their children to private schools also enjoyed significant benefits under the Howard Government.

What of the booming jobs market that had been a boast of the Coalition election campaign? Although the proportion of full-time jobs began to creep up after 2003, much of the jobs growth that had occurred since 1996 for blue- and white-collar workers was low-paid, part-time or casual.[67]

Full-time workers were still working the equivalent of four weeks longer each year when compared to 1983 figures.[68] Nearly one-half of all workers reported 'coming home from work exhausted'.[69]

Property speculation resulting from a favourable tax regime for investors caused many young people to be locked out of the housing market. A spokeswoman from the financial agency Cannex commented two weeks before the election: 'We all know money doesn't stretch as far as it used to, but the fact is wages have been left eating dust in the race towards home ownership.'[70]

Despite unemployment falling to 4 per cent, a 2007 report by the UN Children's Fund found that 10 per cent of young Australians lived in households where no adult was employed, the highest rate of all OECD countries except Hungary. Twelve per cent of Australian children lived in households where total income was inadequate.[71]

All these factors had an impact on mass consciousness. In 2005, 82 per cent of Australians felt that the gap between those with high incomes and those with low incomes was too high.[72] Eighty per cent of workers earning less than $60 000 per year agreed with the statement that 'While the economy is going well, it is a struggle for working people to make ends meet.'[73] A team of Sydney University academics noted in 2007 that:

> The population is evenly split between those reporting that they are living comfortably and those just coping or having difficulty getting by. There are clearly pockets and issues around which discontent is smouldering.[74]

These 'pockets' were revealed vividly in the election results in what had been dubbed 'Howard's Battler' seats in western Sydney and outer south-east Melbourne when these predominantly working-class areas swung heavily to Labor.

The 2007 election result was a major victory from the perspective of the ACTU and its YRW campaign. The campaign had been stunningly successful in focusing public opposition to WorkChoices. It had placed unions once again at the forefront of popular consciousness and reinforced their legitimacy in the eyes of millions. The NDAs brought workers into collective action by the hundreds of thousands. The mobilisation of so many workers on the streets highlighted the power that workers have to stop the central business districts of the major cities, and by implication the day-to-day life of capitalism. They broke down, even if only for a moment, the sense of isolation that often wears down individual unionists, and gave heart to all those who attended. The rallies dominated mainstream political discourse for days either side of the events and struck fear into the hearts of government and employers. The sheer size of the rallies was an undeniable physical representation of workers' power. The rallies also mobilised workers as a *class*, overcoming the sectional divisions within the labour movement between the skilled trades and the unskilled workers, between male-dominated and female-dominated areas, and between blue-collar and white-collar. In addition, they drew in tens of thousands of non-unionists, who understood the significance of the struggle for all workers, pensioners and students.

The ACTU strategy therefore had many strengths. However, it failed the Australian working class on three important grounds. It had allowed the Coalition 18 months to implement WorkChoices without a significant industrial challenge. It had permitted Labor to put forward the most right-wing and anti-union platform that it had ever advanced without serious resistance. And it had not prevented the resumption of rapid decline in union coverage.

Central elements of an alternative strategy would have involved a greater preparedness to use strikes and other forms of militant direct action, an orientation to rank-and-file initiative rather than bureaucratic management of the campaign, and an escalation of struggle as the election neared, not its diminution. The O'Shea campaign of 1969 had demonstrated how anti-union laws could be beaten and the way cleared for a union revival. If anything, the ACTU in 2005 had an even greater opportunity to destroy WorkChoices which, unlike the penal powers that tended to affect only the more militant unions, affected all workers whether in unions or not. Unions were also markedly more popular than in the late 1960s. However, the union leaders for the most part lacked the will to fight, arguing, as they had during the waterfront dispute, that to do so would open the unions up to heavy fines. This was an unconvincing excuse.

In October 2007, 30 000 Victorian nurses showed what was possible when they stood up to WorkChoices and won. The Australian Nursing Federation (Victorian Branch) imposed work bans as part of their campaign to increase wages, improve workloads and resist management attempts to attack their working conditions. While the nurses' union initiated the legal steps necessary under WorkChoices to commence protected industrial action, the Commission ruled that their ballot could not proceed as the union was openly pressing for the same terms and conditions to apply to all Victorian public sector nurses, who were technically employed by 143 separate health authorities. The union instead took the proposed industrial campaign to a mass meeting of 4000 nurses, not a secret ballot, which meant that the bans breached WorkChoices and could not be legal.

The nurses' union was hauled before the Industrial Relations Commission, where it was ordered to lift its bans. When it refused, the Victorian Hospitals Industrial Association launched an action in the Federal Court to prosecute the nurses. Employers docked the pay of nurses who implemented bans and attempted to intimidate them into backing down. The State Labor Government declared the nurses' action unlawful and their union faced the likelihood of substantial fines. Union secretary Lisa Fitzpatrick condemned the Court's action as 'an attempt by the State Government to threaten us and get us to back down. We will not back down. This dispute will not be resolved in the Federal Court.'

The nurses' determined stand and refusal to be bullied forced the Government to improve its pay offer and agree to provide an additional 500 nurses and midwives. Following another mass meeting of 6000 nurses, the union voted to lift the bans in late October. All court action seeking fines and legal sanctions against the union were dropped. The union also recruited 2500 new members out of this campaign. Here was a union, not the most left wing and not the strongest by any means, that demonstrated what was possible even under WorkChoices. Had a serious campaign of industrial action been undertaken by the stronger blue-collar unions – the CFMEU, ETU, AMWU, TWU, MUA and others – WorkChoices could have been wrecked, not left to live on under a Labor Government.

The Victorian nurses proved that unions could defy anti-union laws, as had the thousands of workers who struck in defence of the MUA nine years earlier. A YRW campaign that incorporated some of the bravery demonstrated by the Victorian nurses and MUA supporters could have deterred employers from taking advantage of their new legal firepower and reversed the more than two decades of retreat at the grassroots of the union movement. A more aggressive industrial stance would also have put the ACTU in a much stronger position in relation to the ALP. Instead, the ACTU, by its refusal to defy the laws and by driving the campaign solely towards an election outcome, ensured that workers were left to face an incoming Labor Government with an industrial relations platform almost as draconian as WorkChoices itself and without the industrial confidence among workers, for the most part, to fight it.

Chapter Nine

RESULTS AND PROSPECTS

Australian unionism from flood to ebb tide: a summary of the argument

This book has told the story of Australian unionism over five decades. It is a story filled with drama, from the migrant worker revolt in the car factories to the unprecedented mobilisations against WorkChoices that defeated a government and lost the Prime Minister his own seat. The story of unionism in these years encompasses mass strikes to free Clarrie O'Shea, the Vietnam Moratorium marches, and the emergence of a new generation of women and public sector unionists in the 1970s. It includes a bitter 10-week strike in the Latrobe Valley in the 1970s and work-ins at factories and coal mines. It also includes mass demonstrations against the Kennett Government in Victoria and a six-week strike by Ford workers in defiance of their own union leaders. The story encompasses the militant demonstration at Parliament House in 1996 and mass pickets on the waterfront. During these five decades trade unionists acted in solidarity with working-class communities and social causes on dozens of occasions. Aboriginal activists, students and environmentalists have all had cause to thank unions for their support.

The story of unions is also a chronicle of the 'little' events: the workers who were reinstated due to union action, and the bullying supervisors who had their wings clipped. It is the story of fights for higher wages, paid public holidays, paid maternity leave, decent sick pay and safer workplaces. It is a tale of women winning jobs previously forbidden to them.

If the struggles of unions have been characterised by daring and coura-
geous deeds, unions have also suffered over these years from stifling bureaucracy, passivity and defeats, some self-inflicted and some imposed by their
enemies. If the history includes left-wing union leaders organising hundreds
of thousands of workers to strike in support of O'Shea, it also includes the
Accord, whereby virtually the entire apparatus of the union bureaucracy was
devoted to stifling strikes and holding down wages. If the history encompasses the actions of militants risking dismissal and blacklisting to build
unions, it also includes the personal careers of successive generations of
union leaders keen for a quiet life and a sinecure in parliament or business.
Trade unionism features both self-sacrifice and cynical self-advancement,
struggle and strike-breaking. The balance between the positive and negative
aspects has not remained static but has changed over time.

In the period on which this book focuses, trade unionism passed through
three phases – flood tide, stand-off and ebb tide. The flood tide ran from
1968 to 1974, when Australian workers went on the offensive for higher
wages, improved working conditions and political reform. Nearly 30 years
of full employment and a rapidly expanding workforce had created the
conditions for the breakthrough. The workforce was not just expanding
but was also undergoing a transformation with the entry of millions of
women and migrants. At work these newcomers often encountered poor
working conditions and began to demand better treatment and more pay.
Recovering from the defeats and retreats of the late 1940s and 1950s, and
in many cases with a new generation of job delegates who had not known
the misery of the Depression, increasing numbers of Australian workers
gathered the confidence to take action in the first half of the 1960s, putting
pressure on their union leaders to lead or fall behind. The successful metal
trades campaign against absorption in the summer of 1968 was the breakthrough. There followed a strike wave of proportions not seen since the mid
1940s.

The upsurge in strikes was a challenge to employers, government, tribunals and the courts. It helped push social attitudes to the left and underpinned the emergence of a new generation of social movement activists.
The strike wave was responsible for a massive redistribution of national
income from capital to labour and ensured that workers finally enjoyed
more of the benefits from the postwar boom. It also lifted union membership sharply, from 2.1 million in 1966 to 2.8 million 10 years later,
and reversed a 20-year decline in union coverage. Industrial success was

matched by political achievements and many unions did not hesitate to take up political campaigns, from Vietnam to apartheid and environmental protection. The working-class mobilisation also had echoes inside the Labor Party, which shifted to the left and in 1972 won office for the first time in 23 years. The new Labor Government then enacted reforms of direct benefit to the working class under pressure from this upsurge among the working class and the left.

The flood tide threatened more than the conservative establishment. Because it was driven from below it also shook up the established structures and leaders of the union movement. Right-wing leaders retired, lost their positions, were marginalised by militant workers or had to adjust. Left-wing leaders found it easier to adapt, and sometimes encouraged strikes, but they were just as fearful of the movement slipping out of their hands. They put themselves at the head of worker militancy, the better to control it.

The economic and political crises of 1974–75 heralded the end of the flood tide and the beginning of more bitter struggles between capital and labour. This stand-off, which lasted nearly a decade, occurred in the context of a sharp lift in unemployment and a more aggressive capitalist class, which had begun to regroup. The optimism of the union delegates was replaced by a more sombre perspective; it became clear that winning gains required a serious fight. As a sign of these tougher times, picket lines became more common and some strikes dragged on for many weeks. Even if the Fraser Government *had* won the 1975 and 1977 elections this did not mean that the militants were going to roll over, and attempts by the Government and employers to push unions back often met dogged resistance. The Industrial Relations Bureau failed to curb unionism and the Government's repeated attempts to cut wages by partial indexation eventually exploded in its face with a wages breakout from 1980 to 1982.

While many workers were determined to resist Fraser, the leaders of the ALP retreated at the first sign of the business offensive in 1974–75 and capitulated to the Kerr Coup without a serious fight. They then concluded from the experience of the Whitlam Government that, in the context of economic crisis, they needed a right-wing program that gave business virtually everything that it wanted. The Wran Labor Government in New South Wales, elected in 1976, ushered in three decades of Labor administrations at state and federal level that were hardly distinguishable from their Coalition opponents.

Resistance to business and government attacks was also not forthcoming from many union leaders in the late 1970s. ACTU president Bob Hawke rapidly sought to make peace with the Fraser Government. Most conservative union leaders saw little need to fight – in fact, wage indexation saved them the job of organising strikes to win wage increases. This much might have been expected. However, the left leaders also failed to fight. Indeed, they underwent a marked shift to the right. In particular, the leadership of the union most identified with the flood tide of the late 1960s and early 1970s, the AMWU, increasingly blocked with the right at ACTU Congresses and sold out important struggles. By the early 1980s this process had culminated in the left union leaders developing a full-blown program for social 'consensus', using the unions to discipline workers and facilitate capitalist recovery. On this basis Labor won and held office for the following 13 years.

The introduction of the Accord framework marked the beginning of the ebb tide in Australian unionism. This period was marked by sustained and successful employer and government offensives to revive the rate of profit at the expense of labour. It was accompanied by a 25-year decline in union coverage and strikes. For the first few years, the legacy of the bitter fights of the 1970s and early 1980s was such that the capitalist class could not simply dispense with the union leaders as an agency for delivering labour discipline. In fact, in the 1980s union leaders enjoyed unprecedented access to government circles and were involved in regular round-table discussions with ministers and business leaders. At the grassroots, however, unions began to decline. Strike muscles not used began to atrophy, and union delegate structures fell into decay.

Wage restraint on its own was not enough to drive the capitalist recovery. From 1987 onwards, in response to the first probing efforts by New Right employers, the union leaders took an active role in developing programs to undermine established work practices. The two-tier wages system and the award restructuring that came after it constituted the first moves in this direction, followed in 1991 by enterprise bargaining. The rhetoric of solidarity and uplifting disadvantaged groups, which had been used by union leaders in the early years of the Accord, gave way to the language of business competitiveness. The process that culminated in WorkChoices was set in train: trading off wage rises for employment conditions and work practices established during the postwar boom. Meanwhile, union delegate networks, already in decline, were virtually shattered by the recession of 1990–92.

With union organisation severely weakened at the base, business leaders began to actively circumvent it. The pioneer in this respect, Rio Tinto, was joined over the course of the decade by other companies that ditched their long-standing industrial relations arrangements and sought to operate in a 'union-free' environment. They were helped by anti-union legislation by conservative state governments, most notably in Victoria and Western Australia, but also by the Keating Government. By the time Labor lost power in 1996, union coverage had slumped from 49 per cent in 1982 to 31 per cent, the fastest rate of decline of any Western economy except New Zealand, which had suffered similar attacks.

The Howard Government and its Workplace Relations Act ended the special access that the country's most senior union leaders had enjoyed to government ministers, creating a very cold climate for union leaders and members alike. Employers now had the legal weaponry to directly exclude trade unions. Government ministers spoke quite candidly of destroying union power in its remaining heartlands. However, Howard discovered the union movement was far from dead when his Government was defeated in its attempts to break the MUA by a wave of working-class solidarity.

The MUA dispute showed the *potential* power that could rebuild the union movement. However, this potential was not built upon, either during the dispute or in its aftermath, and union decline continued apace. The union leaders realised that they had to act lest their own position become untenable. Amalgamations in the late 1980s and early 1990s had done nothing to halt the decay, and in 1999 the ACTU announced new strategies. *Unions@work* heralded some minor changes to union practices that may have helped to halt union decline in the early 2000s. However, it did not revive the kind of *militancy* that had underpinned the last period of union revival in the late 1960s. On the contrary, the ACTU demonstrated a marked antipathy to confrontations with employers and government which, with grassroots organisation in a parlous state, rank-and-file workers were not able to overcome.

WorkChoices and the 2007 federal election bring us to the end of our story. The new legislation represented the most drastic attack on work-ers' rights for decades. It compelled the union leaders to resist or face near-annihilation. The ACTU launched the Your Rights at Work campaign which, on four occasions, brought out hundreds of thousands of people onto the streets in nationwide rallies. However, the union campaign was hampered by a deference to the ALP and a hostility to the kind of industrial militancy that had defeated the penal powers nearly four decades previously. The campaign became increasingly dominated by electoral considerations and conventional electoral methods. YRW was a stunning success in channelling public hostility towards WorkChoices and ensuring the defeat of the Coalition. However, it also allowed Labor to coast to power with the most right-wing industrial relations policy in its history and did nothing to prevent employers from using the legislation for more than 18 months. As the new Rudd Government took power, therefore, the ebbing tide showed no signs of slowing.

The challenge facing the unions

At the close of 2007, Australian capitalism had enjoyed more than 15 years of unchecked growth. Yet this growth had not restored profitability to the levels of the 1960s. The advent of a US recession in 2008 and the prospect of this having damaging effects on the world economy brought calls for workers to accept further sacrifice. Business demanded that the wages share of GDP be cut further and did its best to bring this about over the summer of 2008. Major companies such as Telstra, the Commonwealth Bank and BHP Billiton rushed to force through new AWAs en masse before they were outlawed. Qantas, which had just announced an annual profit of $720 million, introduced a new two-tier staffing structure for its long-haul cabin crew, under which new staff were to be paid 25 per cent less and to work 30 per cent longer hours.[1] The airline also announced plans to recruit hundreds of scabs to replace its licensed engineers during a threatened strike.[2]

Business groups were generally comfortable with the election of the new Rudd Government[3] and understood that *Forward with Fairness* was the best that they could have hoped for, given the wave of anti-WorkChoices sentiment. Labor did its best to assure them that it would continue where the 'reforming' governments of Hawke and Keating had left off. Kevin Rudd, a self-described 'economic conservative', spoke of 'a third round of economic reforms to meet the needs of our 21st century economy'.[4] The first round had been the wave of economic deregulation of the 1980s. The second had taken the form of Keating's 1992 National Competition Policy and the Industrial Relations Reform Act of 1993. *Forward with Fairness*, in association with a new round of infrastructure projects and an 'education revolution', would deliver the third round of productivity improvements. The Business Council and Australian Industry Group welcomed the Labor Government's evident commitment to a new wave of economic reform.[5]

If business was to be kept happy, unions were going to be disappointed. This much was already clear from *Forward with Fairness*. Labor's early months in office in 2008 only confirmed that unions were not going to receive any help from Rudd. Despite a record profit share, unions were warned to accept wage restraint. While ruling out new AWAs, Rudd and Gillard brushed aside union requests to retrospectively strike out the hundreds of thousands of extant AWAs. Gillard declared that the Government was not in the business of 'artificially propping up union membership'[6] and took no steps to organise regular meetings with the ACTU executive. By contrast, business representatives were quickly accorded an inside running on policy formation with the establishment of a Business Advisory Council comprising, among others, representatives from union *bêtes noires* Rio Tinto and News Limited. To cap it off, the new Labor Government confirmed the tenure of Barbara Bennett, the Workplace Authority's director, who had appeared in WorkChoices advertisements for the Howard Government.[7]

This was a continuation of the Howard agenda in all but name. It was not what Labor's supporters had voted for in November 2007. The fundamental contradiction in the Australian political scene at the beginning of 2008 was the gulf between Labor's program and the aspirations of millions of Labor voters.

On almost every indicator, the attitudes of ordinary Australian workers had shifted to the left over 20 years. Repeated opinion surveys found most Australians held collectivist values – they favoured more public spending on education and health rather than tax cuts, and they were concerned about rising inequality.[8] Rather than celebrating business 'achievers', most people were suspicious of them.[9] Whatever question was asked by differing survey organisations in a series of separate opinion polls held over 2004–07, approximately three-quarters of all respondents had a negative view about big business.[10] One pollster, Mary Winter, reported: 'Most people see big business as a ruthless, money-making machine that doesn't let anything get in the way of profit except the law – and then occasionally not even that.'[11]

Many middle-aged and older workers did not feel they had benefited from 15 years of economic growth. They worried about their future and that of their children. More than 70 per cent of older workers feared they would not have enough money to retire, 61 per cent were concerned that if they lost their job they would not get another one as good, and 77 per cent said they worried for the next generation of workers.[12] Ms Winter reported 'When they do their sums, they can't see prosperity at the end of it.'[13]

Workers in large numbers voted Labor at the 2007 election, but that did not mean they trusted their traditional party. A 2005 survey of workers earning less than $60 000 found that 71 per cent believed both Labor and Liberal were too close to big business, and 84 per cent of Labor voters said they would like Labor to 'go back to the days when they stood up for workers.'[14] Only 47 per cent felt that 'Labor still seems to care somewhat more for working people than the Liberals.' In these circumstances it was not surprising that more than a million people, including many white-collar public sector unionists, voted for the Greens as a left-wing alternative to Labor at the 2007 Federal election. These sentiments, which evidently run counter to the entire thrust of the Rudd Government, foreshadow a clash between the Government and its support base in coming years. How well prepared is the Australian labour movement for this situation?

Prospects for revival

There are two contradictory dimensions to working-class consciousness in the early 21st century. The first is a widespread sense of *fatalism* – a lack of faith that action by ordinary people can stop the juggernaut of economic reform and work intensification. Workers are unhappy with their economic and working circumstances, but years of work intensification without any significant resistance by unions has created a weary resignation. In focus groups organised by Unions NSW in summer 2005, many workers reported working unpaid overtime, longer and less regular hours, and increasing work intensity. Unions NSW secretary John Robertson reported that:

> Most working families do not see any respite from this increase in work intensity – they see it as something that is inevitable and that they have to manage . . . ideas like a job for life and standard working hours are now a thing of the past – accepted as being so by many of the people we speak to.[15]

Working-class acceptance of what appears to be an unstoppable process also affects many union militants who, after years of retreats and defeats and half-fought battles, have grown cynical about reviving unions and pessimistic about the preparedness of their fellow workers to fight.

The other dimension of working-class consciousness is a *willingness to resist* when a lead is given by their traditional leaders. Employer and government offensives have fuelled discontent and this has been evident on repeated occasions since the early 1990s, from the 150 000 who marched against the Kennett Government in 1992 to the tens of thousands of workers who took action in support of the MUA in 1998 and the hundreds of thousands who rallied against WorkChoices.

If there is a will to resist, why are unionisation rates at a historic low? The most common response, heard from both conservatives and frustrated union militants, is that Australian workers have become complacent and have been 'bought off', more interested in their plasma TVs and overseas holidays than in joining a union. This argument has no basis in fact, as David Peetz has pointed out.[16] Successive Unions NSW surveys demonstrate untapped potential membership among non-unionists; the 2005 survey confirmed that one half of all workers 'would rather be in a union'. A 2007 survey by Brigid van Wanrooy and her Sydney University colleagues found a lower, but still substantial, figure: over 800 000 non-members were interested in joining unions. Had they joined, overall coverage would have climbed to 30 per cent.[17]

Forty-one per cent of non-members reported to Unions NSW that they would like to be in a union but had never been asked.[18] Many of these non-members hold strongly pro-union attitudes – they are as likely as union members to regard trade unions as 'very important for workers' job security' and as essential to prevent a worsening of working conditions for employees.[19] They are actually *more* likely than union members to agree that 'employees will never protect their working conditions and wages without strong unions.'[20] And they are disproportionately young, indicating that sympathy for trade unionism is not restricted to older generations. If unions fought they could easily sign up such non-members, as mass recruitment following every significant public sector strike in the 2000s has demonstrated. As an example of this, over the summer of 2008 25 000 Victorian teachers struck twice for higher wages, better working conditions and a reduction in contract teaching. The Victorian branch of the Australian

Education Union signed up 5200 new members in three months.[21] The problem is that such strikes are the exception rather than the rule and that the strike rate is at record lows.

Workers have demonstrated that they are willing to fight if given a lead. However, they do not have the confidence or the organisation to act on their own initiative, independently of their union leaders. Workplace union organisation has been severely damaged over recent decades by redundancies, anti-union legislation, company attacks and the self-defeating strategies adopted by the union movement. It is not that there are no workplace delegates in existence – according to the study by van Wanrooy et al., there were approximately 115 000, equivalent to one per cent of all employees, in 2007.[22] This estimate is almost certainly on the high side, but even if it were twice the actual figure, this still leaves more than 50 000 trade union delegates, by far the largest pool of potential activists in the Australian population.[23] The problem is not the numbers, but organisation, confidence and politics.

Here Australian unionism confronts its greatest weakness: the failure of the current generation of trade union leaders to channel the latent mass discontent and to organise the workplace delegates who survive into meaningful and sustained campaigns. Some union leaders are aware of this vacuum. Reflecting on the 2005 Unions NSW study, John Robertson concluded that 'a vast majority of workers are crying out for some sort of leadership which allows them to gain a modicum of control over their destiny.'[24] But what leadership did Robertson offer? In the aftermath of the 2007 election, Robertson argued that conflict between business and unions had only been manufactured by the Howard Government and its Work-Choices legislation.[25] Now that Labor was in office, business and unions could return to the 'spirit of cooperation' that had characterised relations when Labor was last in power.[26] Pragmatic calculations of mutual interest would ensure that business felt no need to strip workers' penalty rates, and unions no need to fight for their right to represent members:

> ... working with industry to create secure, well-paid jobs is the No. 1 priority. For business ... getting on with business will mean dealing with workers and their representatives again. This imperative of cooperation will not be limited to workplace relations but will include broader industry and, indeed, economic projects.[27]

Sharan Burrow concurred:

> WorkChoices and the lazy approach of the Howard–Costello [*sic*] to managing the economy are the main cause of Australia's stagnating productivity . . . We need to achieve better results on skills, infrastructure, and create better and more flexible workplace environments that promote greater cooperation and trust between employers and workers to generate higher levels of productivity. The union movement is determined to achieve higher productivity and better results for both the Australian economy and working people.[28]

The Accord may be dead, and with no prospect of disinterment, but senior union leaders are determined to pursue the same political agenda that had such disastrous consequences for unions in the 1980s and 1990s.

This is not to say that the union leaders *never* fight – examples in the past two decades have been cited in previous chapters where they have done just that. But when they have fought they have tended to do so in such a limited and hesitant fashion that their actions do little to rebuild union activism. And they fight with one arm tied behind their backs, because they are as committed as the employers to ensuring that Australian capitalism is efficient and competitive. They mobilised thousands to defend the MUA in 1998 but, once the union was back on the wharves, they traded away conditions that had been fought for and won over decades in the name of waterfront efficiency. They organised demonstrations of hundreds of thousands around WorkChoices, yet support the Rudd Government's promises of a new 'productivity revolution', taking up where Hawke and Keating left off.

The union leaders are able to continue this self-limiting strategy because today they are under little organised pressure from below. But here we come to a quandary. If rank-and-file unionists lack the confidence to fight unless given a lead by their officials, and the latter refuse to provide it, is Australian unionism doomed to a downward spiral?

There is a potential circuit breaker in the dynamics of capitalism itself. Workers fight not because they like to but because capitalism *requires* them to fight if they are to improve their pay and conditions or, increasingly, simply to defend them. When industrial struggles break out they invariably draw in new members, rebuild dormant union structures or create them from scratch. Examples include the Mount Isa workers in 1964, who had to contend not just with the bosses but with the hostility of their own union leaders. Their first step in 1964 was to threaten to strike in protest at the poor state of the washing facilities. Just the threat was sufficient to force the company to install new facilities. Having been emboldened by this victory, the Mount Isa workers then went on to demand increased pay and thence to wage the famous struggle over the summer of 1965 discussed in Chapter 1. As they did so, a rank-and-file committee was established and attendance at union meetings exploded from a couple of dozen to 1500.

Another example of these processes is that of workers at Kortex, a textile company based in Melbourne in the early years.[29] In December 1981, the 300-strong workforce, predominantly female and migrants from southern Europe and the Middle East, walked out on strike at the company's Brunswick plant. They wanted a $25 wage rise and their union leaders were doing nothing to help them get it, so they took things into their own hands. Very quickly they began to raise other demands as well: an end to the unfair bonus system, a canteen, tea breaks, the right to take toilet breaks when needed, and an end to 'voluntary' donations to buy the bosses birthday presents.

But to make the most from such outbursts of struggle, workers need leaders who can articulate their grievances, have some notion of how to take the struggle forward and can establish structures within the workplace – and across workplaces and even industries – to sustain the momentum. In the past, such leaders have commonly had some prior experience of organising, either in other workplaces, or as student or community activists. They may also have had experience with leftist groups. Again, this was demonstrated in the Mount Isa strike in 1964. At the heart of the miners' struggle was Pat Mackie, a semi-itinerant union militant and self-described 'Wobbly', with a history of involvement in struggle in the US, New Zealand and Australia over 30 years.[30] Likewise, a small number of militants at the Kortex plant belonged to the Victorian Turkish Labourers' Association, a communist group that had been involved in the strike at Ford Broadmeadows only a few months earlier. These militants knew how to organise a strike. They set up the picket lines, produced leaflets in several languages and encouraged the previously fearful workers to make a stand. Neither Pat Mackie nor the Turkish Labourers' Association *caused* the strikes at Mount Isa and Kortex – company management were responsible for that – but it is likely that the strikes would not have happened without them. Or, if they had occurred, they would have collapsed quickly.

The major problem holding back the union movement in 2008 is the absence of networks of experienced left-wing activists capable of taking any outbreak of struggle to its full potential. The best historical precedent for such a current in Australia is the Minority Movement of the early 1930s. Facing savage wage cuts, mass unemployment and entrenched union leaders who refused to fight the effects of the Great Depression, the Minority Movement was founded by the Communist Party and grew to include 3000 members, 60 job groups and eight shop committees.[31] The Minority Movement rebuilt unions, most obviously in the coal mines but also in the Queensland canefields, the Victorian textile factories, the New South Wales railway workshops and a number of public works projects.[32] In 1934 it led an important strike to victory at the Wonthaggi state coal mine in Victoria.

The CPA was beginning to sink deeper roots into the Australian working class in the 1930s.[33] Its members were committed socialists dedicated to the overthrow of Australian capitalism. Party activists made the Minority Movement a home and organising base for hundreds of non-party workers. But at the same time the CPA recruited hundreds of workers from its rank-and-file union work and this laid the basis for the party to win leadership positions in the unions. Something like the Minority Movement is needed today. It will need to involve a combination of radical politics, an emphasis on building from below rather than seeking bureaucratic positions, and a commitment to struggle at the point of production.

A revival of unionism will inevitably be part of a broader surge of activity in the working class, as it was in the late 1940s and early 1970s. Whether this collapses back quickly or is sustained will depend on the outcome of sharp debates between those forces trying to rein it in and those that want to take it forward.

The current union leaders are not likely to countenance the kinds of struggles needed to rebuild trade unions, and the organised left in Australia is weaker than at any time since the late 19th century. Nonetheless, a revival is neither impossible nor without precedent. In the 1890s union coverage fell from 20 per cent to less than 5 per cent of the workforce. Yet by 1901 membership had begun to rise again and by 1911 coverage had grown to 28 per cent. In the Great Depression, union coverage fell by over 10 percentage points but subsequently recovered.[34] On both occasions the intervention of organised socialist groups provided the crucial driving force to recruit and rebuild.[35] Consolidating a sizeable socialist organisation and rebuilding the networks of militants are the crucial tasks in the struggle to revive trade unionism in Australia today.

NOTES

1 Trade unionism in the postwar boom, 1945–67

1 T. Sheridan, *Mindful Militants: The Amalgamated Engineering Union in Australia 1920–72*, Cambridge, 1975, p. 167.

2 The account that follows of the CPA in the postwar years draws heavily from T. O'Lincoln, *Into the Mainstream: The Decline of Australian Communism*, Stained Wattle Press, Sydney, 1985.

3 Award wages had two components at this time. The basic wage, with its origins in the Harvester Judgment of 1907, fit for a man, his wife and three children to live a life of 'frugal comfort', and the margin that was paid on the basis of the particular skill or occupation. The Arbitration Court adjusted both at periodic intervals.

4 Cited in Sheridan, *Mindful Militants*, p. 185.

5 Kenny's union activities are discussed in M. Dodkin, *Brothers: Eight Leaders of the Labor Council of New South Wales*, UNSW Press, Sydney, 2001.

6 J. Hutson, *From Penal Colony to Penal Powers*, AEU, 1966, p. 199.

7 J. Kuhn, 'Grievance machinery and strikes in Australia', *Industrial and Labor Relations Review*, 7, 1954, pp. 170–6.

8 K. Hince, 'Unions on the shopfloor', in J. Isaac & G.W. Ford (eds), *Australian Labour Relations Readings*, 2nd edn, Sun Books, Melbourne, 1974, pp. 193–4.

9 Virtually all trades-qualified workers in the metal and engineering industry were male at this stage; hence the use of the term 'tradesmen'.

10 Sheridan, *Mindful Militants*, p. 207.

11 ibid., p. 238.

12 ibid., p. 238.

13 L. Perry, 'Trends in Australian strike activity: 1913–1978', *Australian Bulletin of Labour*, 6 (1), 1979, p. 45.

14 The following analysis of trends in the CPA draws heavily from O'Lincoln, *Into the Mainstream*, chapter 4.

15 Cited in D. Rawson, *Unions and Unionists in Australia*, Allen and Unwin, Sydney, 1978, p. 105. Monk and Broadby were ACTU president and secretary respectively.

16 Cited in Rawson, *Unions and Unionists*, p. 106.

17 O'Lincoln, *Into the Mainstream*, p. 83.

18 ibid., p. 99.

19 ibid., pp. 83–4.

20 Sheridan, *Mindful Militants*, pp. 207, 226.

21 ibid., pp. 169, 180, 228.

22 P. George, 'Power politics: a study of industrial conflict in the NSW power industry', BA Honours thesis, Department of Government, Sydney University, unpublished, 1975.
23 Sheridan, *Mindful Militants*, p. 266.
24 ibid., p. 266.
25 C. Fox, *Working Australia*, Allen and Unwin, Sydney, 1991, p. 146.
26 ibid., p. 147.
27 Sheridan, *Mindful Militants*, p. 6.
28 VBEF Federal Council minutes, 1965.
29 I use the term 'foremen' in this period advisedly.
30 Interview, Sol Marks, 1989.
31 G.W. Ford et al., 'A study of human resources and industrial relations at the plant level in seven selected industries', in Policies for the Development of Manufacturing Industry: a Green Paper (the Jackson Committee Report), vol. 4, *Commissioned Studies*, AGPS, 1976, p. 49.
32 ibid., p. 87.
33 A.G.L. Shaw, *The Economic Development of Australia*, Longman, Melbourne, 1973, p. 184.
34 C. Lever-Tracy & M. Quinlan, *A Divided Working Class*, Routledge & Kegan Paul, London, 1988.
35 N.F. Dufty, *Industrial Relations in the Australian Metal Industry*, West Publications, Sydney, 1972, p. 19.
36 J. Collins, 'Political economy of post-war immigration', in T. Wheelwright & K. Buckley (eds), *Essays in the Political Economy of Australian Capitalism*, vol. 2, ANZ Books, Sydney, 1975, p. 120. Although worker migrants from anglophone backgrounds continued to constitute the majority, they suffered from no specific oppression as migrants. Henceforth the term 'migrant' is used to refer to migrants from non-English-speaking backgrounds.
37 Ford et al., 'A study of human resources', pp. 20–7.
38 Fox, *Working Australia*, p. 152.
39 See Lever-Tracy & Quinlan, *A Divided Working Class*, for evidence of the problems facing migrants from non-English-speaking backgrounds in Australian unions.
40 R. Tierney, 'The Australian automotive industry, 1939 to 1965: a sociological study of some aspects of state intervention, managerial control and trade union organisation', PhD thesis, Macquarie University, 1991, p. 264.
41 Sheridan, *Mindful Militants*, p. 288.
42 Hutson, *From Penal Colony*, p. 207.
43 Interview, Les Perrett, Industrial Relations manager, Borg Warner, 1985.
44 O. Foenander, *Shop Stewards and Shop Committees: A Study in Trade Unionism and Industrial Relations in Australia*, Melbourne University Press, Carlton, 1965, pp. 122–3.
45 AMIA executive minutes, 1 November 1962.
46 ibid.
47 ibid.
48 Cited in Foenander, *Shop Stewards*, p. 79.
49 VBEF Victorian Branch minutes, 19 February 1964.
50 *Sydney Morning Herald*, 15 April 1964.

51 *AEU Monthly Journal*, August 1964.

52 ACTU interstate executive minutes, 6 September 1964.

53 Hince, 'Unions on the shopfloor', p. 199.

54 See Hutson, *From Penal Colony*, pp. 220–6.

55 ibid., p. 223.

56 The following account of the 1964 GMH strike is drawn from Tierney 'The Australian automotive industry'; J. Arrowsmith & G. Zangalis, *The Golden Holden: The Story of General Motors in Australia*, International Bookshop, Melbourne, 1965; and VBEF records.

57 Tierney, 'The Australian automotive industry', p. 333.

58 Interview, Theo Zianas, 1989.

59 Dufty, *Industrial Relations*, table 6.7.

60 The following account of the dispute at Mount Isa is based on P. Mackie, *Mount Isa: The Story of the Dispute*, Hudson, Hawthorn, 1989.

61 Metal Trades Employers' Association, *Metal Trades News*, cited in *Industry Today*, October–November 1967, p. 42.

62 R.M. Martin, 'The ACTU Congress of 1965', *Journal of Industrial Relations*, 7 (4), 1965, pp. 323–4.

63 Cited in *MTEA News Bulletin*, no. 55, 29 September 1966.

64 The following account of union involvement in the anti-Vietnam war campaign is drawn from M.J. Saunders, 'The trade unions in Australia and opposition to Vietnam and conscription: 1965–73', *Labour History*, 43, 64–82, 1982.

65 The story of the expulsion of the 27 rebel unions is told in D. Plowman, 'The VTHC split: a study of inter-union conflict', *Labour History*, no. 36, May 1979.

2 The union upsurge, 1968–74

1 D. Fieldes, 'Industrial relations laws made to be broken', *Socialist Alternative* (Melbourne), August 1999.

2 The account of the struggle against absorption and the penal powers draws from Chapter 2 of D. Fieldes, '"Some are more equal than others" – Australian trade union campaigns for equal pay, 1968–75', PhD thesis, University of New South Wales, School of Industrial Relations and Organisational Behaviour, 2002.

3 J. Hutson, *Six Wage Concepts*, AEU, Sydney, 1971, p. 201.

4 Rawson, *Unions and Unionists*, p. 101.

5 J. Baird, 'Skill and fines and "rock and roll": the Metal Trades Margins Campaign of 1967–8', *The Hummer* (Sydney), 2 (7), 1997.

6 ibid.

7 ibid.

8 Hutson, *Six Wage Concepts*, p. 203.

9 A.E. Woodward, 'A review of industrial relations, 1968/9', *JIR*, 11 (2), 1969, p. 89.

10 MTEA press release, 'Employers call for action to halt wave of strikes', 10 March 1969.

11 Fieldes, 'Some are more equal', p. 17.

12 C. O'Shea, speech to the 'Communists and the Labour Movement' conference, Melbourne, 1980. Tapes of the conference held by State Library of Victoria. Transcript of tape by Liz Ross. The Melbourne Trades Hall Council was renamed the Victorian Trades Hall Council in 1968.

13 Fieldes, 'Industrial relations laws'. It was widely suspected at the time that Mr Dudley McDougall was, in fact, 'put up' by the Government to pay the fine.

14 Decisions of the ACTU Special Executive Meeting, 21–22 May 1969, second session.

15 ibid.

16 Hutson, *Six Wage Concepts*, p. 204.

17 A.E. Woodward, 'Industrial relations in the 70s', *JIR*, 12 (2), 1970, p. 115.

18 Cited in A. Lavelle, 'In the wilderness: federal Labor in opposition', PhD thesis, Griffith University, 2004, p. 83.

19 P. Bentley, 'Australian trade unionism, 1970–71', *JIR*, 13 (4), 1971, p. 405.

20 P. Bentley, *Industrial Relations: A Study*, CEDA Monograph no. 40, Melbourne, 1975, p. 26.

21 George, 'Power politics', p. 32.

22 MTIA (NSW branch), Report on the Newcastle Workers Control Conference, April 1973, mimeo.

23 This account is based on George, 'Power politics', pp. 39–40.

24 P. Thomas, *The Nymboida Story: The Work-ins that Saved a Coal-mine*, Miners' Federation, Sydney, 1975.

25 L. Caldwell & M. Tubbs, 'The Harco Work-In: an experience of workers' control', National Workers' Control Conference, 1973.

26 *Courier-Mail*, 14 August 1969.

27 George, 'Power politics', p. 57.

28 AEU Report, Jim Scott, SA State Secretary, March 1970. Reported to National Workers' Control Conference, Newcastle, April 1973.

29 The story is told in P. True, *Tales of the BLF . . . Rolling the Right! The Battle of the Builders Labourers Rank and File in NSW 1951–1964*, Militant Publications, Parramatta, 1995.

30 O'Lincoln, *Into the Mainstream*, pp. 140–1.

31 Report by NSW BLF to the National Workers' Control Conference, Newcastle, April 1973.

32 Woodward, 'Industrial relations in the 70s', p. 124.

33 *AEU Monthly Journal*, 'Metal workers accept challenge: Employers threaten workers, blackball strikers, deregister unions', July 1970, 16–19, p. 16.

34 ibid.

35 Interview, Chris Burns industrial relations manager, Hoover, 1985.

36 Interview, Mike Holland, industrial relations manager, GMH Elizabeth, 1990.

37 For more on the role of unions in the Vietnam campaign, see M.J. Saunders, 'Vietnam' and T. Duras, 'Trade unions and the Vietnam War', at the Marxist Interventions web site: www.anu.edu.au/polsci/marx/interventions/workers.htm.

38 Saunders, 'Vietnam', p. 69.

39 ibid, p. 69.

40 Cited in B. Scales, *'Draftmen go free': A History of the Anti-Conscription Movement in Australia*, self-published, Melbourne, 1989, p. 50.

41 M.J. Saunders, 'Vietnam', p. 70.

42 ibid, p. 74.

43 'Peaceful call for peace', *The Australian*, 9 May 1970, p. 1.

44 Saunders, 'Vietnam', p. 81.

45 See C. Harman, *The Fire Last Time*, Bookmarks, London, 1988.

46 Bentley, *Industrial Relations*, p. 31.

47 Lavelle, 'In the Wilderness', p. 39.

48 C.P. Mills, 'A review of developments in industrial relations, 1970–71', *JIR*, September 1971, p. 221.

49 M. Burgmann & V. Burgmann, *Green Bans, Red Union: Environmental Activism and the NSW Builders Labourers' Federation*, UNSW Press, Sydney, 1998, p. 128, cited in Fieldes, 'Some are more equal', p. 39.

50 L. Russell, 'Today the students, tomorrow the workers! Radical student politics and the Australian labour movement, 1960–1972', PhD thesis, University of Technology Sydney, 1998, p. 396, cited in Fieldes, 'Some are more equal', p. 39.

51 I. MacPhee, 'Industrial relations – 1970', *JIR*, 13 (1), 1971, p. 55.

52 Saunders, 'Vietnam', p. 75.

53 ibid., p. 66.

54 O'Lincoln, *Into the Mainstream*, pp. 112–16.

55 The CPA's stronghold was in Victoria where, in addition to holding key positions in the metal trades, it also had officials in the Liquor Trades, the SUA, the Railways, the WWF, the Meatworkers, the Clothing Trades, Technical Teachers and Ship Painters and Dockers, among others. In NSW, the party held leadership positions in the NSW Teachers' Federation, the BLF, the Miners' Federation, the WWF, FEDFA and the Meatworkers, and in Queensland they controlled the BWIU and were influential also in the Meatworkers.

56 O'Lincoln, *Into the Mainstream*, Chapter 2.

57 Saunders, 'Vietnam', p. 71.

58 Cited in Bentley, 'Australian trade unionism 1970–71', p. 406.

59 ibid., pp. 412–13.

60 Saunders, 'Vietnam', p. 71.

61 C. Ferrier & R. Pelan (eds), *The Point of Change: Marxism, Australia, History, Theory*, Australian Studies Centre, University of Queensland, 1998, pp. 45–46, cited in Fieldes, 'Some are more equal', p. 38.

62 Burgmann & Burgmann, *Green Bans, Red Union*.

63 See L. Cupper & J. Hearn, 'Australian union involvement in "non-industrial" issues: the Newport dispute, 1971–78', in G.W. Ford, J. Hearn & R. Lansbury (eds), *Australian Labour Relations*, 3rd edition, Macmillan, Melbourne, 1980.

64 T. O'Lincoln, *Years of Rage: Social Conflicts in the Fraser Era*, Bookmarks Australia, Melbourne, 1993, p. 89.

65 R.D. Williams, 'The white collar strikes', *JIR*, 15 (2), 1973, pp. 216–17, cited in Fieldes, 'Some are more equal', p. 28.

66 P. Bentley, 'Australian trade unionism in 1969–70', *JIR*, 12 (3), 1970, pp. 379–80.

67 G. Griffin, *White Collar Militancy: The Australian Banking and Insurance Unions*, Croom Helm, Sydney, 1985.

68 Bentley, 'Australian trade unionism in 1969–70', p. 379.

69 Williams, 'The white collar strikes', p. 216. See also D. Fieldes, 'Equal pay: the insurance industry struggle, 1973–75', in S. Bloodworth & T. O'Lincoln (eds), *Rebel Women in Australian Working Class History*, Red Rag, Melbourne, 2008 (orig. 1998).

70 Mills, 'A review of developments', p. 224.

71 Important exceptions included the Clerks and the Shop Assistants.

72 R. Lansbury, 'The growth and unionization of white collar workers in Australia: some recent trends', *JIR*, 19 (1), 1977, p. 39.

73 ibid.

74 The account that follows is based on R. Wilkinson, 'Militant Ford workers: class consciousness or sheer frustration?', BA (Hons) thesis, La Trobe University, 1983; C. Lever-Tracy, 'The segmentation and articulation of the working class: an exploration of the impact of postwar Australian immigration', PhD thesis, Flinders University, 1984; L. Townsend, 'Ford dispute report, 1973', VBEF federal office, Melbourne, 1973; and my own interviews with AMWU stewards Sol Marks and Ronnie Gent in 1989.

75 J. Hearn, 'Migrant participation in trade union leadership', in Ford, Hearn & Lansbury, *Australian Labour Relations*, p. 159.

76 ibid., p. 160.

77 O. Covick, 'The Australian labour market', *Australian Bulletin of Labour*, 6 (1), 1979, pp. 9–10.

78 The following account of the equal pay campaign is drawn from D. Fieldes, 'Fighting for equal pay: the Australian metal industry 1969–1972', on the Marxist Interventions website: www.anu.edu.au/polsci/marx/interventions/.

79 M. Bevege, 'The history of women's struggle to become tram drivers in Melbourne, 1956–1975', *Women and Labour Conference Papers, volume 2: The Experience of Work*, May 1978.

80 Fieldes, 'Equal pay', p. 116.

81 Rawson, *Unions and Unionists*, p. 32.

82 Fieldes, 'Equal pay', p. 118.

83 Australian Conciliation and Arbitration Commission, National Wage Case April 1975, Reasons for Decision, 30 April 1975, p. 7.

84 See D. Scott, 'Metal Trade Award campaign best ever in the industry', AMWU *Monthly Journal*, May 1974, p. 4, and D. Scott, 'Urgent! Consider claims now for 1975 award negotiations', AMWU *Monthly Journal*, December 1974, p. 20.

85 Combined Research Centre of the AEU and BBS, *Labour Force Survey*, mimeo, Sydney, May 1970, p. 1.

86 D. Plowman, 'Australian trade unions: some vital statistics', in Ford, Hearn & Lansbury, *Australian Labour Relations*, pp. 212–16.

87 ibid.

88 D. Rawson, 'A note on manual and non-manual union membership in Australia', *JIR*, 16 (4), 1974, pp. 394–6.

89 P. Bentley, 'Australian trade unionism, 1971–72', *JIR*, 14 (4), 1972, pp. 439–46.

90 Plowman, 'Australian trade unions', in Ford, Hearn & Lansbury, *Australian Labour Relations*, pp. 212–16.

91 Lansbury, 'White collar unionism', p. 44.

92 Cited in Lavelle, 'In the Wilderness', p. 80.

93 ibid., pp. 81–2.

94 ibid., p. 83.

95 Cited in Bentley, 'Australian trade unionism, 1969–70', p. 379.

96 C. Cameron on 'Productivity and the community', speech to House of Representatives, Parliamentary Debates, 1 April 1971, reproduced in AEU *Monthly Journal*, June 1971, p. 22.

97 Cited in Bentley, 'Australian trade unionism, 1970–71', p. 414.
98 ibid., p. 415.
99 ibid., p. 416; Lavelle, 'In the Wilderness', pp. 92–3.
100 Bentley, 'Australian trade unionism, 1971–72', p. 445.
101 C. Johnson, *The Labor Legacy: Curtin, Chifley, Whitlam, Hawke*, Allen and Unwin, 1989, p. 52–3.
102 ibid., p. 56.
103 C.P. Mills, 'Legislation and Decisions affecting industrial relations 1973', *JIR*, 16 (2), 1974, p. 165.
104 R. Lansbury, 'Performance against promise: the Labor Government and industrial relations', *JIR*, 17 (3), 1974, p. 290.
105 K. Hancock & J. Isaac, 'Australian experiments in wages policy', *BJIR*, 30 (2), 1992, pp. 217–18.
106 AMWU *Monthly Journal*, November 1973, p. 24.
107 'Interview with Frank Cherry', *Link* newsletter, AMWU Eastern Suburbs branches, Melbourne, February 1974, p. 4.

3 Economic crisis and the halting of the flood tide, 1974–75

1 See C. Harman, *Explaining the Crisis*, Bookmarks, London, 1984, for an explanation of the factors underpinning the postwar boom and the subsequent bust.
2 K.T. Davis & M.K. Lewis, 'Inflation first: an evaluation of recent economic policies', *Australian Bulletin of Labour*, 6 (1), p. 23.
3 M. Derber, 'Changing union-management relations at the plant level in Australian metal-working', in Ford, Hearn & Lansbury, *Australian Labour Relations*.
4 Burgmann & Burgmann, p. 273.
5 O'Lincoln, *Years of Rage*, pp. 34–35.
6 P. Bentley, 'Australian trade unionism, 1973–74', *JIR*, 16 (4), 1974, p. 382.
7 ibid., p. 384.
8 ibid., p. 384.
9 *The Battler* (Melbourne), 15 February 1975.
10 Johnson, *The Labor Legacy*, p. 74.
11 ACTU, 'Decisions of the ACTU executive meeting, 26–30 August 1974', Melbourne.
12 167 *Commonwealth Arbitration Reports* 18, p. 39.
13 ACTU executive resolution on the April 1975 National Wage Case, reproduced in the AMWU *Monthly Journal*, July 1975, p. 4.
14 *Link* newsletter (AMWU Eastern Suburbs, Melbourne), June 1975, p. 1.
15 O'Lincoln, *Years of Rage*, p. 23.
16 R.M. Martin, 'The ACTU Congress of 1975', *JIR*, December 1975, p. 385.
17 B. Carr, 'Australian trade unionism in 1975', *JIR*, December 1975, p. 413.
18 C. Donn, 'The economic policy of the ACTU', *JIR*, December 1975, p. 397.
19 ibid., p. 398.
20 ibid.
21 Carr, 'Australian trade unionism in 1975', p. 415.
22 ibid.
23 ibid., p. 422.
24 AMWU, 'General statement on the economic crisis, 15 August 1975', AMWU *Monthly Journal*, September 1975, p. 13.

25 See R. Kuhn, 'Class analysis and the left in Australian history', in R. Kuhn & T. O'Lincoln (eds), *Class and Class Conflict in Australia*, Longman, Melbourne, 1996.

26 AMWU 'General statement'. See also L. Carmichael, 'Multinationals and the economic crisis in the 1970s', AMWU *Monthly Journal*, September 1975, pp. 14–15; and AMWU *Monthly Journal*, October 1975, pp. 17–18.

27 J. Baird, 'Commonwealth Council resolution: Call for action on the economy', AMWU *Monthly Journal*, May 1975, p. 5.

28 O'Lincoln, *Years of Rage*, p. 37.

29 Editorial 'Wage demands and economy', AMWU *Monthly Journal*, March 1975, p. 1.

30 George, 'Power politics', p. 64.

31 ibid., p. 74.

32 ibid., p. 75.

33 *The Battler* (Melbourne), 16 August 1975.

34 ibid., 11 October 1975.

35 ibid., 5 April 1975.

36 ibid., 26 March 1975.

37 Johnson, *The Labor Legacy*, p. 83.

38 Carr, 'Australian trade unionism in 1975', p. 422.

39 P. Griffiths, 'Strike Fraser out! The labour movement campaign against the blocking of supply and the sacking of the Whitlam Government, October–December 1975', Marxist Interventions website, www.anu.edu.au/polsci/marx/interventions/ p. 2. The account that follows draws heavily from this source.

40 ibid., p. 3.

41 Carr, 'Australian trade unionism in 1975', p. 422.

42 Griffiths, 'Strike Fraser out!', p. 4.

43 O'Lincoln, *Years of Rage*, p. 49.

44 Cited in Griffiths, 'Strike Fraser out!', p. 9

45 Cited in *The Canberra Coup*, Workers News, Sydney, 1976, p. 21.

46 Griffiths, 'Strike Fraser out!', p. 10.

47 ibid.

48 B. Hawke, 'The Labor powerbroker', *The Weekend Australian Magazine*, 5–6 November 2005, p. 27.

49 'Election vital to trade unions', AMWU *Monthly Journal*, December 1975, p. 1.

50 Carr, 'Australian trade unionism in 1975', p. 422.

4 Unionism in the Fraser years

1 This account of union activity in the period from 1976 to 1980 draws heavily from A. Kahn, 'The industrial struggle since 1975', *International Socialist*, 11, 1981, and O'Lincoln, *Years of Rage*, Bookmarks Australia, Sydney, 1993.

2 O'Lincoln, *Years of Rage*, p. 57.

3 The following account of the Medibank dispute is based on Kahn, 'The industrial struggle', pp. 5–6 and O'Lincoln, *Years of Rage*, pp. 59–66.

4 Cited in Lavelle, 'In the Wilderness', p. 167.

5 B. Carr, 'Australian trade unionism in 1977', *JIR*, 20 (1), 1978, p. 79.

6 Lavelle, 'In the Wilderness', p. 167.

7 ibid., p. 113.

8 ibid., p. 128.
9 ibid., p. 169.
10 The following is drawn from O'Lincoln, *Years of Rage*, pp. 69–77.
11 B. Carr, 'Australian trade unionism in 1976', *JIR*, 19 (1), 1977 p. 83.
12 ibid.
13 ibid., p. 84.
14 PKIU militants, led by the head of chapel, Don Paget, did respect the journalists' picket line in 1980 but they were unable to persuade their fellow printers, angry with the journalists for their betrayal in 1976, to do the same.
15 The following draws from O'Lincoln, *Years of Rage*, p. 77–88.
16 Carr, 'Australian trade unionism in 1977', p. 78.
17 J. Benson & D. Goff, 'The 1977 Latrobe Valley SECV maintenance workers' strike', *JIR*, June 1979, p. 227; O'Lincoln, *Years of Rage*, p. 85.
18 *Tribune*, 2 November 1977, cited in O'Lincoln, *Into the Mainstream*, p. 161.
19 O'Lincoln, *Years of Rage*, p. 86.
20 Kahn, 'The industrial struggle', p. 7.
21 Carr, 'Australian trade unionism in 1977', pp. 77–78; Kahn, 'The industrial struggle', p. 6.
22 O'Lincoln, *Years of Rage*, p. 214.
23 Interview, Neal Tamblyn, industrial relations manager Mitsubishi Motors, 1990.
24 The story of events at Chrysler is drawn from interviews with the VBEF leaders and militants from the time, the South Australian *VBU News* (n.d.) issued a week after the sackings and G. Hill, 'Anatomy of an industrial struggle', *Solidarity Motor Bulletin*, no. 9, London, n.d. The *Adelaide Advertiser*, 14 and 16 July 1977 and 8 October 1977, also covered events and their aftermath. The legal case that followed can be found at *Hyde v Chrysler Australia* (1977) 30 FLR 318; 1978 AILR ¶14).
25 The following account of rising public service militancy and the activities of the ACOA Reform Group draws heavily on R. Kuhn, 'Thin cats and socialism: class struggle within the state', *International Socialist*, 10, 1980.
26 Source for the following information is long-time VSTA activist Tess Lee-Ack.
27 See Kahn, 'The industrial struggle', pp. 8–9 and O'Lincoln, *Years of Rage*, pp. 199–200.
28 This account of union political activity from 1976 to 1980 draws heavily on Kahn, 'The industrial struggle', and also O'Lincoln, *Years of Rage*, Chapter 6.
29 Carr, 'Australian trade unionism in 1976', p. 81.
30 Cited in S. Ryan, 'Secret plans for troops on the wharves', *The Australian*, 1 January 2008, p. 7.
31 Lavelle, 'In the Wilderness', p. 279.
32 Carr, 'Australian trade unionism in 1976', p. 83.
33 O'Lincoln, *Years of Rage*, p. 91.
34 ibid., p. 92.
35 ibid., p. 93.
36 ibid., p. 101.
37 ibid., p. 101.
38 B. Carr, 'Australian trade unionism in 1978', *JIR*, 21 (1), 1979, p. 98.
39 ibid.
40 ibid.
41 ibid., p. 99.

42 Kahn, 'The industrial struggle', p. 8; O'Lincoln, *Years of Rage*, p. 124.
43 O'Lincoln, *Years of Rage*, p. 124.
44 *The Battler* (Melbourne), 9 September 1978.
45 Carr, 'Australian trade unionism in 1978', p. 97.
46 ibid.
47 O'Lincoln, *Years of Rage*, p. 207.
48 Lever-Tracy, 'The segmentation and articulation of the working class', p. 349.
49 VBEF federal executive minutes, 8 October 1981.
50 Melbourne *Herald*, 30 October 1981.
51 The following account of women in the unions is based on O'Lincoln, *Years of Rage*, pp. 172–75.
52 ibid., p. 172.
53 ibid., p. 173.
54 ibid., p. 175.
55 ibid., p. 221.
56 Carr, 'Australian trade unionism in 1978', p. 98.
57 AMWSU, 'Consolidated decisions of biennial national conferences, 1973–1980', AMWSU, Sydney, p. 59.
58 *Sydney Morning Herald*, 4 April 1982, cited in O'Lincoln, *Years of Rage*, p. 218.
59 Kahn, 'The industrial struggle', p. 11.
60 The following analysis of AMWU economic policy in the late 1970s and early 1980s draws heavily on R. Kuhn, *Militancy Uprooted: Labour Movement Economics, 1974–1986*, Socialist Action, Melbourne, 1986.
61 ibid., p. 1.
62 Mark Burford, 'Prices and incomes policy and socialist politics', *Journal of Australian Political Economy*, no. 14, 1983, p. 25.
63 Lavelle, 'In the Wilderness', p. 161 and p. 96.
64 Communist Party of Australia, 'A strategy for the metal industry in the 1980s', Sydney, 1982, cited in Kuhn, *Militancy Uprooted*, p. 17.
65 Lavelle, 'In the Wilderness', p. 163.
66 Interview, industrial relations manager, Betts Electric Motors, 1985.
67 J. Hearn, 'Australian trade unionism in 1982', *JIR*, 1983, p. 97.
68 ibid.; O'Lincoln, *Years of Rage*, p. 126.
69 O'Lincoln, *Years of Rage*, p. 126.
70 ibid., p. 127.
71 S. Deery & D. Plowman, *Australian Industrial Relations*, 2nd edn, McGraw-Hill, Sydney, 1985, p. 308.
72 Hearn, 'Australian trade unionism 1982', p. 94.
73 ibid.

5 The ALP–ACTU Accord, 1983–90

1 At his farewell speech to the 1995 Congress, ACTU president Martin Ferguson told delegates that 'When the history of the 1980s and '90s is written, industrially and politically it will be one of record achievements.' P. Gahan, '(Re)organise! Recruit! Survive? The 1995 ACTU Congress' *JIR*, 37 (4), 1995, p. 611.
2 'Statement of the Accord by the Australian Labor Party and the Australian Council of Trade Unions regarding Economic Policy', February 1983 (henceforth 'The Accord').

3 ibid.

4 ibid.

5 Cited in Lavelle, 'In the Wilderness', p. 170.

6 B. Dabscheck, *Australian Industrial Relations in the 1980s*, Oxford University Press, Melbourne, 1989, p. 53.

7 National Economic Summit Conference, 'Communique', April 1983.

8 ibid.

9 ibid.

10 Speech by Mr W.J. Kelty to the National Economic Summit, April 1983.

11 Economic Summit, 'Communique'.

12 VBEF *Federal Newsletter*, 19 April 1983.

13 I. Hampson, 'Rethinking union strategy? Reflections on a critique of "left productivism"', *Labour and Industry*, 17 (2), 2006, p. 32.

14 I am grateful to Jeff Sparrow for research assistance on the education unions.

15 Interview, 25 March 1999.

16 Interview, 28 April 1999.

17 T. Gnatenko, 'Education Officer's Report for the Year Ending 31.12.89', AMWU South Australian State Council, mimeo, 1990, p. 10.

18 T. Gnatenko, 'Education Officer's Report', p. 10.

19 Cited in J. McPhillips, *The Accord and its Consequences*, Socialist Party of Australia, Sydney, 1985, p. 12.

20 *Australian Financial Review*, 15 October 1984, cited in J. McPhillips, *The Accord*, p. 27.

21 Interview, industrial relations manager, Betts Electric Motors, 1985.

22 A. Petridis, 'Wages policy and wage determination in 1985', *JIR*, 28 (1), 1986, p. 130.

23 Business Council of Australia: 'Restrictive Work Practices', submission to the Economic Planning Advisory Council, 5 September 1986.

24 The following account of the Furnishing Trades and Food Preservers' campaigns draws heavily on McPhillips, *The Accord*.

25 Cited in ibid., p. 24.

26 M. Gardner, 'Australian trade unionism in 1986', *JIR*, 29 (1), 1987, p. 104.

27 O'Lincoln, *Into the Mainstream*, p. 176.

28 ibid., p. 186. The following section on the fate of the CPA is drawn from pp. 174–88 of this book.

29 ibid., p. 188.

30 *The Metal Worker*, vol. 5, no. 7, August 1984, p. 1.

31 ibid., p. 2.

32 J. Halfpenny, 'The effectiveness of the Accord', *JIR*, 27 (2), 1985, p. 236.

33 Cited in Evatt Foundation, *Unions 2001: A Blueprint for Union Activism*, Sydney, 1995, p. 261.

34 The changing position of the BLF on the Accord is discussed in L. Ross, *Dare to Struggle, Dare to Win! Builders Labourers Fight Deregistration 1981–94*, Vulgar Press, Melbourne, 2004, pp. 276–7.

35 The following account of the BLF deregistration is drawn from Ross, *Dare to Struggle*.

36 The BLF continued to function as a registered union in the other four states, until one by one the union branches amalgamated with the BWIU to form in 1993 the new Construction, Forestry, Mining and Energy Union (CFMEU).

37 The nurses' story is told in L. Ross, 'Dedication doesn't pay the rent! The 1986 Victorian nurses' strike' in Bloodworth & O'Lincoln, *Rebel Women*.

38 Cited in McPhillips, *The Accord*, p. 75.

39 Details of the SEQEB dispute are drawn from E. Petersen, 'From the Plague to Reith: the legal antecedents of the Workplace Relations Act', published at the Marxist Interventions website: www.anu.edu.au/polsci/marx/interventions.

40 J. Minns, *Hawke, Class Struggle and the Left*, International Socialists, Sydney, 1988, p. 21.

41 M. Burgmann, 'Australian trade unionism in 1985', *JIR*, 28 (1), 1986, p. 140.

42 Details of the Mudginberri Abattoirs picket are drawn from Petersen, 'From the Plague to Reith'; and B. Brian, 'Mudginberri revisited: a case study of a secondary boycott', *Green Left Weekly*, 4 December 1986.

43 Details of the Dollar Sweets picket are drawn from Petersen, 'From the Plague to Reith'; and P. Costello 'The Dollar Sweets Story', in 'In Search of the Magic Pudding', The Proceedings of a Conference of the H.R Nicholls Society at Lorne 5–7 August 1988, published at www.hrnicholls.com.au/nicholls/nichvol5/vol5cont.htm#Pageone.

44 Nearly 80 per cent of metal industry plants with more than 50 workers reported union density of more than 75 per cent among manual workers in 1984. Source: S. Frenkel, 'Management and labour relations in the metal industry: towards joint regulation?', in S. Frenkel (ed.), *Union Strategy and Industrial Change*, University of NSW Press, Sydney, 1987.

45 Cited in D. Rawson, *Unions and Unionists in Australia*, 2nd edition, Allen and Unwin, Sydney, 1986, p. 103.

46 *Financial Review*, 4 September 1986.

47 Cited in Minns, *Hawke, Class Struggle*, p. 29.

48 Confederation of Australian Industry, *Industrial Review*, November 1986, cited in R. Evans, 'A Retrospective', H.R. Nicholls Society, 1996, www.hrnicholls/nichvol17/volxv014.htm, accessed 9 March 2008.

49 *Financial Review*, 5 September 1986.

50 Gardner, 'Australian trade unionism in 1986', p. 109.

51 The following draws on Gardner, 'Australian trade unionism in 1986', pp. 106–7.

52 N. Way, 'Robe River: how not to tame a union', *Business Review Weekly*, 23 January 1987, cited in Minns, *Hawke, Class Struggle*, p. 28.

53 A notable feature of the Hawke Government was the reversal in the normal meaning of the word 'reform'. Hitherto understood as a measure that in some way advanced the material or political interests of the working class, from the early 1980s 'reform' was used in elite political discourse to mean a measure that benefited the capitalist class instead. In my use of the word 'reform' in this and subsequent chapters, I am using it in its contemporary meaning.

54 T. McDonald & M. Rimmer, 'Award restructuring and wages policy', in J. Nevile (ed.), *Wage Determination in Australia*, Committee for Economic Development of Australia, Melbourne, 1989.

55 *The Australian*, 9 August 1986; *Sydney Morning Herald*, 17 October 1986.

56 Australian Conciliation and Arbitration Commission, *National Wage Case, March 1987*, Melbourne, 1987, p. 9.

57 ibid., p. 6.

58 E. Davis, 'The 1987 ACTU Congress: restructuring Australia?', *JIR*, 30 (1), 1988, p. 124.

59 *Sydney Morning Herald*, 15 August 1988.

60 C. Briggs, 'Australian exceptionalism: the role of trade unions in the emergence of enterprise bargaining', *JIR*, 43 (1), 2001, p. 40.

61 K. Spooner, 'Australian trade unionism in 1988', *JIR*, 31(1), 1989, p. 119.

62 ibid.

63 ibid., p. 125.

64 R. Willis, *Labour Market Reform: the Industrial Relations Agenda*, AGPS, Canberra, 1988, p. iii.

65 ibid., p. 2.

66 Australian Conciliation and Arbitration Commission, *National Wage Case, August 1988*, Melbourne, 1988, p. 5.

67 J. Hutson, 'Productivity bargaining agreements', AMWU *Monthly Journal*, March 1974, p. 13.

68 ibid., p. 15.

69 ACTU, *Future Strategies for the Trade Union Movement*, ACTU, Melbourne, p. 5.

70 R. Sharp, 'Reconstructing Australia', *Arena*, 82, 1988, p. 75.

71 Letter to the *Sydney Morning Herald*, 22 October 1988.

72 'Labor's five years: counsel for the defence: an interview with Laurie Carmichael', *Australian Left Review*, no. 109, 1989.

73 ibid.

74 Davis, 'The 1987 ACTU Congress', p. 122.

75 R. Callus, A. Morehead, M. Cully & J. Buchanan, *Industrial Relations at Work*, Department of Industrial Relations, AGPS, Canberra, 1991, p. 331.

76 ibid.

77 M. Rimmer & J. Zappala, 'Labour market flexibility and the second tier', *Australian Bulletin of Labour*, 14 (4), 1988, pp. 564–91.

78 ibid.

79 Evatt Foundation, *Unions 2001: A Blueprint for Union Activism*, Sydney, 1995, p. 35.

80 *Financial Review*, 30 July 1987.

81 Rimmer & Zappala, 'Labour market flexiblity'.

82 Federation of Vehicle Industry Unions, 'Mid-term report of Industrial Relations working party', VBEF federal office, 4 December 1990, p. 13.

83 ibid.

84 These findings were, by and large, in line with Callus et al., *Industrial Relations*, pp. 132–6.

85 ibid., p. 135.

86 ibid.

87 Minns, *Hawke, Class Struggle*, p. 9.

88 Gardner, 'Australian trade unionism in 1986', p. 153.

89 Callus et al., *Industrial Relations*, p. 271.

90 ibid.

91 ibid., p. 102.

92 ibid., p. 288.

93 ibid., p. 340.

94 Gnatenko, 'Education Officer's Report', p. 4.

95 G. Singleton, *The Accord and the Australian Labour Movement*, Melbourne University Press, 1990, cited in A. Learmonth, 'Government policy, aviation deregulation, and the 1989 pilots' dispute', AIRAANZ conference paper, Sydney University, 2004, p. 111.

96 Data sourced from I. Campbell, 'Globalization and changes in employment conditions in Australia', unpublished mimeo, June 2007, table A2.

97 ibid., table A8.

98 *Business Review Weekly*, 'Rich 200' lists, May editions 1984 and 1990. Data provided by G. Murray (personal communication).

6 Enterprise bargaining and a revived employer offensive, 1990–96

1 G. Dumenil & D. Levy, 'The profit rate: where and how much did it fall? Did it recover? (USA 1948–2000)', *Review of Radical Political Economics*, 34, 2002, pp. 437–61.

2 Evatt Foundation, *Unions 2001: A Blueprint for Union Activism*, Sydney, 1995, p. 141.

3 *Australian Financial Review*, 15 July 1994.

4 The *Australian*, 11 July 1994.

5 R. Macklin, M. Goodwin & J. Docherty, 'Workplace bargaining in Australia', in D. Peetz, A. Preston & J. Docherty (eds), *Workplace Bargaining in the International Context*, Department of Industrial Relations, Commonwealth of Australia, 1993, p. 37.

6 C. Briggs, 'Australian exceptionalism'.

7 ibid., p. 34.

8 ibid., p. 36.

9 ibid., p. 30.

10 S. Jamieson, 'Trade unions in 1991', *JIR*, 34 (1), 1992, p. 163.

11 J. Hewson & T. Fischer, *Fightback! It's Your Australia*, Liberal and National Parties, Canberra, November; *Fightback! Fairness and Jobs*, Liberal and National Parties, Canberra, December.

12 J. Kelsey, *The New Zealand Experiment*, Auckland University Press, Auckland, 1995.

13 M. Ferguson, 'Building effective unions', speech delivered to the Australian Hotels Association National Convention, 9 August 1993.

14 ibid.

15 Department of Industrial Relations, *Workplace Bargaining: The First 1,000 Agreements*, Commonwealth of Australia, Canberra, 1993; Department of Industrial Relations, *Enterprise Bargaining in Australia, Annual Report 1994*, AGPS, Canberra, 1995. Much of the information on the agreements that follow is drawn from these sources.

16 Department of Industrial Relations, *Enterprise Bargaining*, p. 219.

17 Evatt Foundation, *Unions 2001*, p. 81.

18 ibid., p. 83.

19 The examples that are used in the following discussion are drawn from the two government surveys, unless otherwise indicated.

20 Department of Industrial Relations, *Enterprise Bargaining*, p. 224.

21 S. Jamieson, 'Australian trade unions in 1992', *JIR*, 35 (1), 1993, p. 162.

22 ibid., p. 163.

23 ibid., p. 162.

24 D. Kelly, 'Trade unionism in 1993', *JIR*, 36 (1), 1994 p. 144.

25 D. Kelly, 'Trade unionism in 1994', *JIR*, 37 (1), 1995, p. 137.

26 B. Pocock, 'Trade unionism in 1995', *JIR*, 38 (1), 1996, p. 139.

27 R. Waldersee & L. Blackstock, *Organisational Change in Australia: What's Really Happening?* Centre for Corporate Change, University of New South Wales, 1993. All quotes that follow are from this source.

28 These figures are compiled from data published in the ACTU's 1994 *National Union Directory*. The figure for average annual income was calculated from data provided by eight of these 11 unions – the remaining three did not provide this information.

29 ABC Radio National, Background Briefing, 'Coles Myer', 22 October 1995, www.abc.net.au/rn/talks/bbing/stories/s10786.htm.

30 For more on industrial relations staffing at Qantas, see *The Australian*, 11 July and 1 August 1994.

31 This figure covers only workplaces with more than 20 staff. A. Morehead, M. Steele, M. Alexander, K. Stephen & L. Duffin, *Changes at Work: the 1995 Australian Workplace Industrial Relations Survey*, Longman, Melbourne, 1997, p. 327.

32 G. Griffin, 'Recognition, bargaining and unions in Australia', in G. Gall (ed), *Union Recognition: Organising and Bargaining Outcomes*, Routledge, London, 2006.

33 Morehead et al., *Changes at Work*, p. 151.

34 Ferguson, 'Building effective unions'.

35 P. Gahan, '(Re)organise! Recruit! Survive? The 1995 ACTU Congress', *JIR*, 37 (4), 1995, p. 618.

36 M. Ferguson, opening speech, ACTU Congress, 27 September 1995.

37 P. Saunders & T. Hill, 'Mr Howard and the Gini Coefficient', *Dialogue 27*, Academy of the Social Sciences, 2008, p. 51.

38 Data sourced from Campbell, 'Globalization and changes in employment conditions, pp. 48 and 50.

39 Average working hours rose from 38.4 in 1983 to 41.1 in 1996. Data sourced from Campbell, 'Globalization and changes in employment conditions', table A8.

40 S. Mohun, 'The Australian rate of profit: 1985–2001', *Journal of Australian Political Economy*, no. 52, 2003.

7 Unionism in a cold climate, 1996–2004

1 Throughout the period under review in this chapter, between one-fifth and one-quarter of workers were concerned that they could lose their jobs within 12 months. Roy Morgan poll: www.roymorgan.com/news/polls/2007/4256, accessed 26 March 2008.

2 *The Australian*, 10 August 1996.

3 ACTU, *Unions@work: A Report of the ACTU Overseas Delegation, August 1999*, Melbourne, 1999.

4 G. Campbell, 'A union view of the Accord', in K. Wilson, J. Bradford & M. Fitzpatrick (eds), *Australia in Accord*, South Pacific Publishing, Melbourne, 2000, p. 50.

5 Cited in B. Pocock & P. Wright, 'Trade unionism in 1996', *JIR*, 39 (1), 1997, p. 123.

6 Cited in S. Long, 'The new Australian militancy', *Australian Financial Review*, 18 March 2000.

7   The following account of the ACTU's response to the Workplace Relations Bill draws heavily on the BA Honours thesis by Luke Deer, '"Precisely because it was the seat of government": The Parliament House riot of 1996', Department of Political Science, Australian National University, 1998. This is excerpted on the Marxist Interventions website: www.anu.edu.au.polsci/marx/interventions/riot.htm, accessed 3 October 2007. No page numbering.

8   ibid.

9   ibid.

10 ibid.

11 B. Pocock, 'Trade unionism in 1997', *JIR*, 40 (1), 1998, p. 143.

12 L. Ross, 'Building unions and government "reform": the challenge for unions', *Journal of Australian Political Economy*, 56, 2005, pp. 172–85.

13 The following account of the waterfront dispute draws on 'War and peace: an Age special report', *The Age*, 17 June 1998, pp. 11–14; Parliament of Australia *Current Issues Brief 15 1997–98*: 'Outline of the waterfront dispute', Canberra, May 1998; S. Svensen, 'Chronology of the Patrick dispute', unpublished mimeo, 1998; M. Gillespie, 'The 1998 waterfront dispute: a Marxist analysis', BA (Hons) thesis, Faculty of Arts, Griffith University, 1999; contemporary news media; and personal observation. See also T. Bramble, *War on the Waterfront*, Socialist Alternative, Melbourne, 2007 (originally 1998).

14 Cited in Gillespie, 'The 1998 waterfront dispute', p. 5.

15 ibid., p. 56.

16 The following story is told in J. Small, 'The war on the waterfront – ten years on', *Socialist Alternative* (Melbourne), April 2008.

17 ibid.

18 R. Hodder, 'Workers rally against Reith's second wave', *Green Left Weekly*, 18 August 1999.

19 J. Fetter, 'The strategic use of individual employment agreements: three case studies', Centre for Employment and Labour Relations Law Working Paper No. 26, Melbourne University, 2002.

20 B. Ellem, 'Trade unionism in 1998', *JIR*, 41 (1), 1999, p. 134.

21 M. Bray & P. Waring, 'The rise of managerial prerogative under the Howard government', *Australian Bulletin of Labour*, 32 (1), 2006, pp. 45–61; C. Briggs, 'The return of the lockout in Australia: a profile of lockouts since the decentralisation of bargaining', *Australian Bulletin of Labour*, 30 (2), 2004, pp. 101–12.

22 Fetter, 'Individual employment agreements'.

23 Ross, 'Building unions', p. 174.

24 ibid., p. 176.

25 ibid., p. 177.

26 M. Windisch, '10 000 workers rally for union organiser', *Green Left Weekly*, 5 November 2003.

27 S. Rosewarne, 'Workplace "reform" and the restructuring of higher education', *Journal of Australian Political Economy*, no. 56, 2005, pp. 190–2.

28 ibid., p. 193.

29 ibid., pp. 195–7.

30 ibid., p. 197.

31 *Business Review Weekly*, 24 March 1997, pp. 96–7; Community and Public Sector Union, *Our Voice*, March 1997, p. 1.
32 See for example K. Bronfenbrenner, S. Friedman, R. Hurd, R. Oswald & R. Seeber (eds), *Organizing to Win: New Research on Union Strategies*, Cornell University Press, Ithaca, 1998.
33 See B. Carter & R. Cooper, 'The organizing model and the management of change', *Relations Industrielles*, 57 (4), 2002; and G. Griffin, R. Small & S. Svensen, 'Trade union innovation, adaptation and renewal in Australia: still searching for the holy membership grail', in P. Fairbrother & C. Yates (eds), *Trade Unions in Renewal: A Comparative Study*, Continuum, London, 2003.
34 R. Cooper, 'Organise, organise, organise! ACTU Congress 2000', *JIR*, 42 (4), 2000, pp. 582–94.
35 B. Ellem, 'New unionism in the old economy: community and collectivism in the Pilbara's mining towns', *JIR*, 45 (4), 2003, pp. 423–41.
36 ibid.
37 The Star City Casino campaign is described in detail by M. Crosby, 'Union renewal in Australia', 2000. Accessed online at www.actu.asn.au/educationnews/unionrenewal.html on 28 March 2007.
38 D. Peetz, *Unions in a Contrary World*, Cambridge University Press, Melbourne, 1999.
39 One estimate suggests that the proportion of 'conscripts' among union members fell from 33 per cent to 15 per cent between 1979 and 2005. G. Meagher & S. Wilson, 'Are unions regaining popular legitimacy in Australia?', in D. Denemark, G. Meagher, S. Wilson, M. Western & T. Phillips (eds), *Australian Social Attitudes 2: Citizenship, Work and Aspirations*, UNSW Press, Sydney, 2007, p. 213.
40 AMWU, 'Keep the heart of the Victorian economy beating', Victorian Branch, Melbourne, 1999.
41 ibid.
42 D. Fieldes, 'From exploitation to resistance and revolt: the working class', in R. Kuhn (ed.), *Class and Struggle in Australia*, Longman, Melbourne, 2005, p. 63.
43 R. Cooper, 'Trade unionism in 2003', *JIR*, 46 (2), 2004, pp. 213–25.
44 ibid.

8 WorkChoices and the defeat of the Howard Government

1 G. Combet, speech to the National Press Club, Canberra, 30 June 2005.
2 ibid.
3 ibid.
4 K. Beazley, 'Opposition Leader's Statement – Workplace Relations', Parliament House, 7 June 2005.
5 ibid.
6 Labor's industrial spokesperson, Stephen Smith, cited in *Workers Online*, December 2004, Labor Council of NSW.
7 Beazley, 'Opposition Leader's Statement'.
8 T. Bramble, 'Contradictions in Australia's "Miracle Economy"', *Journal of Australian Political Economy*, no. 54, 2004, pp. 5–31.

9 International Monetary Fund, *Staff Report for the 2005 Article IV Consultation*, Washington, 2005, p. 18; World Bank, *Doing Business in 2006: Creating Jobs*, World Bank, Washington, 2005.

10 See D. Fieldes, '"We've got this new legislation": a review article on Australia@Work and other 2007 reports on WorkChoices', *Economic and Labour Relations Review*, 18 (1), 2007 for a review of the findings from 14 studies of the impact of WorkChoices.

11 A. Roan, T. Bramble & G. Lafferty, 'Australian Workplace Agreements in practice: the "hard" and "soft" dimensions', *JIR*, 43 (4), 2001, pp. 387–401.

12 M. Davis, 'Workers' rights lost with AWAs', *The Age*, 17 April 2007, p. 1.

13 Fieldes, '"We've got this new legislation"', p. 146.

14 E. Hannan, 'Meatworkers "forced into contracts"', *The Australian*, 3 March 2008, p. 7.

15 M. Shaw, 'Rocky road for sweet shop casuals in AWA firing line', *The Age*, 30 March 2007, p. 3.

16 J. Elton, J. Bailey, M. Baird, S. Charlesworth, R. Cooper, B. Ellem, T. Jefferson, F. Macdonald, D. Oliver, B. Pocock, A. Preston & G. Whitehouse, *Women and Work-Choices: Impacts on the Low Pay Sector: Summary Report*, Centre for Work and Life, Adelaide, p. 7.

17 E. Hannan, 'Pay row exposes IR law loophole', *The Australian*, 3 August 2007, p. 7.

18 ACTU, 'One year on: the impact of the new IR laws on Australian working families', 27 March 2007.

19 ibid.

20 ibid.

21 Fieldes, '"We've got this new legislation"', p. 147.

22 B. Van Wanrooy, S. Oxenbridge, J. Buchanan & M. Jakubauskas, *Australia at Work Report*, Workplace Research Centre, University of Sydney, 2007, cited in Fieldes, '"We've got this new legislation"', p. 147.

23 The results of a Galaxy poll by the Sydney *Sunday Telegraph*, 31 December 2006, cited in ACTU 'One year on'.

24 B. Norington, 'Employers caught out on fairness', *The Weekend Australian*, 29–30 September 2007, p. 1.

25 ABS, *Industrial Disputes Australia*, September 2007, cat. no. 6321.0, Table 1.

26 G. Matthews, 'Miners petition against AWAs', *Green Left Weekly*, 15 June 2007.

27 ibid.

28 Ross, 'Building unions', p. 179.

29 ibid.

30 E. Clancy, 'ABCC: Howard's ideologically driven "dirt unit"', *Green Left Weekly*, 7 November 2007.

31 'Railway workers fined $10,000 for striking', *Sydney Morning Herald*, 21 December 2007.

32 M. Franklin, 'Gillard ponders waste', *The Australian*, 29 May 2008, p. 4.

33 Essential Media Communications, 'ACTU *WorkChoices* Campaign Case Study', 2007. Accessed from www.essentialmedia.com.au, 5 February 2008.

34 Ross, 'Building unions', p. 182.

35 C. Jackman, *Inside Kevin 07: The People. The Plan. The Prize*, Melbourne University Press, Melbourne, 2008, p. 122.

36 Essential Media Communications, 'ACTU *WorkChoices* Campaign'.
37 Meagher & Wilson, 'Are unions regaining popular legitimacy?', in Denemark et al., *Australian Social Attitudes 2*, p. 201; ANU Australian Election Study 2007.
38 M. Bachelard & M. Grattan, 'Work laws still disliked', *The Age*, 26 March 2007, p. 1.
39 ibid.
40 L. Sinclair, 'Voters fearful of IR laws', *The Australian*, 3 August 2007.
41 ibid.
42 Angela Knox, 'Fear and loathing in Australia: gauging employee responses to the *WorkChoices* Act 2005', paper presented to the 2007 AIRAANZ conference, Auckland, February 2007.
43 Sharan Burrow, speech to 'Australia at the Crossroads', Just Peace public forum City Hall, Brisbane, 8 August 2007.
44 M. Bachelard & M. Shaw, 'New weapons in the workplace revolution', *The Age*, 26 March 2007, p. 7.
45 Interview, ABC radio, *PM* show, 30 June 2005.
46 ACTU, 'Liberal Party advertisement is insulting to working families, says ACTU', press release, 18 October 2007.
47 Julia Gillard, Q&A at National Press Club Speech, Canberra, 30 May 2007.
48 P. Karvelas, 'ALP offers carrot to contractors', *The Australian*, 2 October 2007, p. 5.
49 ACTU, 'Labor's IR policy offers a balanced IR system for a strong economy and fair workplaces: says ACTU', ACTU press release, 28 April 2007.
50 ibid.
51 'Miners cheer Rudd's improved IR policy', *The Australian*, 29 August 2007, p. 19.
52 Cited in T. Cook, 'Rudd tries to fudge Labor's agreement with *WorkChoices*', World Socialist website, www.wsws.org, 19 October 2007.
53 ACTU, 'Labor policy an important step towards better rights for working families, says ACTU', ACTU press release, 28 August 2007.
54 M. Davis, 'Rudd's work choice – the AWA clone', *Sydney Morning Herald*, 4 September 2007.
55 B. Norington, 'Rudd acts to soothe IR nerves', *The Australian*, 29 August 2007, p. 1.
56 A. West, 'End to business-class politics', *Sydney Morning Herald*, 1 September 2007.
57 E. Hannan, 'Ads aim at "evils" of *WorkChoices*', *The Australian*, 16 October 2007, p. 5.
58 'ALP outlines second phase of IR strategy', *The Age* on line, 28 August 2007.
59 P. Kelly & D. Shanahan, 'Leader prepared to fight unions', *The Australian*, 23 November 2007, p. 1.
60 SBS News on line, 'Rudd slams union bosses', 20 April 2007.
61 Two years before the election, it was apparent that greater knowledge of Work-Choices only accentuated hostility to it. See B. van Wanrooy, 'The quiet before the storm? Attitudes towards the new industrial relations system', in Denemark et al., *Australian Social Attitudes 2*, p. 185. At the election itself, 69 per cent of voters reported that WorkChoices was an important consideration in determining their vote, and 62 per cent disapproved of the Government's new work laws (Australian Election Study 2007, accessed at the Australian Social Science Data Archive via www.assda.anu.edu.au, 28 May 2008).
62 Essential Media Communications, 'Myth-Busters – it's not always the economy, stupid!', 17 December 2007, accessed at www.essentialmedia.com.au, 5 February 2008.

63 A.B. Atkinson & A. Leigh, 'The distribution of top incomes in Australia', Centre for Economic Policy Research Discussion Paper no. 514, Australian National University, 2006.

64 ibid.

65 L. Gettler, 'In the politics of pay, it's up to us to show them the money', *The Age*, 19 May 2007, Business Day, p. 6.

66 ibid.

67 Campbell, 'Globalization and changes in employment conditions', tables A5–A7.

68 ibid, table A8.

69 B. van Wanrooy, 'The quiet before the storm?', p. 178.

70 Cannex Media release, 'Are we reaching peak unaffordability?', www.cannex.com.au, 7 November 2007.

71 Cited in C. Catalano, 'Australia middling good for children', *Sydney Morning Herald*, 15 February 2007.

72 S. Wilson & G. Meagher, 'Howard's welfare state: How popular is the new social policy agenda?', in Denemark et al., *Australian Social Attitude 2*, p. 273.

73 Labor Council of NSW, 'Thumbs down for union busters', *Workers Online*, 1 April 2005.

74 B. van Wanrooy et al., *Australia at Work Report*, p. 94, cited in Fieldes, '"We've got this new legislation"', p. 150.

9 Results and prospects

1 T. Cook, 'Qantas-union deal will set a new benchmark to cut pay and conditions', World Socialist Website, www.wsws.org, 7 December 2007, accessed 27 January 2008.

2 S. Creedy, 'Qantas fires first shots in pay fight', *The Australian*, 28 December 2007, p. 11.

3 *The Australian* had editorialised for a Labor victory at the November 24 election, as did the liberal *Sydney Morning Herald*. *The Age* hedged its bets.

4 K. Rudd & J. Gillard, *Forward with Fairness: Labor's Plan for Fairer and More Productive Australian Workplaces*, April 2007, p. 1.

5 ABC Inside Business, 'New era for business under Labor rule', ABC Online, 25 November 2007; J. Hewitt, 'Rudd revitalises reform hopes', *The Australian*, 26 November 2007, p. 33.

6 B. Norington, 'No Rudd rescue of unions', *The Australian*, 15 April 2008, p. 2.

7 B. Norington & E. Hannan, 'Anger as Howard IR chief stays on', *The Australian*, 27 December 2007, p. 1.

8 S. Wilson, G. Meagher & T. Breusch, 'Where to for the welfare state?', and M. Pusey & N. Turnbull, 'Have Australians embraced economic reform?', both in S. Wilson, G. Meagher, R. Gibson, D. Denemark & M. Western (eds), *Australian Social Attitudes: The First Report*, UNSW Press, Sydney, 2005; ANU Australian Election Study 2007.

9 N. Shoebridge, 'We use them but we love to abuse them', *Australian Financial Review*, 9 October 2006, p. 56.

10 Three-quarters of Australians believed that big Australian corporations abused their power. The same proportion thought that Australian corporations were 'probably'

abusing human rights, and 84 per cent felt that chief executives were overpaid (all figures sourced from a poll conducted in 2006 by STW Communications Group, reported in Shoebridge, 'We use them', p. 56). In three successive ANU Australian Election Studies (2001, 2004 and 2007), 70 per cent of respondents thought that big business had too much power (data accessed online at Australian Social Sciences Data Archive: www.assda.anu.edu.au). A mere 15 per cent of Australians polled in 2006 believed that company executives had high standards of ethics and honesty (Roy Morgan polling).

11 Shoebridge, 'We use them', p. 56.
12 J. Robertson, 'State of the Union', *Workers Online*, April 2005.
13 N. Shoebridge, 'Unhappy days are here again', *Australian Financial Review*, 9 October 2006, p. 56.
14 Robertson, 'State of the Union'.
15 ibid.
16 D. Peetz, *Brave New Workplace*, Allen and Unwin, Sydney, 2006, Chapter 2.
17 B. van Wanrooy et al., *Australia at Work Report*, p. 95.
18 'Thumbs down for union busters', Workers Online, Unions NSW, 1 April 2005.
19 Meagher & Wilson, 'Are unions regaining popular legitimacy', in Denemark et al., *Australian Social Attitudes 2*, p. 200.
20 ibid.
21 M. Moustafa, 'Victorian teachers demand fair pay', *Socialist Alternative* (Melbourne), March 2008, p. 17.
22 van Wanrooy et al., *Australia@Work Report*, p. 91.
23 An authoritative survey in 1991 estimated a total union delegate population of 50 000 in that year. Callus et al., p. 102.
24 Robertson, 'State of the Union'.
25 J. Robertson, 'After 11 years of war, we can all share peace', *The Australian*, 27 November 2007, p. 14.
26 ibid.
27 ibid.
28 ACTU, 'Australia's decline in productivity is a result of WorkChoices and skills neglect under the Coalition Govt. [sic]', ACTU press release, Melbourne, 6 March 2008.
29 The following is drawn from S. Bloodworth, 'Sweatshop rebels: the 1981 Kortex strike', in Bloodworth & O'Lincoln, *Rebel Women*.
30 The Wobblies (more properly known as the Industrial Workers of the World) were a militant group of syndicalist unionists active in Australia, the United States and several other countries in the 1910s. See V. Burgmann, *Revolutionary Industrial Unionism: The Industrial Workers of the World in Australia*, Cambridge, Melbourne, 1995; M. Armstrong, *The First Revolutionary Alternative to Labor: The Industrial Workers of the World in Australia*, Socialist Alternative, Melbourne, 1997.
31 O'Lincoln, *Into the Mainstream*, p. 43.
32 T. O'Lincoln, *The Militant Minority: Organising Rank and File Workers in the Thirties*, available at Marxist Interventions: www.anu.edu.au/polsci/marx/interventions/minority.htm, accessed 25 January 2008.

33 O'Lincoln, *Into the Mainstream*, p. 43.

34 Deery & Plowman, *Australian Industrial Relations*, 3rd edn, McGraw-Hill, Sydney, 1991, p. 226.

35 I. Turner, *Industrial Labour and Politics: The Dynamics of the Labour Movement in Eastern Australia, 1900–1921*, Hale and Iremonger, Sydney, 1979 [orig. 1965]; O'Lincoln, *The Militant Minority*.

INDEX